Paul Jebbott

WEST MIDLANDS POLICE

M3 SOCO

SIG

DATE

SCIENTIFIC SUPPORT

Scientific *and* Legal Applications *of*
BLOODSTAIN PATTERN INTERPRETATION

Edited by
Stuart H. James

CRC Press

Boca Raton   Boston   London   New York   Washington, D.C.

Acquiring Editor: Becky McEldowney
Project Editor: Carol Whitehead
Cover design: Denise Craig
PrePress: Kevin Luong
Manufacturing: Carol Royal

Library of Congress Cataloging-in-Publication Data

Scientific and legal applications of bloodstain pattern interpretation
/ edited by Stuart H. James.
      p. cm.
    Includes bibliographical references and index.
    ISBN 0-8493-8108-8
    1. Bloodstains.   2. Forensic hematology.   3. Evidence, Expert.
  I. James, Stuart H.
  HV8077.5.B56S25   1998
  363.25'62--dc21   98-13654
                                      CIP

Preface

The emergence of bloodstain pattern interpretation in modern times began in 1955 when Dr. Paul Kirk presented his affidavit regarding his findings in the *State of Ohio v. Samuel Sheppard*. As we approach the year 2000, the current high level of acceptance of bloodstain pattern interpretation in forensic science and the courts has its roots in the efforts of renowned criminalist, Herbert Leon MacDonell, Director of the Laboratory of Forensic Science in Corning, New York.

Professor MacDonell's contributions to the advancement of research and applications of bloodstain pattern interpretation since 1971 have been unsurpassed. He has shared his research and knowledge with many of us in the forensic community through his instructing basic and advanced Bloodstain Institutes over the years and has consulted and testified throughout the U.S. and abroad in major criminal and civil cases.

I have been a student of Professor MacDonell and have worked bloodstain cases with him as well as on the opposing side within the legal system. In all cases he has adhered to the scientific method approach to case analysis and has not been an advocate for the prosecution or defense, but rather an advocate of the evidence and credibility as an expert witness. These qualities should be within the soul of every bloodstain analyst. This book strives to combine some of the scientific approaches and developments in bloodstain pattern interpretation with a comprehensive overview of its applications and acceptance within the legal system, which is the ultimate test in forensic science.

The growth of the discipline of bloodstain pattern interpretation has not been without controversy with respect to qualifications of individuals as bloodstain analysts as well as some of the expert testimony that has been offered at trials. Differences of opinion have emerged as to the degree of educational background and experience required for individuals to render expert opinions on bloodstain pattern interpretation in a court of law. One view is that, in order to be considered an expert, an individual should possess a college degree in either the sciences or criminal justice that includes some science courses such as biology, chemistry, or physics. Most forensic scientists acknowledge the importance of a scientific educational background but also opine that practical experience in analyzing bloodstain patterns is crucial.

Because the courts are given broad discretion in qualifying experts, no clear standard exists which defines a sufficient degree of expertise. Therefore, individuals with a variety of educational and experience levels have been qualified as experts in this discipline. It should be noted that neither the Federal Rules of Evidence nor existing case law require degrees in formal education for this type of expert testimony. The courts have accepted bloodstain pattern testimony from forensic scientists with backgrounds in chemistry, biology, physics, serology, and pathology. The courts have also accepted bloodstain pattern testimony from law enforcement personnel including crime scene investigators, evidence technicians, and detectives, who do not necessarily possess a scientific background. In many cases, these individuals — though not scientists — have successfully completed basic and advanced courses in bloodstain pattern interpretation. Coupled with practical experience at crime scenes, these individuals can attain expertise in the discipline and render credible testimony in courts of law.

Unfortunately, the misinterpretation and overinterpretation of bloodstain evidence does occur in the courts. This has happened with experts possessing academic degrees as well as with those who do not possess a degree but rely upon his or her experience. Anyone involved in the interpretation of bloodstain patterns should recognize his or her own limitations, whether it be in education and/or experience, and avoid going beyond his area or level of expertise. There should be no speculation or overstating of the facts of a case nor ignoring or not considering other forensic evidence that does not support one's conclusion. A competent expert will recognize that bloodstains at a crime scene may have been produced by a number of mechanisms. All possibilities should be explored and given consideration when drawing conclusions concerning bloodstain patterns at a crime scene.

A bloodstain pattern interpretation report recently received for review stated:

> "The number and focus of the wounds, the apparent restriction of the victim by more than one person, the apparent tortuous, and tortuous nature of the wounds, and the confinement of the bloodletting to a small area suggests this act was deliberate and methodical. There are insufficient castoff patterns, spatter patterns, and ambulation in the blood to infer this to be spontaneous and/or a frenzied act. The fact that there are no readily detectable trails of blood drops or transfer from the assailants as they departed the scene would indicate extraordinary care by the assailants in cleaning themselves before departure or an inexplicable fluke."

Clearly this type of expert opinion is speculative, extends well beyond the scope of scientific method and the discipline of bloodstain pattern interpretation, and shows a lack of objectivity.

In another case a few years earlier, an expert testified that based upon the bloodstain evidence that he was "110% certain that the defendant was the killer." The defendant was ultimately acquitted. Laurens van der Post, a South African writer was quoted as saying, "Human beings are perhaps never more frightening than when they are convinced beyond doubt that they are right."

Situations such as these may be avoided if the courts and the attorneys educate themselves and have a better understanding of bloodstain pattern interpretation. As Professor Andre A. Moenssens stated in an article entitled, "Novel Scientific Evidence in Criminal Cases" published in the *Journal of Criminal Law and Criminology* in 1993, attorneys have the responsibility to learn about the scientific evidence that they wish to admit. If the attorneys who are questioning and cross-examining the expert witnesses have a working knowledge of bloodstain pattern interpretation, they will be better equipped to distinguish between those experts with sufficient qualifications and those without them. Also, attorneys will be able to more capably critique an expert's testimony and limit or eliminate conclusions that are speculative or overstated. Unless attorneys know what questions to ask during cross-examination, much of what the witness testifies to will go unchallenged.

The production of this text, *Scientific and Legal Applications of Bloodstain Pattern Interpretation,* has evolved as a companion to the second edition of the text, *Interpretation of Bloodstain Evidence at Crime Scenes* by James and Eckert (CRC Press, 1999). The Editor has brought together some of the respected and noted experts in forensic science, the law, and bloodstain pattern interpretation as contributing authors to provide a comprehensive overview of the discipline with respect to research, applications, and the current view of bloodstain pattern interpretation within the legal system at the trial and appellate court levels. Chapters written by contributing authors include "Defining the 'Address' of Bloodstains and Other Evidence at the Crime Scene" and "Utilizing Bloodstains in Accident Reconstruction" by William C. Fischer, "Bloodstain Pattern Analysis with a Computer" by Alfred L. Carter, "Presumptive Testing for Blood" by T. Paulette Sutton, "Approach to Case Evaluation and Report Writing" by Paul Erwin Kish, "Legal and Ethical Aspects of Bloodstain Pattern Evidence" by Carol Henderson, and "Bloodstain Pattern Interpretation: A Post-Conviction Analysis" by Marie Elena Saccoccio.

Novel features of this text are the inclusion of a color atlas of bloodstains in conjunction with a glossary of terms and an outline of basic laboratory experiments that are commonly used in the discipline for basic bloodstain pattern training.

Finally, the Appendix section includes the original affidavit of Paul Leland Kirk for the State of Ohio v. Samuel Sheppard, an illustrative testimony of a motion in limine for the admissibility of bloodstain evidence, and updated appellate court decisions relating to bloodstain pattern interpretation and presumptive tests for blood.

It is hoped that this book will provide useful information to prosecutors and defense attorneys as well as investigators and forensic scientists within the discipline of bloodstain pattern interpretation.

Stuart H. James
Ft. Lauderdale, Florida

List of Authors

Alfred L. Carter
Physics Department
Carleton University
Ottawa, Ontario
Canada

William C. Fischer
Fischer Bureau of Investigations
Endicott, New York

Carol Henderson
Nova Southeastern University
Shepard Broad Law Center
Fort Lauderdale, Florida

Stuart H. James
James and Associates
    Forensic Consultants, Inc.
Fort Lauderdale, Florida

Paul Erwin Kish
Laboratory of Forensic Science
Corning, New York

Marie Elena Saccoccio
Attorney
Cambridge, Massachusetts

T. Paulette Sutton
Department of Pathology
Division of Forensic Pathology
University of Tennessee
Memphis, Tennessee

About the Authors

Alfred L. Carter, Ph.D. is a retired Professor of Physics at Carleton University in Ottawa, Canada. He has done extensive work in computer analysis of bloodstains and developed computer programs for this application. He is a member of the International Association of Bloodstain Pattern Analysts. Dr. Carter has worked with the Royal Canadian Mounted Police in Ottawa, Canada and has instructed computer analysis of bloodstains both in Canada and the U.S.

William C. Fischer is a private investigator and owner of Fischer Bureau of Investigations in Endicott, New York where he specializes in homicide investigation and automobile accident reconstruction. He received a B.S. degree in Criminal Justice from the State University of New York in Binghamton, New York and attended the Traffic Institute at Northwestern University in Evanston, Illinois. Mr. Fischer is retired from the New York State Police and has consulted and testified in numerous states throughout the country. He is a member of the Society of Accident Reconstructionists and the International Association of Bloodstain Pattern Analysts.

Carol Henderson is a Professor of Law at The Shepard Broad Law Center, Nova Southeastern University in Fort Lauderdale, Florida, where she teaches Scientific Evidence Workshop, Professional Responsibility, and Criminal Law. She is a Fellow in the American Academy of Forensic Sciences and has served on the Board of Directors. She is the author of *Scientific Evidence in Civil and Criminal Cases* (4th Edition, The Foundation Press, Inc., Westbury, NY, 1995) with Moenssens, Starrs, and Inbau as well as the author of more than 35 articles on scientific evidence and ethics.

Stuart H. James is a forensic consultant with James and Associates Forensic Consultants, Inc. in Fort Lauderdale, Florida and has worked with Professor Herbert MacDonell both at the Institute on the Physical Significance of Human Bloodstain Evidence and the Laboratory of Forensic Science in Corning, New York. He has been consulted as a bloodstain analyst on criminal and civil cases in numerous states throughout the continental U.S. as well as in Australia, Canada, South Korea, and the U.S. Virgin Islands. He has testified in many of these jurisdictions for prosecution and defense attorneys. Mr. James is a member of the American Academy of Forensic Sciences and a charter member of the International Association of Bloodstain Pattern Analysts.

Paul Erwin Kish is a Research Associate with the Laboratory of Forensic Science under the direction of Herbert Leon MacDonell in Corning, New York and an adjunct instructor of Forensic Science and Criminal Justice at Elmira College in Corning, New York. He is a private consulting bloodstain pattern analyst and has been consulted by agencies in Australia, Canada, Denmark, New Zealand, Sweden, and throughout the United States, and qualified as an expert in many courts of law. He holds an M.S. degree in education and a B.S. degree in criminal justice from Elmira College. Mr. Kish has lectured extensively and authored various articles on the topic of bloodstain patterns. He is a member of several scientific organizations including the American Academy of Forensic Sciences and the International Association of Bloodstain Pattern Analysts.

Marie Elena Saccoccio is an alumna of the New England School of Law and Yale Law School and is a practicing attorney in Cambridge, Massachusetts concentrating on appellate/postconviction matters. She is admitted to the bars of Colorado, Florida, and Massachusetts where she works as a sole practitioner. She is the former judicial law clerk to the Honorable Wade Brorby of the U.S. Court of Appeals for the Tenth Circuit.

T. Paulette Sutton is an Associate Professor of Clinical Laboratory Sciences and supervisor of the Forensic Serology Section of the Department of Pathology, Division of Forensic Pathology at the University of Tennessee in Memphis. Ms. Sutton has lectured extensively for the National District Attorneys' Association and contributed to the second edition of the text, *Interpretation of Bloodstain Evidence at Crime Scenes* (CRC Press, 1999).

Acknowledgments

The completion of this book would not have succeeded without the work ethic and dedication of the contributing authors. They are all highly respected professionals in their fields and have shared their expertise and helped to merge the scientific and legal aspects of bloodstain pattern interpretation into a book that should complement the current texts in bloodstain pattern interpretation and the forensic sciences. The Editor expresses his sincere thanks and appreciation for their excellent chapters contributed to *Scientific and Legal Applications of Bloodstain Pattern Interpretation.*

The Editor and the contributing authors recognize and thank the following individuals for their efforts and assistance with the production of this text:

Victoria Wendy Hilt, R.N., of Fort Lauderdale, Florida for her support and patience with editing and typing, and for providing moral support throughout the development of this book.

Erik Joyce of Welleby Photographics in Sunrise, Florida for his expert assistance with many of the color photographs which appear in the section "Bloodstain Atlas and Terminology."

Sgt. Pat Laturnus of the Royal Canadian Mounted Police Central Forensic Laboratory in Ottawa, Canada for his assistance to Dr. Alfred L. Carter in the preparation of "Bloodstain Pattern Analysis with a Computer;" Inspector Ed Podworny of the Royal Canadian Mounted Police who, in addition to his strong support, collaborated in a number of crucial experiments in 1989 and 1990, which proved the efficiency and accuracy of this procedure for bloodstain pattern analysis; and Inspector Herb Leroy, Officer in Charge, Forensic Identification Research and Review Section of the R.C.M.P. in Ottawa, for a five-month research contract in 1992 to work exclusively on blood spatter analysis.

Roger Cruz, Toby Perl, Cathy Williams, and Dori Stibolt, law students at Nova Southeastern University in Fort Lauderdale, Florida, for their research assistance to Carol Henderson with "Legal and Ethical Aspects of Bloodstain Pattern Evidence."

Josepha Parente and Anthony Pierro, law students at New England School of Law, for their research assistance to Marie Elena Saccoccio with "Bloodstain Pattern Interpretation: A Post-Conviction Analysis."

Table of Contents

8   Outline of Basic Laboratory Experiments for Bloodstain Pattern Interpretation   157

Stuart H. James

Bloodstain Atlas and Terminology

Scientific *and* Legal Applications *of*

BLOODSTAIN PATTERN INTERPRETATION

Defining the "Address" of Bloodstains and Other Evidence at the Crime Scene[1]

1

WILLIAM C. FISCHER

Contents

Introduction

Acts of extreme violence often produce a dispersion of blood volumes forced from a wound site. Gunshot and other high-energy impacts, such as blunt force beatings, may disperse these blood volumes along relatively flat trajectories.

---

[1] Portions originally presented at the 10th training conference of the International Association of Bloodstain Pattern Analysts, October 1993.

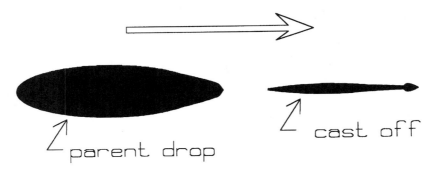

Figure 1.1

Molecular cohesion creates surface tension at the boundaries of these blood volumes. Surface tension causes the drop volumes to assume nearly spherical shapes in free flight. These drops result in bloodstain evidence being deposited on the floor, walls, ceiling, or other surfaces or objects within a crime scene.

Interpretation of the resulting stain patterns may permit an analyst to approximate the three-dimensional point of origin. This chapter develops an equation and a methodology for calculating that point.

It is a common observation that the path of a liquid drop is aligned with the long axis of the resulting stain (Figure 1.1). The flight direction of the drop is toward the tapered end of the stain. In a 1971 paper, MacDonell and Bialousz[1] demonstrated that a predictable relationship exists between the length-to-width ratio of a bloodstain and the angle at which it strikes a *static* surface (Figure 1.2).

$$\text{IMPACT ANGLE} = \arcsin\left(\frac{\text{Width}}{\text{Length}}\right) \qquad (1.1)$$

MacDonell further demonstrated that the approximate three-dimensional point of origin can be reestablished by running several tautly stretched strings. Each string is aligned with the long axis of a particular stain and angled from the surface according to the width/length relationship of the stain.

In a 1986 paper Pizzola and DeForest[2] demonstrated that a predictable relationship exists between the length-to-width ratio of a stain and the velocity of a target surface moving perpendicular to the path of a falling drop (Figure 1.3).

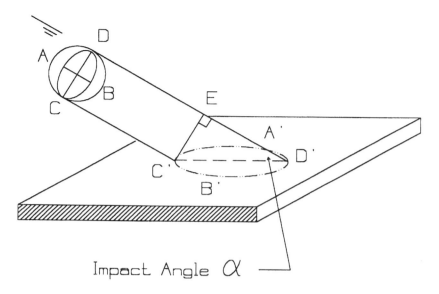

Figure 1.2

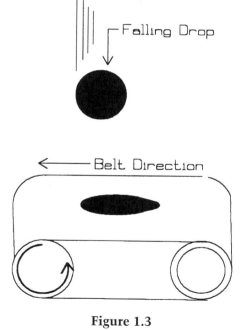

Figure 1.3

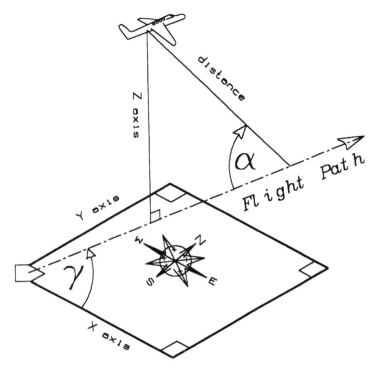

Figure 1.4

Methodology

- Establish an orthogonal coordinate axis system at a crime scene.
- Identify, address, and database the location, size, and orientation of bloodstains and other items of physical evidence within a crime scene.
- Calculate the three-dimensional point of origin in a *fixed* environment.

Two Angles and a Distance

To locate a single point in three-dimensional space requires knowledge of two angles and a distance. Imagine an observer in left field at a baseball park who hears a plane flying overhead. The field is oriented such that the third base line (Y axis) heads due north. The first angle, gamma (γ), is formed between the first base line (X axis) and the flight path. (Figure 1.4).

The second angle, alpha (α), is formed between the ground and the airplane at the position of the observer. The distance is the hypotenuse of

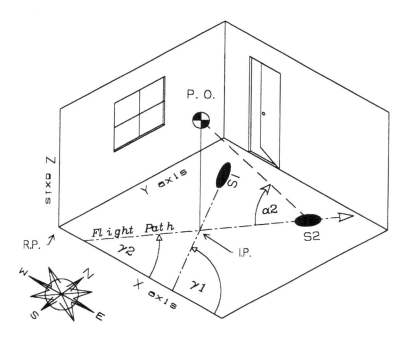

Figure 1.5

the right triangle formed by the observer, the plane, and the ground. In similar fashion, we can approximate the point source of related bloodstains at a crime scene. The analysis is based upon three variables:

1. The width/length ratio of several stains on a common surface;
2. The distance of each stain to a common point, that being the intersection point, or IP, of their flight paths over the two-dimensional surface upon which they appear;
3. The distance of each stain to the point of origin.

Attributes

The crime scene depicted in Figure 1.5 shows two bloodstains, S_1 and S_2, which are located on the floor of a room. Each stain has nine specific attributes of location, geometry, and orientation which identify it as unique from any other in the crime scene. *Note:* stains have no height!

1. The surface designation of the plane on which the stains appear;
2. The X coordinate of each stain;

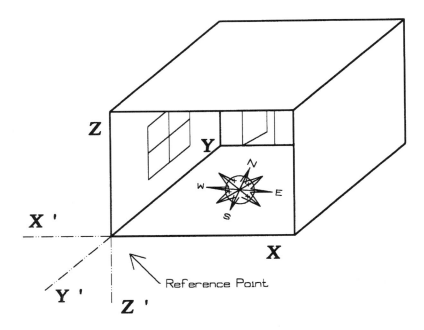

Figure 1.6

3. The Y coordinate of each stain;
4. The Z coordinate of each stain;
5. The height of objects only;
6. The width of each stain;
7. The length of each stain;
8. The flight path of each stain designated as gamma (γ);
9. The angle of impact of each stain designated as alpha (α);

Orientation

First, an orientation must be assigned to the crime scene (Figures 1.5 and 1.6). For ease of explanation our hypothetical crime scene is oriented with the compass. In practice, any bottom corner of the crime scene can be designated as the reference point, or RP. An orthogonal system is thus established from the three primary axes at the RP. This method operates on the premise that most building construction joints meet at right angles. Where this is not the case, a base line can be struck to ensure the data integrity.

Surface Designation

Next, surface designations are established for all surfaces within the crime scene (Figures 1.7 and 1.8). This can be facilitated by mentally unfolding the

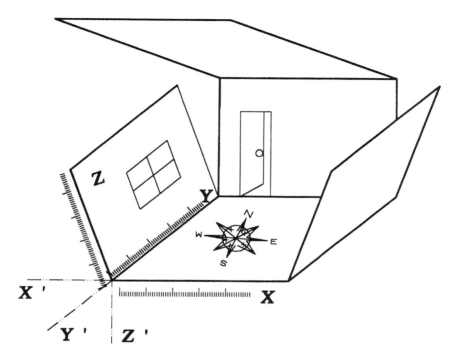

Figure 1.7

room in which the crime scene is located. It is not uncommon to find bloodstains on the undersides of ceilings, tables, doors, kitchen counters, etc.

- All top surfaces are Z.
- All bottom surfaces are Z'.
- All East exposures are X.
- All West exposures are X'.
- All North exposures are Y.
- All South exposures are Y'.

All measurements will be located with respect to the RP. Thus, two coordinate measurements are necessary to locate an object on the surface of any plane.

Establishing the Flight Path

The flight path is projected back along the stain and measured counterclockwise from a designated base line or axis on the surface (Figure 1.9). Stains with a flight path angle greater than 180° are measured from a relocated axis parallel to the designated axis (Figure 1.10). (Or add 180° to the angle measured from the primary axis.)

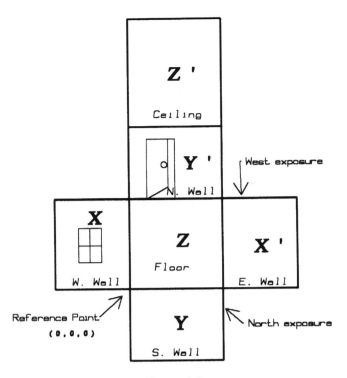

Figure 1.8

Solving for the Slope of the Flight Path

Because the flight path is measured counterclockwise from a designated axis, it is equivalent to the slope of the line. Recall that the slope is the tangent of the angle formed with the designated axis.

$$\text{SLOPE} = m = \frac{y_2 - y_1}{y_2 - x_1} = \frac{\text{opposite}}{\text{adjacent}} \qquad (1.2)$$

In Figure 1.11 the two stains on the floor of the crime scene have been plotted as S_1 and S_2. The coordinates of S_1 are ($x = 40.0$, $y = 25.1$). The flight path of S_1 forms an angle of 79.8° with the X axis as measured at the scene. The slope of the flight path is the tangent of 79.8 or 5.56. The coordinates of S_2 are ($x = 10.0$, $y = 30.0$). The flight path of S_2 is 133.9°. The slope is −1.04.

Databasing

By using a form similar to the one in Figure 1.12, the data for each stain or item in the crime scene are recorded. Underline one of the coordinate values of the stain to designate the axis from which the flight path is measured.

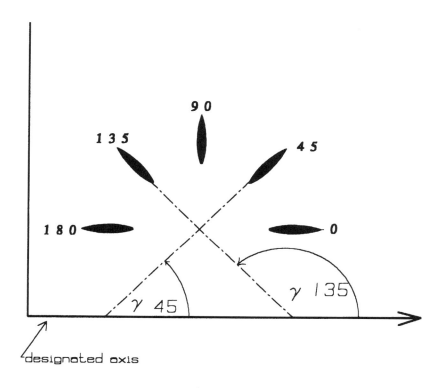

Figure 1.9

Solving for the Impact Angles

Stain 1	Stain 2	
$\alpha1 = \arcsin\left(\dfrac{w}{l}\right)$	$\alpha1 = \arcsin\left(\dfrac{w}{l}\right)$	
$\alpha1 = \arcsin\left(\dfrac{14.3}{20}\right)$	$\alpha1 = \arcsin\left(\dfrac{12}{23}\right)$	
$\alpha1 = 45.6^0$	$\alpha1 = 31.4^0$	(1.3)

Solving for the Point of Intersection

Rewriting the equation (1.2) for the flight path allows us to solve for the coordinates of the IP using two simultaneous equations.

$$\left(y_2 - y_1\right) = m\left(x_2 - x_1\right) \tag{1.4}$$

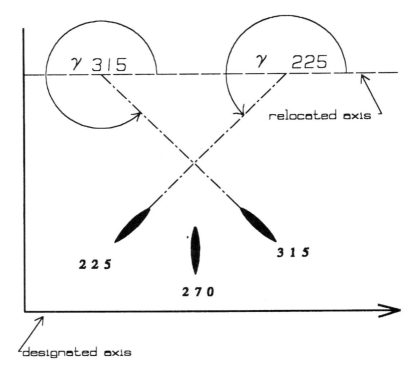

Figure 1.10

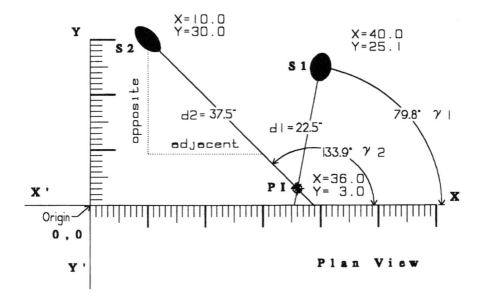

Figure 1.11

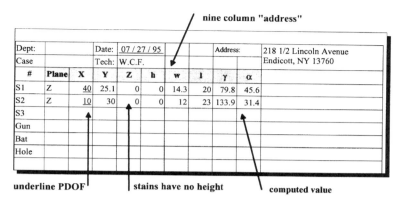

Figure 1.12

First substitute the slope values in the equation of each line and solve for y_2:

Line 1

$$(y_2 - y_1) = m_1(x_2 {}_- x_1)$$
$$(y_2 - 25.1) = 5.56(x - 40.0)$$
$$y_2 - 25.1 = 5.56x - 222.31$$
$$y_2 = 5.56x - 197.21$$

Line 2

$$(y_2 - y_1) = m_2(x_2 - x_1)$$
$$(y_2 - 30) = m(x - 10)$$
$$(y_2 - 30) = -1.04x + 10.39$$
$$y_2 = -1.04x + 40.39$$

Next set the values of $y_2(S_1)$ equal to $y_2(S_2)$, as they are equal at the IP. Solve for x:

$$5.56x - 197.2 = -1.04x + 40.39$$
$$6.6x = 237.6$$
$$x = 36$$

Now substitute the value of x into the equation for either flight path. Solve for y:

$$y = 5.56x - 197.21$$
$$y = 200.2 - 197.21$$
$$y = 3$$

Distance to the IP

Using the Pythagorean theorem we can solve for the distance between a stain and the IP. (See Figure 1.13).

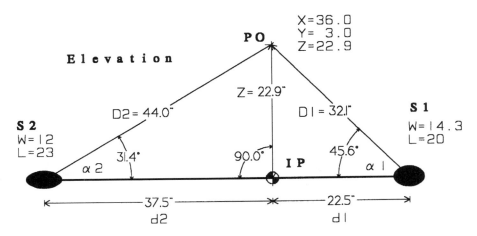

Figure 1.13

$$d_n = \sqrt{\left(x_2 - x_1\right)^2 + \left(y_2 - y_2\right)^2}$$

$$S_1 d_1 = \sqrt{\left(40 - 36\right)^2 + \left(25.1 - 3\right)^2} = 22.5$$

$$S_1 d_2 = \sqrt{\left(10 - 36\right)^2 + \left(30 - 3\right)^2} = 37.5 \qquad (1.5)$$

Calculating the Value of the Third Coordinate

Now that values for both the impact angles and distances across the plane from each stain to IP have been determined, we can calculate the value of the third coordinate above the plane on which the stains appear.

In our hypothetical crime scene (Figure 1.5), the surface of the floor has a Z designation and the unknown third coordinate has a Z value. The equation for calculating the third coordinate is

$$Z_{\left(\text{Point of Origin}\right)} = \left[d\right]\left[\left(\tan\right)\left(\alpha\right)\right] \qquad (1.6)$$

Expanding:

$$Z = \left[\sqrt{\left(X_s - X_{\text{PI}}\right)^2 + \left(Y_s - Y_{\text{PI}}\right)^2}\right]\left[\left(\tan\right)\left(\arcsin\frac{w}{1}\right)\right]$$

Solving for $Z_{(PO)}$ of S_1:

$$Z_{PO} = \left[\sqrt{(40-36)^2 + (25.1-3)^2} \right] \left[(\tan)\left(\arcsin \frac{14.3}{20} \right) \right]$$

$$Z_{PO} = \left[\sqrt{4^2 + 22.1^2} \right] \left[(\tan)(45.64) \right]$$

$$Z_{PO} = (22.45)(1.02) = 22.97$$

Solving for Z_{PO} of S_2:

$$Z_{PO} = \left[\sqrt{(10-36)^2 + (30-3)^2} \right] \left[(\tan)\left(\arcsin \frac{12}{23} \right) \right]$$

$$Z_{PO} = \left[\sqrt{(-26^2) + (27)^2} \right] \left[(\tan)(31.45) \right]$$

$$Z_{PO} = (37.48)(0.61) = 22.92$$

Calculating the Distance from Stain to PO

Again, the Pythagorean theorem is used to calculate D_1 and D_2.

Stain 1   Stain 2

$$D = \sqrt{(22.5)^2 + (22.9)^2} \qquad D = \sqrt{(37.5)^2 + (22.9)^2}$$

$$D_1 = 32.1 \qquad\qquad D_2 = 43.9$$

Units

The use of metric units are far easier to work with in the scene layout. If English units are used, the feet must be converted to decimal equivalents.

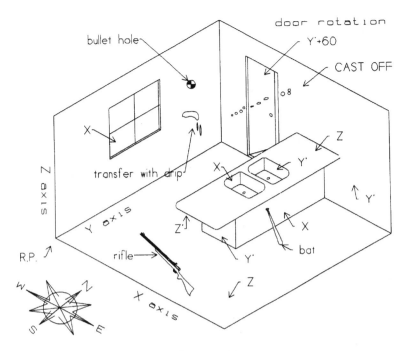

Figure 1.14

Other Objects and Surfaces

The same system of nine attributes can be used to "address" and plot virtually any other object in the crime scene. As with bloodstains, the address both locates and orients the object within the crime scene. Used in conjunction with photographs, this system fully documents the spatial relationship of evidentiary objects.

Note: In Figure 1.14, the door was open at the time of bloodshed. Its angle of rotation can be established by the difference between the impact angles on the door and the impact angles on the wall surrounding the jamb.

Observations

- If the flight paths of any two stains are not identical (parallel flight paths), they will intersect somewhere in the plane, but not necessarily within the crime scene.
- The flight path of any two stains on a plane may intersect, but they may not converge three dimensionally.

Dept:			Date:	07 / 27 / 95			Address:	218 1/2 Lincoln Avenue Endicott, NY 13760
Case			Tech:	W.C.F.				
#	**Plane**	**X**	**Y**	**Z**	**h**	**w**	**l**	**γ**	**α**	
S1	Z	40	25.1	0	0	14.3	20	79.8	45.6	
S2	Z	10	30	0	0	12	23	133.9	31.4	
door	Y+60	n/a	2'6"	n/a	80"	32"	n/a			right hand
Gun	Z	5'7"	1'6"	0	n/a	n/a	32"	155	0	12 ga. Ithaca pump, left side up
Bat	Z	9'0"	8'0"	0	n/a	n/a	30"	180	120	leaning on cabs.behind sink
Hole	X	0	10'5"	5'8"	n/a	3 mm	5 mm	5	36.8	

Figure 1.15

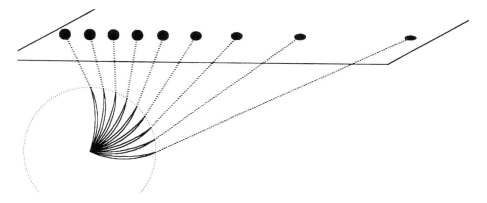

Figure 1.16

- Many stains converging at the same point indicate that they originated from the same event.
- When the flight paths of a series of apparently related stains do not converge, the source is moving.

References

1. MacDonell, H. L. and Bialousz, L. F., Flight Characteristics and Stain Patterns of Human Blood, Washington, D.C., U.S. Dept. of Justice, Law Enforcement Assistance Administration, National Institute of Law Enforcement and Criminal Justice, November 1971.

2. Pizzola, P. A. and DeForest, P. R., Blood Droplet Dynamics II, *Journal of Forensic Sciences,* JFSCA, Vol. 31, No. 1, Jan. 1986, pp. 50–64.

Bloodstain Pattern Analysis with a Computer

2

ALFRED L. CARTER

Contents

Introduction

Bloodstain pattern analysis with a computer combines the well-known laws of projectile motion, the mathematics of three-dimensional geometry, and a computer to study bloodstain patterns found at the scene of violent crimes. The object of the analysis as described here is to discover how many separate blows or bloodletting events took place, and where these events occurred, i.e., was the victim standing or lying on the floor.

This chapter discusses, in some detail, how the traditional "string method" of bloodstain pattern analysis can be adapted to a desktop or a laptop computer with excellent results. We begin with a brief description of the string method.

This ingenious use of strings is based on a simple discovery, explained later in this chapter (Part 1), that enables one to compute the direction of motion of the blood droplet at the instant it strikes a surface. One end of a string is fastened to the surface at the position of the stain and then stretched in the computed direction of motion. This is repeated for a number of individual bloodstains. The result is a pattern of strings extending away from the bloodstain pattern.

A fast-moving droplet has a flat, stringlike trajectory through the air before striking the surface. Therefore, the strings attached to the stains produced by these fast droplets will point back toward the source of the blood.

In principle, only two perfect strings are needed to locate the source position, i.e., the intersection point of the two strings.

In practice, because of the curvature of the flight paths, the impact directions do not point directly at the source but at a point above the source. The height of this point above the source depends on the curvature of the flight path, and the curvature depends on factors that are generally unknown to the analyst, i.e., droplet speed and size. However, by choosing a number of suitable stains for stringing (fast upward-moving droplets), one can usually produce a string pattern that contains a point of convergence of the strings.

It is reasonable to assume that the point of convergence is located somewhere above the source and therefore can be used as an upper limit for the height of the source. The horizontal location of the point of convergence does not depend on the curvature of the flight paths. The correctness of the horizontal position of the point of convergence depends on the accuracy of the measurements of the stain to find the string direction and the precision of the placement of the strings. The string placement consumes most of the time required for the analysis and probably produces most of the errors.

The use of a computer eliminates these errors and also eliminates the considerable time required for the placement of the strings. The computer draws "virtual strings," which are computed precisely to match the data. The computer enables the virtual string pattern to be viewed in three dimensions from different angles. The most important view, for locating the position of the source of the blood, is the top view or bird's-eye view. This is due to the fact that, normally, the flight paths of all droplets, regardless of their sizes or speeds, appear as straight lines when viewed from above.

It would appear, therefore, that the bird's-eye view of the string pattern is the most critical one. The converging patterns of the virtual strings, when seen from above, indicate possible locations of the sources of the blood, and what is most important, these source locations are unbiased by the unknown factors such as the parabolic arcing due to gravitational forces, air resistance, sizes, and speeds of the droplets. Because the curvature of the flight path does not appear in the top view, all flight paths have equal importance for determining the location of the source. Bloodstains that would not be suitable for real strings can be utilized by the computer. Virtual strings can be drawn for all the bloodstains on a surface, thereby increasing the amount of stains available for analysis.

Comparing virtual strings with real strings, we see a number of advantages: a major saving in effort and time by eliminating the need for stringing the bloodstain pattern and error-free placement of the virtual strings. Virtual strings are perfectly straight and mathematically defined. This means that numerical values can be computed for the best estimate of the location of the blood source as revealed by the virtual string point of convergence. Virtual

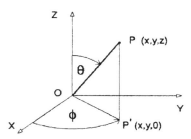

Figure 2.1   The rectangular X,Y,Z coordinate system. The direction of point P, OP, is defined by the two angles θ and φ .

strings drawn by a computer have another important advantage over real strings; i.e., the mathematically precise top view projection of the virtual string pattern can be utilized for analysis. This, the most useful view of the string pattern, is practically impossible to obtain with real strings. Thus, it is fair to say that virtual stringing with a computer overcomes a major limitation in the usefulness of the conventional string method for bloodstain pattern analysis.

The remainder of this chapter is divided into three parts. Part 1 discusses the method for computing the virtual string direction for an individual bloodstain. Part 2 discusses some of the physical properties of moving blood droplets and their flight paths. The program Tracks is used to illustrate some of the important relationships between actual flight paths and their virtual strings. In Part 3 an actual bloodstain pattern produced in the laboratory is analyzed with the program BackTrack/Win.

Part 1 — Computing the String Direction

We begin by considering some of the basic properties of three-dimensional space. Figure 2.1 depicts the conventional rectangular, X,Y,Z coordinate system. The three axes are perpendicular to each other. In this work, only the positive portions of the three axes are used. It is useful at this point to define a scheme for relating the X,Y,Z coordinate system to the walls of a room containing the crime scene.

Point O, where the three axes intersect, is called the origin and the values of X,Y,Z are assumed to be zero at this point. The Z axis extends from the floor toward the ceiling which would normally define the maximum value for Z. The most convenient location for the origin is at a corner of the room on the floor. Thus, all stains located on the floor would have a Z value equal to zero. All stains located on the forward wall would have X values equal to zero and all stains located on the left wall would have Y values equal to zero. By this scheme every bloodstain at the crime scene would have unique values

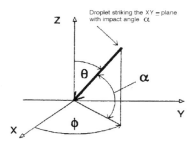

Figure 2.2   The impact angle alpha (α) is shown for a droplet striking the floor while making an angle theta (θ) with the perpendicular or Z axis.

for X,Y, and Z. The computer calculates the string direction appropriate for a particular stain and attaches the virtual string to the point defined by the values of X,Y,Z.

Also in Figure 2.1, a point P is shown with coordinates X,Y,Z, and the point P′, directly below on the floor, has the same values for X and Y but the Z value is zero. A line joins the origin O with the point P. This line is said to have a "direction" defined by the two angles θ and φ. It is a basic property of three-dimensional space that two angles are necessary to define a direction in space. The two angles, alpha (α) and phi (φ), shown in Figures 2.1 and 2.2, are the conventional angles defined in most mathematical texts. Here, it is more convenient to make use of the two angles that occur naturally with bloodstains, i.e., the impact angle which we will call alpha (α) and the directionality angle or glancing angle which we will call gamma (γ).

In Figure 2.2 the arrow pointing toward the origin of the X,Y,Z axis represents the impact direction for a droplet striking the floor with an impact angle alpha (α). It can be seen that in this instance $α = 90 − θ$. A common definition of the impact angle is "the angle between the direction of motion of the droplet upon impact and the surface of impact." The possible values of alpha range from close to zero for an oblique impact, to 90° for a direction of motion perpendicular to the surface.

The empirical relationship between the shape of a bloodstain and the value of the impact angle can be demonstrated by Figures 2.3 and 2.4. In Figure 2.3 we see a spherical droplet of blood falling toward a flat inclined plane with an impact angle of α degrees. The projection of the spherical drop onto the inclined plane is an ellipse of width W, equal to the diameter of the drop. The length of the ellipse, L, will depend on the impact angle.

This dependence can be seen in Figure 2.4 which is a side view of the inclined plane. It is assumed, for the purpose of this discussion, that the blood droplet, upon striking the inclined plane with the impact angle α degrees, will produce a stain that resembles the projected ellipse whose width is equal to the diameter of the spherical drop. From Figure 2.4 one can see

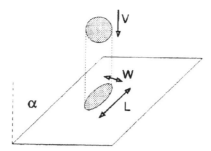

Figure 2.3 A spherical droplet of blood is free-falling onto an inclined plane with an impact angle of alpha (α) degrees. The projection of the sphere is an ellipse of width W and length L.

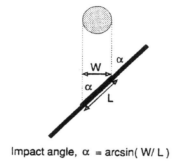

Impact angle, α = arcsin(W/ L)

Figure 2.4 The side view of Figure 2.3 depicts the empirical relationship sin (α) = W/L.

that the ratio of the width to the length is equal to the sine of the angle α; i.e., α = arcsin (W/L).

Of course the stains are not perfect ellipses. However, the arcsin relationship is easily verified as reasonable and useful by laboratory experiments with free-falling droplets. This is a standard exercise in most courses on bloodstain pattern analysis. By calibrating the impact angles with actual stains, one can determine the appropriate length for a particular shape of stain. The first experimental confirmation of the validity of the arcsin relationship for stains on a vertical surface, with a computer, was reported by the author at the training conference of the International Association of Bloodstain Pattern Analysts in Dallas, Texas in November 1993.

A second angle gamma (γ) is needed to define the string direction. This is the so-called directionality angle, which is the direction indicated by the main axis of the stain. This is relatively easy to measure with a protractor. In this work we adopt the following convention for stains on a vertical surface. Droplets moving straight upward when they strike the surface produce stains

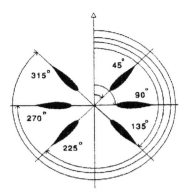

Figure 2.5   The directionality angle gamma (γ) defined.

with gamma angles equal to 0°. Droplets that strike the surface while moving straight downward produce stains with gamma angles equal to 180° in the clockwise sense. This convention is depicted by Figure 2.5 which shows six possible stains on a vertical surface with gamma angles equal to 45, 90, 135, 225, 270, and 315°.

So far we have defined the impact angle alpha (α) for a bloodstain and explained the theory behind the relationship $\alpha = \arcsin(W/L)$ where W and L are the width and length, suitably chosen, of the stain. We have also defined a second angle gamma (γ) for the stain, the directionality angle. With these two angles we can compute the direction of the droplet at the instant it strikes the vertical surface. This direction is also the direction of the virtual string to be attached to the stain and then displayed by the computer. This procedure is repeated with a number of carefully chosen individual stains from the bloodstain pattern under investigation.

The result is a number of virtual strings emanating from the bloodstain pattern. The top view projection of the pattern of virtual strings is examined for convergent strings. Each separate convergent string pattern indicates a possible position for a source of blood droplets. The object of the virtual string analysis is to discover (1) how many blood-spilling events (sources) took place and (2) their location.

Figure 2.6 examines in detail a bloodstain which is the result of a blood droplet striking a vertical surface (the Y–Z plane) with a value for the directionality angle (γ) equal to 45°, i.e., the main axis of the stain makes an angle of 45° measured clockwise from the vertical. The impact angle alpha (α) has a value equal to 60°. The large arrow labeled V represents the speed and direction of the droplet at the instant of impact. The three smaller arrows labeled V_x, V_y, and V_z are the X,Y,Z components of the velocity vector V. These three components of V must add up to be equal to V and their directions must be pointing in the directions of their respective axes. Referring to

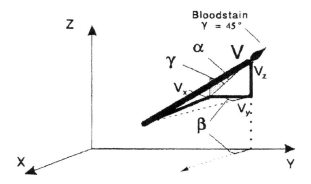

Figure 2.6 This stain is produced by a droplet striking the wall with $\gamma = 45°$ and $\alpha = 60°$. The virtual string for this stain projects onto the floor with $\beta = 67.8°$.

Figure 2.6, the arrows **V** and V_x originate at the same point. Then V_y is added to V_x by drawing V_y starting where V_x ends. V_z is added by drawing V_z starting where V_y ends. It is seen that the end of V_z coincides with the end of **V**. The vector sum of the three components of V is said to be equal to V. The important properties of these component vectors for this work are that (1) the ratios of the lengths of these three components determine the direction, in three dimensions, of the velocity V, and (2) the same ratios depend on the values of the two angles alpha and gamma. Given the values of alpha and gamma, one can compute the three components of V and then discover the direction of V. The details of how this is done is beyond the scope of this chapter.

Referring to Figure 2.6 again, we see a third angle defined with the label beta (β). This angle defines the direction of the projection of V (the virtual string) onto the floor. Thus, by knowing the value of the angle beta, the top view projection of the virtual string can be drawn. It can be shown that the value of beta is related to the values of alpha and gamma by the relationship

$$\tan(\beta) = \tan(\alpha)/\sin(\gamma)$$

Those interested in learning more about this relationship are referred to "Bloodstain Pattern Analysis with a Scientific Calculator" by A. L. Carter and E. J. Podworny, in *Journal of the Canadian Society of Forensic Science,* Vol. 24, No. 1, 1991 or *IABPA News,* Mar. 1991.

Part 2 — Actual Flight Paths Compared with Virtual Strings

In Part 2 we will consider some of the laws of projectile motion in air that are important for our study of blood droplets in flight. With a computer program called Tracks©[1,] we can simulate actual flight paths of droplets of varying sizes and speeds. These flight paths include the effects of air resistance, and, when the droplets impact with a vertical surface, the computer calculates the positions of the stains and the appropriate values for the impact angles α and the directionality angles γ.

The virtual strings defined by these values of α and γ do not contain experimental errors and therefore they all pass through a point above the source of the blood droplets. This allows one to simulate a bloodstain pattern on a vertical surface, observe the actual flight paths, and compare them with the virtual strings. The convergent pattern of the virtual strings can be related to the known position of the source of the blood droplets. We will see that the only unbiased view of the string pattern is from above, the bird's-eye view.

In Figure 2.7 we see the main screen of Tracks showing the flight paths of three droplets originating from a point 50 cm from the target wall, 100 cm above the floor, and 250 cm from the left wall. The target wall is the YZ plane which is marked off with a 50-cm grid. The INITIAL VALUES for DROP01 show that it has a volume of 5.0 µl (about 5 mg mass) and was launched with a speed of 800 cm/s (26.2 ft/s) with an elevation of 45° and a direction of 45° to the right.

The IMPACT VALUES show that the speed upon impact is 570.0 cm/s (18.7 ft/s). The loss in speed is due to air resistance and gravity. It hits the wall with a height of 161.9 cm and a horizontal position of 300.0 cm. The impact angle alpha is 34.9° and the directionality angle is 44.2°. On the left is an idealized image of the stain with the direction of 44.2° and a width and length ratio corresponding to an impact angle of 34.9°.

The flight paths, observed from the bird's-eye view, the side view, and the end view or camera view are shown on the right. The curvature of the flight paths due to gravity and air resistance can be seen in the side and end views. These views can be expanded to full-screen size.

Figure 2.8 shows the side view expanded to fill the screen. At the X position equal to 50 cm, a vertical line extends upward 100 cm. The top of this line is the launching point of the droplets. The three droplets fly through the air to strike the wall between 150 and 200 cm above the floor. The curvature of the flight paths is due to the action of gravity and air resistance forces during the flight. Also shown are the virtual strings. The direction of each virtual string has been computed to equal the direction of each droplet at the instant of impact.

There is no convergence of the strings to be seen from the side view of this pattern. On the contrary, in this case, there is a divergence of the strings.

---

[1]   Copyright 1992 by A. L. Carter and Carleton University. Tracks was created by the author to teach the physics of projectile motion and bloodstain formation to members of the Royal Canadian Mounted Police.

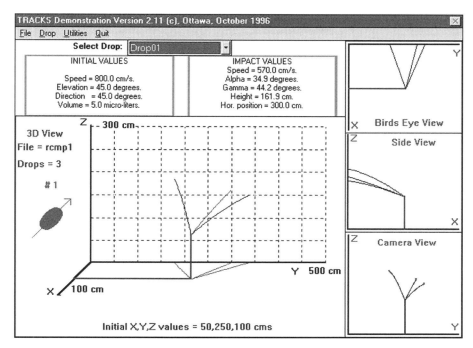

Figure 2.7 The main screen of the program Tracks. Three droplets are launched toward the wall with the 50-cm grid. The flight paths are computed with air resistance and gravity taken into account. The impact angles, directionality angles, impact speed, and position are computed for each stain.

A convergent pattern is rarely seen from the side view. Note that all the virtual strings pass above the launching point. The distance above the launching point will depend on the curvature of the corresponding flight path at the point of impact. The side view of the virtual string pattern is useful for determining a reasonable upper limit for the height of the source point above the floor. This is demonstrated below in Part 3 where we analyze a bloodstain pattern with the program BackTrack®[2]/Win.

Figure 2.9 shows the bird's-eye view expanded to full-screen size. It is important to realize that all flight paths viewed from above are straight lines. Therefore, in this case, they must converge to a common point. Here, it can be seen that the ideal strings, seen from this view, coincide with the flight paths and therefore have the same common point. This common point locates the launching point (the source of the blood droplets).

Thus, we see that the virtual strings that belong to stains from a common source, viewed from above, must converge toward the source position. This

---

[2] Registered trademark by A. L. Carter and Carleton University, 1992.

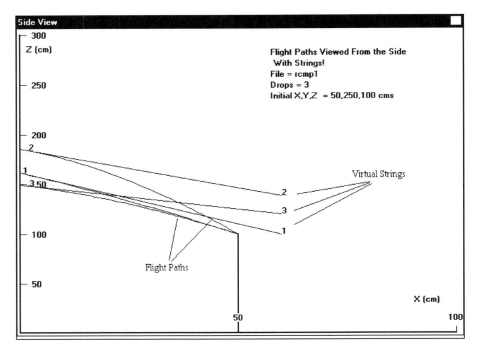

Figure 2.8 Side view showing the flight paths and the virtual strings.

is true regardless of the different sizes and different speeds of the various stains.

The convergence pattern, viewed from above, can be studied with precision only by means of a computer. In the author's opinion, this is the most important advantage that a computer offers to the bloodstain pattern analyst, in addition to the saving in time and effort.

Figure 2.10 shows the end view or camera view of the bloodstain pattern. This is the view of the bloodstain that would be captured by a photograph. Because this simple, three-droplet stain is a result of a computer simulation, the flight paths are known and can be seen projected onto the wall for comparison with the virtual strings. The positions of the three stains and their directionality angles gamma (γ) are equal to the computed values. The width and length of each idealized stain have the correct ratio to match the impact angle alpha (α); i.e., $\sin(\alpha) = W/L$.

All the virtual strings project back to the launching point, as they must. However, due to the curvature of the flight paths caused by gravity and air resistance, all the strings lie above the launching point. This is true for all stains resulting from the same event. Therefore, there will always be a converging string pattern of sorts appearing in the end view projection. However,

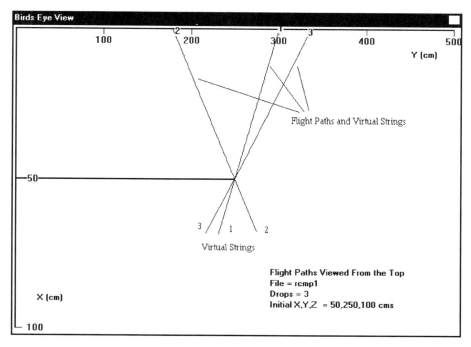

Figure 2.9 The top view of the flight paths and the virtual strings.

this convergence is a false convergence in the sense that it does not converge onto the position of the source of blood. This false convergence can be quite misleading; e.g., one cannot assume that the perpendicular to the wall at this false convergence passes through the location of the bloodletting event. One can only assume (1) that this false point of convergence is always higher than the true source point and (2) that it is horizontally displaced to the right or to the left by an unknown amount.

In Figure 2.10, the true source point is located at Y = 250 cm and Z = 100 cm. The false convergence point for the virtual strings is located at Y = 274 cm and Z = 133 cm, i.e., 33 cm above and 24 cm to the right of the true source point.

To summarize: when working with photographs of bloodstain patterns, it should be realized that, although the convergent pattern obtained by drawing lines through the individual stains may look impressive, the convergence point will always overestimate the height and will be horizontally displaced to the left or to the right by some unknown distance. Whenever possible, the analyst is advised to measure positions, widths, lengths, and gamma angles of the individual stains, directly at the crime scene or, later, from photographs of the bloodstains. Then, with a program like BackTrack/Win, study the top

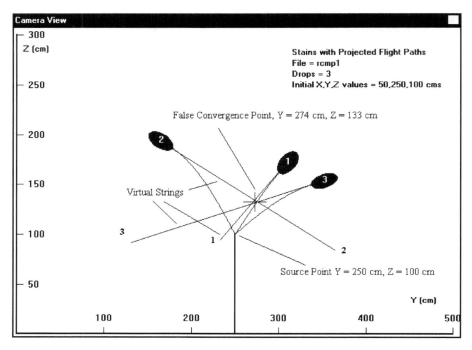

Figure 2.10   End view or camera view, showing the stains, the flight paths, and the virtual strings. The virtual strings do not converge onto the source point.

view of the virtual strings. The top view virtual strings must all point back toward their respective sources. Therefore, the bloodstains that have a common source will produce virtual strings with a convergent pattern. The point of convergence locates the horizontal position of the source.

Part 3 — The Virtual String Analysis of a Bloodstain Pattern Using BackTrack/Win

A bloodstain pattern was produced on a vertical surface in the laboratory[3] by striking a sharp blow to 15 ml of blood with a hammer. From the many stains on the wall, 12 were selected for this analysis. Figure 2.11 shows the data for these stains as displayed by BackTrack/Win with the VIEW DATA command. The measured values of the width, length, directionality angle gamma, and the coordinates X, Y, Z are entered into this spreadsheet. Each stain has a status value. In this example, all the stains reside on the main wall

---

[3]   This work was carried out in 1993 at the Central Forensic Laboratory, Ottawa, as part of a research contract for the Forensic Identification Research and Review Services of the Royal Canadian Mounted Police. The author was assisted by RCMP Sgt. Pat Laturnus.

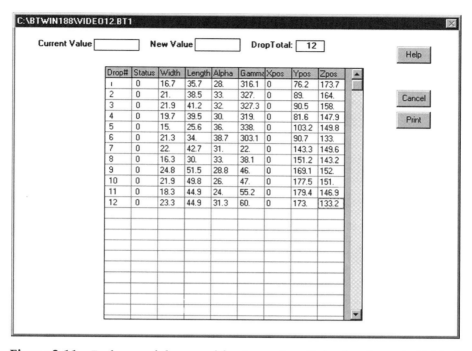

Figure 2.11 Each row of the spreadsheet contains all the data for an individual stain and the corresponding virtual string. These data can be entered via the keyboard and saved as a file on the hard disk.

and have a status value equal to 0 and an X value equal to 0. Bloodstains can occur on any of the four walls, the floor, the ceiling, and offsets to these surfaces, a total of 12 possible surfaces. The status value along with the X,Y,Z coordinates locates the position of each stain in the crime scene. The unit of measurement for the width and length of each stain is 0.1 millimeters. The data are entered into the appropriate cells of the spreadsheet. When the width and length is entered via the keyboard, the alpha angle is computed and updated automatically. Each row defines a stain and the virtual string for that stain. This data file can also be produced by BackTrack/Images,[4] which analyzes digital images of the stains. The digital images are single frames of a video recording of the bloodstain pattern.

Figure 2.12 shows the top view of the virtual strings that are defined for the 12 stains. The convergent pattern is clearly present. The cross marks the computed average of the intersections of the 12 virtual strings (AutoCPxy command). The X and Y coordinates of the convergence point as marked by the cross are CPx = 34.7 cm and CPy = 121.4 cm.

---

[4]   BackTrack/Images was created in 1993 along with a new procedure for blood spatter analysis that utilizes digital cameras or video camcorders.

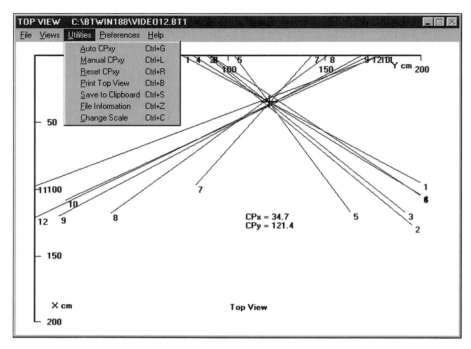

Figure 2.12 Shows the top view of the virtual strings that are defined for the 12 stains. The convergent pattern is clearly present. The cross marks the computed average of the intersections of the 12 virtual strings (AutoCPxy command). The X and Y coordinates of the convergence point as marked by the cross are CPx = 34.7 cm and CPy = 121.4 cm.

In order to obtain a reasonable estimate of the height (Z position) of the source of the blood, one must observe the side view of the 12 virtual strings and look for virtual strings belonging to fast, upward-moving blood droplets. A procedure called Manual CPz enables one to draw a box around such strings and mark the intersections of these strings with the CPx position. The CPx position is indicated in the side view by a vertical line. Figure 2.13 shows the result of such an analysis. The height of the source of the blow calculates to be 104.8 cm. The true height is 100 cm.

Figure 2.14 shows an end view of the projections of the virtual strings. Sometimes an investigator's only evidence is a photograph of lines drawn on the pattern showing the direction of the individual stains. The figure shown here represents such a photograph. It is noted that a fairly acceptable convergence is seen which could be used to estimate the source point. However, by studying the pattern with regard to the white cross marking the location of the source point, one can see that the center of the intersections of the virtual line projections does not quite agree with the source point that was

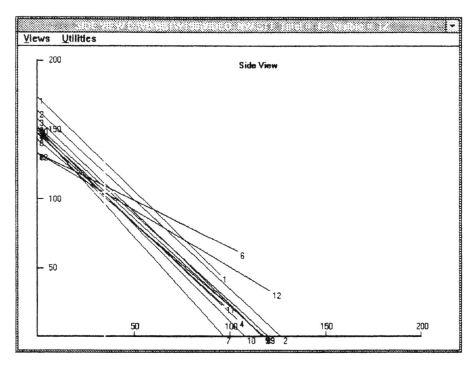

Figure 2.13 Shows the side view of the virtual strings. An estimate of the height of the source of the blood can usually be estimated by computing the average intersection of virtual strings belonging to fast, upward-moving blood droplets with the CPx line. These droplets have flat trajectories with stringlike properties.

analyzed starting with the top view. The investigator should be aware of the possible bias that can exist in the end view projections of the virtual strings or photographs of line patterns.

This concludes the examination of the traditional string method and its adaptation for use with a computer. The virtual string analysis of 12 stains are used as an example for this discussion. The true values of CPx, CPy, and CPz are 30, 124, and 100 cm, respectively, compared with the analyzed values of 34.7, 121.4, and 104.8 cm, respectively.

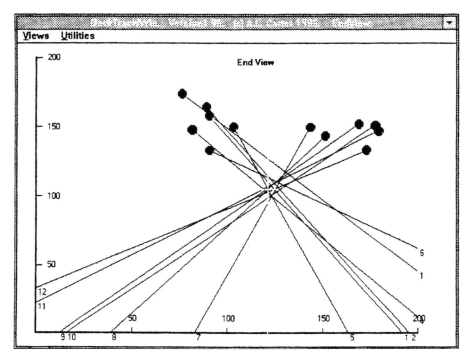

Figure 2.14   The XY projection of the virtual string pattern, often called the camera view.

Utilizing Bloodstains in Accident Reconstruction

3

WILLIAM C. FISCHER

Contents

Introduction

Blood is a fluid commonly associated with vehicular collisions. Reconstruction techniques can be augmented by the interpretation of bloodstain evidence to resolve and/or confirm such significant issues as

1. Seatbelt usage
2. Centerline issues
3. Accident vs. homicide
4. Occupant dynamics
5. Pedestrian dynamics
6. Principal direction of force
7. Mechanism of injury
8. Questioned driver identification
9. Conscious pain and suffering

Relative Motion

The theories and methods of bloodstain evidence interpretation have, for the most part, originated in the context of a crime scene where the frame of reference is static; i.e., the floor, ceiling, and walls do not move. It is the geometry of the bloodstain patterns on static surfaces that allows the analyst to infer the dynamic motions of persons and objects within that fixed frame. In accident reconstruction, roadways, guide rails, poles, signs, etc. remain fixed. Therefore, the relative motion of pedestrians struck by motor vehicles, and motions of occupants separated from motor vehicles during collision, may also be inferred from bloodstains appearing on the fixed objects in the surrounding environment, using traditional stringing methods to determine the three-dimensional area of origin.

However, for bloodstains which appear both within and on the vehicle, two other variables must be factored:

- Relative motion between blood source and vehicle and
- Laminar flow.

Relative motion between occupant and vehicle is itself dependent upon other variables, including

- Centered vs. eccentric collisions
- Principal direction of force
- Multiple impacts
- Occupant position within the vehicle
- Restrained vs. unrestrained occupant

Laminar flow results from the adhesion of air molecules to the surface of the car. Molecules in direct contact with the surface do not move relative to the vehicle, while the air several molecular layers above the surface moves at the relative velocity of the vehicle. This phenomenon will significantly distort bloodstain geometries on vehicles moving at normal highway speeds. The result is that bloodstains on striking vehicles which result from pedestrian impacts may be skewed in the direction of relative motion. A further source of distortion may result from the partial vacuum created by the trailing vortex of many square-backed vehicles. Thus, attempting to determine the area of origin from outside the car using traditional techniques may lead to significant error.

Pattern Recognition

Several types of bloodstain patterns commonly associated with vehicle collisions may be differentiated by their unique geometries. Understanding the

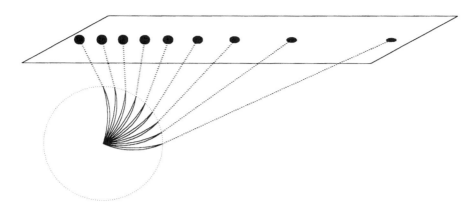

Figure 3.1

genesis of these characteristic patterns permits inferences to be drawn about the dynamic events which created them.

1. Arterial spurting patterns result when an artery is breached near the surface of the skin. The patterns may show the rise and fall of systolic rhythm. Several such patterns may be found superimposed, or closely spaced. A progressive decrease in the amplitude of the pattern corresponds with a pressure drop resulting from catastrophic blood loss.

2. Expirated patterns result from blood forcefully expelled from the mouth, nose, or a wound opening connected to the airway. If the lung itself is injured, the blood may be mixed with air, such that characteristic bloody bubbles are deposited on surrounding surfaces. Such stain patterns are commonly associated with broken ribs and flailed chest injuries, resulting from contact with the steering wheel in frontal impacts. Expirated stain patterns have been found wheezed onto the interior of window glass that has been rolled down during rescue efforts.

3. Cast-off patterns result when blood is released from the surface of an object that is experiencing a change in its motion. Release occurs when the acceleration force acting on a blood mass exceeds the restraining force of surface adhesion. When the change in velocity is angular, the resulting pattern is characterized by a linear dispersion of distinctly separate stains whose individual length-to-width ratios increase in the direction of motion (Figure 3.1). This type of pattern, often associated with whiplash subsequent to a head injury, is commonly found on the headliner. Coffee, cola, and other beverage stains which may be found on the headliner also give clues as to occupant motion during the collision sequence.

4. Dripped patterns result when a bleeding occupant moves about in, gets out of, or is removed from a motionless vehicle. Dripped blood may be conclusive in determining whether or not the occupant was wearing a restraint at the time of bloodshed. If inspection of the seat belt and shoulder harness webbing show drip patterns on those portions which are exposed *only* when pulled from the retractor, it is a significant indication that the restraint was in use. This finding may be especially significant in low-speed collisions which do not leave other indicia, such as loading marks on the webbing or "D" ring. On the other hand, a retracted seat belt with bloodstains of any pattern type extending only to the retractor aperture indicates that the occupant was not wearing the restraint. This is true regardless of whose blood may be on any given piece of webbing. This is especially true when an occupant seat exhibits a void, or shadow pattern, created when blood is dripped onto the entire seat surface except where the occupant's body has protected it from exposure.

5. Patterns of blood dripped into blood occur when an injured occupant remains relatively motionless within a vehicle. Such patterns may clearly indicate the final position of an unconscious or disabled occupant within the vehicle after impact.

6. Splashed blood patterns result from the release of substantial quantities of pooled blood. These are usually associated with an already bleeding and exposed wound site being forcefully decelerated. The pattern is usually elliptical. The leading edge is often feathered in the direction of motion. An intermittent series of these stains is sometimes observed on the roadway surface when an injured pedestrian rolls and tumbles to final rest position. Splashed blood patterns are usually found on the road surface or low to the ground on vertical faces, such as on curbing. They are occasionally found on guide rails.

7. Slide patterns occur when the initial velocity of a bleeding body sliding on asphalt causes the first few contact stains to appear as "drag marks." The length of the stain is much greater than its width. As the body slows with each successive road contact, the width-to-length ratio of the stains tends to increase in the direction of motion. The location of splashed blood or slide patterns may indicate the first point at which a pedestrian contacted the ground after having disengaged from the vehicle. This establishes the "throw distance," which is a critical variable in a number of different pedestrian impact speed equations.

8. Transfer patterns occur when an already bloody object comes in contact with another surface. A transfer pattern frequently mirrors the shape of the object which makes it. Fingerprints in blood and other transfer patterns may lead the investigator to discriminate between accident and homicide. Bloody fingerprints have also been used to differentiate the identity of the driver successfully. Placement of the print is, of course, critical to the analysis. Identifying prints may be found on the rim of the steering wheel or on the inboard seat belt buckle in such an attitude that it could be made only by one sitting in the driver's seat.

9. *Runoff patterns* are seen when a bleeding body comes to rest on a sloped surface. Such patterns made by oil, ethylene glycol, hydraulic or brake fluid have long been used to establish the final rest position of vehicles. Similar patterns in blood establish the final rest position of a pedestrian or "ejected" occupant. Large quantities of blood that have soaked into the asphalt may appear very similar to an oil stain several days after a collision.

10. *Rising bloodstain patterns* can sometimes be observed on the windshield of a car involved in a pedestrian impact. The speed required to make blood flow "up" a windshield is dependent upon the slope of the windshield, the speed of the car, and any surface contaminants on the windshield. Thus, the minimum speed at impact may be determined by experimenting with a similar vehicle. This is a phenomenon not observed at static crime scenes. The windshield angle can be measured with an inclinometer or researched in proprietary databases when the vehicle is no longer available.

11. *Void or shadow patterns* occur when the blood is prevented from reaching a distant surface due to an intervening object. For example, voids are often seen when a bleeding occupant's legs cover portions of the seat over which the occupant is dripping blood. Rearview mirrors and other objects prevent blood from reaching the interior of the windshield. Thus, the void may also assist in determining the direction from which the blood came. Voids and shadows may also establish the position and identity of an object which has been moved before the scene or vehicles are documented. A break in a stain pattern on one object may permit the repositioning of another object on which the stain pattern continues.

Case Examples

Case 1 — Expired Blood

Figure 3.2 shows the deceased driver sitting behind his steering wheel. Spots of expired blood can be seen on the knuckles of his right hand. The black beam in front of his face is the left frame rail of a brick truck which had stopped in the road directly in line with a low afternoon sun which was skirting in and out of passing cloud cover. A significant issue at trial was

Figure 3.2

whether or not the victim experienced conscious pain and suffering. Medical testimony by the defense indicated that the brain stem had been transected, causing immediate death. Testimony that the expired bloodstains belied such a conclusion was denied on the basis of foundation. The case was taken on appeal. The appellate court found that there was indeed sufficient basis to permit bloodstain testimony on the issue of pain and suffering, and a second trial was scheduled. Between the first and second trials an eyewitness to the event was located, who later testified that he had heard the driver moan, "Help me!"

Case 2 — Hit and Run

An early morning collision with a retaining wall left the operator of a Chevrolet Prism dead in the eastbound driving lane about 45 ft from his car. He was alone and unrestrained. He had a blood alcohol content of 0.15% . There were tire imprints across his torso, and his shirt was up around his nipple line. A door on the car was open. No scene photographs were taken by police, but one of the responding patrolmen did take excellent field measurements of significant items at the scene, including two bloodstains on the road. "There was no blood in the vehicle but there was an extensive amount on the pavement." The collision was unwitnessed. A detective opined that the deceased may have been both thrown from and run over by his own vehicle. Polaroid photos of the three different types of tires on the car were sent to the state police laboratory for comparison with another Polaroid of the diffuse tire imprints on the torso. The laboratory technician concluded that "any one of the tires 'could' have made the tracks on the body." Due to the conclusions reached by the police investigation, the insurance company refused to pay benefits to the widow on the premise that the driver had caused his own death due to intoxication.

The police measurements were plotted to produce Figure 3.3. Note that the bloodstains are in line with each other, and in line with the final rest position of the body. A line extended back through the bloodstains does not intersect the path of the car prior to its colliding with the retaining wall. Thus, there were no deceleration forces which could have "ejected" the driver in line with the bloodstains. Given the open door of the car, the alignment of the stains with the body, the position of the shoe, the tire marks on the torso, and the shirt pulled up around the nipples, it is apparent that the driver got out of the car after it stopped, and was then run over by another vehicle in the eastbound passing lane.

Case 3 — Ejection/Cast-Off Blood

Airborne and *ejection* are two terms commonly misused when applied to motor vehicle collisions. Air cannot bear the weight of a car; cars merely fall. Even the "spoilers" found on supermodified racing cars are inverted to create a greater down-force. Ejection seats only appear in James Bond movies. What does occur in collisions is that unrestrained occupants will tend to maintain their original speed and direction (inertia), while the car in which they ride changes its speed and or direction. Thus, the occupant becomes separated from the vehicle when two events occur simultaneously:

1. The vehicle experiences a significant change in acceleration (usually due to impact).
2. The occupant's velocity vector is aligned with an exit portal.

In the nearly right-angle intersection collision illustrated in Figure 3.4, a northbound Monte Carlo was struck in the right front corner. Post-impact, the car spun counterclockwise toward the northwest corner, striking an 8-in. curb, and coming to rest facing east. The right front door was opened during disengagement from the initial impact. All other doors and windows remained intact. The deceased driver, the sole occupant, had been unrestrained and was found on the ground alongside the left rear corner of his car. He had sustained a massive open head wound with partial brain evisceration. Blood, hair, and small pieces of brain tissue were found spattered

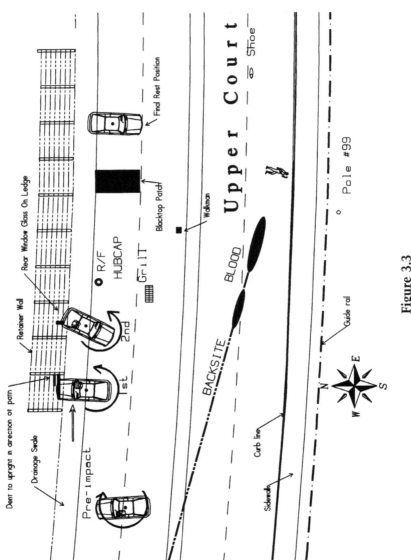

Figure 3.3

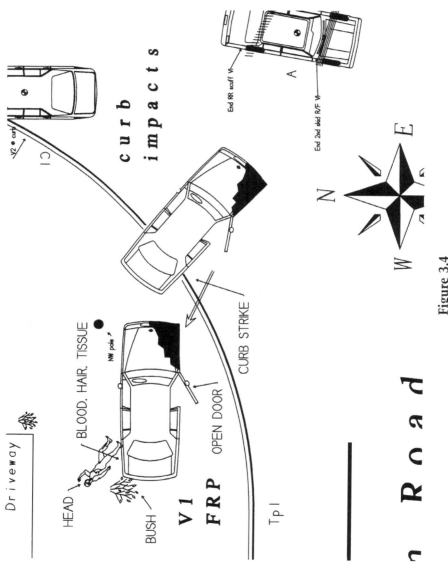

Figure 3.4

Figure 3.5

over the right rear corner. Close inspection of at-scene photographs showed that the bloodstains were nearly round, indicating an impact perpendicular to the fender surface.

The issue to be determined: since the driver had obviously been separated through the right front door, how did the blood, brain, and hair get deposited on the left rear fender? The answer lay in the bush next to the left rear corner of the car. The driver came out through the open passenger door when the car, traveling rearward, struck the high face curb with the left rear tire. This deceleration effectively "ejected" the driver out the door and through the bush. His massive open head wound deposited blood and brain tissue on the stiff, but flexible branches. The car followed the driver to final rest position. The car crashing into the bush caused cast-off spatters from the branches to the fender.

Case 4 — Questioned Driver

Both occupants were intoxicated when a pickup truck struck a pole at the right front corner (Figures 3.5 and 3.6). The passenger door was jammed shut by damage. The driver's door partly opened with force. Both occupants got out of the driver's door prior to the arrival of police. Neither suffered apparent injury. Each denied being the driver. An exhaustive search of the truck's interior was made for trace evidence on the following day.

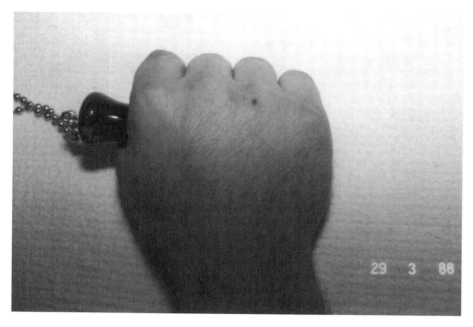

Figure 3.6

One small elliptical bloodstain was found on the interior of the driver's side door. It was about halfway back from the jamb, near the center of a padded bolster just below the window. The stain was lifted with tape and transferred to a 3" × 5" card. When both occupants were examined, one was found to have a small fresh scab between the third and fourth knuckle on the right hand. The scab was a mirror impression of the lifted stain. At impact with the pole, the back of the driver's hand was nicked by the keys hanging from the ignition switch. When confronted with the evidence, the driver confessed.

Case 5 — Pedestrian Dynamics — Final Rest Position

This nighttime collision illustrated in Figures 3.7 and 3.8 resulted when a northbound pedestrian was struck 15 ft from the curb line by an eastbound sedan. Fatal injuries included "a broken pelvis, right arm and shoulder and severe head injuries." The driver was arrested for speed too fast for conditions. Police took measurements of precollision skid marks. They did not, however, locate the final rest position of the victim.

Figure 3.7 shows the bloodstains left by the victim as she rolled off the right side of the car and struck the ground. The slide mark begins at the rear bumper of the car. The pooled blood at the end of the slide mark establishes the final rest position of the victim's head. Runoff from the pool is due to the crown of the road. Splashed blood can be seen on the front passenger

Figure 3.7

Figure 3.8

Figure 3.9

door trim strip, which establishes the path of the victim off the car. Figure 3.8 shows the front of the car. Two dents located on the right side of the hood, two windshield impacts, hair located on the lower windshield guard, the injury pattern to the victim, and the splashed blood on the front passenger door detailed the dynamics of the pedestrian's movements. She was turning clockwise and attempting to head back to the curb when struck.

The point of impact was established by a spreading of the right front tire skid. The beginning of the bloody slide mark, as measured from the point of impact, determined the throw distance. Measurements from the car itself provided the drop height. As a result of both the precollision skid marks and the bloodstain patterns, the speed of the car could be accurately estimated.

Case 6 — Seatbelt Issue

A right front collision to the Trans Am shown in Figure 3.9 caused the unbelted driver to pitch forward and to the right. A helmet-shaped depression in the underside of the "T" top bar showed where his head stopped after a fatal "elevator ride" on top of the deploying air bag. Transfer and drip patterns on the webbing of the retracted, door-mounted restraint are only found on those portions of the webbing exposed when the belt is retracted. It is only when the belt is retracted that the drip patterns are vertical. Drips and cast-off patterns can also be seen on the window bolster and interior door panel.

Presumptive Testing for Blood

4

T. PAULETTE SUTTON

Contents

0-8493-8108-8/99/$0.00+$.50

Introduction

Conventional forensic serology utilizes a two-step analytical approach. The first step that must be taken is the identification of the body fluid making up the unknown or questioned stain. Only after the identity of the body fluid has been confirmed scientifically are tests undertaken which will potentially link a body fluid stain to an individual, such as ABO typing, polymorphic protein analysis, and/or DNA typing. In general terms, the steps in the identification of blood are (1) visual examination, (2) presumptive testing, (3) confirmation testing, (4) species identification, and (5) individualization testing.

In situations where the bloodstains in question are wet or very fresh, a visual examination is certainly simplified. In actual practice, though, bloodstains will often be diluted, aged, or degraded to the point that their appearance is no longer characteristic or even predictable. Of the steps listed above, only the visual examination and the presumptive testing lend themselves to use outside of the laboratory setting. By combining the visual examination and the presumptive testing results, the forensic scientist has a much better chance of collecting stains which will later be confirmed as being blood.

Presumptive Tests for Blood

There are several presumptive, or screening, tests for blood available. Historically, benzidine was probably one of the most widely used catalytic screening tests for blood since its introduction in 1904 by Rudolf and Oscar Adler.[1] Since benzidine has subsequently been identified as a carcinogen,[2] its use as a presumptive testing reagent has been largely discontinued. The tetramethylbenzidine[1] and o-tolidine[3] presumptive testing methods for blood also require the use of carcinogenic chemicals. At the present time, the phenolphthalein, leucomalachite green, and luminol presumptive tests for blood continue to enjoy widespread use.

Presumptive Test Mechanism

The benzidine, tetramethylbenzidine, o-tolidine, phenolphthalein, leucomalachite green, and luminol presumptive tests for blood are classified as catalytic tests. These tests are based upon the peroxidase-like activity of hemoglobin and its derivatives. In the living cell, peroxidase functions to remove hydrogen peroxide which could prove toxic to the cell.

$$2\,H_2O_2 \xrightarrow[\text{Catalase}]{\text{in the presence of}} 2\,H_2O \;+\; 2\,O_2$$

Enzymes that catalyze the peroxide-mediated oxidation of organic compounds *in vivo* are called peroxidases. By the definition that an enzyme is a protein with catalytic functions, hemoglobin cannot be classified as an enzyme, and, therefore, it cannot be called a peroxidase.[7] Because of this, whenever hemoglobin or its other derivatives exhibit this catalytic property, they are said to have "peroxidase-like activity."

The general peroxidase reaction is

AH$_2$ (the donor) + ROOH (the peroxide) → A + ROH + H$_2$O

Hydrogen peroxide (H_2O_2) is commonly employed as the peroxide in the presumptive tests for blood, and the AH_2 is a reduced, colorless substrate which will yield a colored product A when it is oxidized.

The basic reaction for the presumptive tests for blood is

$$H_2O_2 \xrightarrow[\text{Hydroxyls seeking } H_2]{\substack{\text{in the presence}\\ \text{of Heme}}} 2\,[OH^-]$$

$$\underset{\substack{\text{Colorless}\\\text{Reagent}}}{AH_2} + 2\,[OH^-] \longrightarrow \underset{\substack{\text{Colored}\\\text{Product}}}{A} \;+\; 2\,H_2O$$

Benzidine Test

As previously discussed, benzidine is a recognized carcinogen. It should be employed only in conjunction with appropriate safety and health precautions. The substitution of an alternative presumptive test is strongly recommended.

Benzidine Test Reagent, Single Stage

Reagent Preparation

Solution 1:

1. Prepare a saturated solution of benzidine, free base in 2 ml of glacial acetic acid.
2. Add 2 ml of 3% hydrogen peroxide.
3. Prepare reagent fresh for each use.[4]

Method of Use

1. Elute a small sample of unknown stain onto a cotton-tipped swab or filter paper moistened with distilled water.
2. Add 1 to 2 drops of benzidine, single-stage reagent.
3. Observe for deep blue color formation (positive reaction) within 10 s.[4]

Benzidine Test Reagent, Two Stage

Reagent Preparation

Solution 1:

1. Dissolve 0.25 g of benzidine, free base in 175 ml of absolute ethanol.
2. Add 5–10 drops (250 to 500 µl) of glacial acetic acid.
3. Store refrigerated in amber bottle.

Solution 2:

1. Prepare a 3% solution of hydrogen peroxide in a separate bottle.[5]

Method of Use

1. Elute a small sample of unknown stain onto a cotton-tipped swab moistened with distilled water.
2. Add 1–2 drops of benzidine reagent.

3. Observe for any color changes. Color changes at this step would indicate the possible presence of oxidative contaminants.
4. Add 1–2 drops of 3% hydrogen peroxide.
5. Observe for deep blue color formation (positive reaction) within 30 s.[5]

Interpretation

The rapid development of a deep blue color formation is considered a positive benzidine test. A lack of color change, or the formation of a dirty blue to brown color after 1 to 2 min is a negative benzidine test.[5] With the two-stage benzidine test, color changes which occur prior to the addition of hydrogen peroxide indicate the possibility that the unknown contains oxidative contaminants which would be considered a "false positive." Reported sensitivity ranges for the benzidine screening test range from 1:100[5] to 1:300,000 to 500,000.[4]

o-Tolidine Test

Note: o-Tolidine may be carcinogenic. Proper safety and health precautions should be taken if o-tolidine is used as a reagent in the screening test for blood. Substitute methods are recommended.

Reagent Preparation

Solution 1:

1. Add 1.6 g of o-tolidine base to 40 ml of absolute ethanol.
2. Add 30 ml of glacial acetic acid.
3. Add 30 ml of distilled water.
4. Store refrigerated.

Solution 2:

1. Prepare a 3% solution of hydrogen peroxide.

Method of Use

1. Elute a small sample of unknown stain onto a cotton-tipped swab or filter paper moistened with distilled water.
2. Add 1 to 2 drops of o-tolidine reagent.
3. Observe for any color changes. Color changes at this step would indicate the possible presence of oxidative contaminants.
4. Add 1 to 2 drops of 3% hydrogen peroxide.
5. Observe for deep blue color formation (positive reaction) within 10 s.

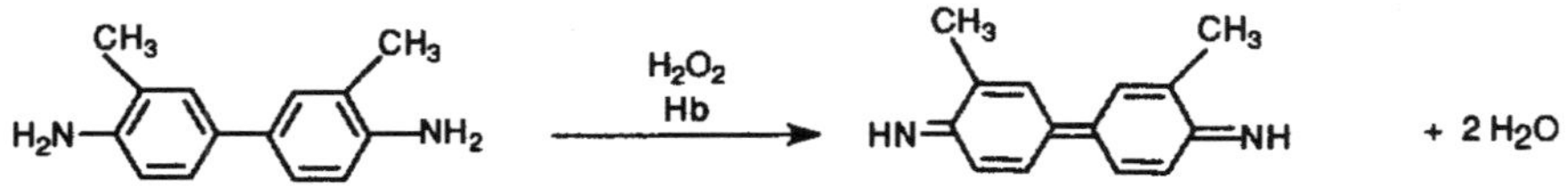

Figure 4.1

Interpretation

The rapid development of a deep blue color is considered a positive *o*-tolidine test (Figure 4.1). Any color changes which occur prior to the addition of hydrogen peroxide indicate the possibility of oxidative contaminants and would be considered a "false positive." This color should develop within 10 s. Reported sensitivity ranges for the ortho-tolidine test are similar to those of benzidine.[4]

Hemastix® Test

Hemastix® are plastic reagent strips manufactured by Ames (Miles, Inc., Diagnostic Division, Elkhart, IN). In the clinical laboratory, these strips are utilized for the detection of occult blood in urine. They are used as a presumptive test for blood in forensic science. The test is based upon the peroxidase-like activity of hemoglobin that catalyzes the reaction of diisopropylbenzene dihydroperoxide and 3,3′,5,5′,tetramethylbenzidine. The resulting color change is from orange to green/blue.

Method of Use:

1. Elute a small sample of unknown stain onto a cotton-tipped swab or filter paper moistened with distilled water.
2. Press reagent area of Hemastix® strip onto swab or filter paper.
3. Observe for rapidly developing deep blue-green color formation (positive reaction) within 10 s.

Leucomalachite Green Test

Single Stage

Reagent Preparation

Reagent 1 (Sodium Perborate:Leucomalachite Green Mixture):

1. Thoroughly mix 0.32 g of sodium perborate and 0.1 g of leucomalachite green using a mortar and pestle.
2. If desired, aliquot the sodium perborate:leucomalachite green mixture into quantities desired for later use. (A convenient quantity of test reagent is 0.14 g of the sodium perborate:leucomalachite green mixture added to 4 ml of the acetic acid:water mixture.)
3. Store at room temperature.

Reagent 2 (Acetic Acid:Water):

1. Slowly add 8 ml of glacial acetic acid to 4 ml of distilled water.

Working Reagent:

1. Pipet 4 ml of Reagent 2 (acetic acid:water) in reagent bottle.
2. Add 0.14 g of Reagent 1 (sodium perborate:leucomalachite green mixture).
3. Prepare working reagent fresh daily.

Method of Use

1. Elute a small sample of unknown stain onto a cotton-tipped swab or filter paper moistened with distilled water.
2. Add 1 to 2 drops of working reagent.
3. Observe for rapidly developing deep blue-green color formation (positive reaction) within 10 s.

Two Stage
Reagent Preparation

Reagent 1:

1. Slowly add 8 ml of glacial acetic acid to 4 ml of distilled water.
2. Pipet 10 ml of the acetic acid:water dilution prepared in step 1 in a reagent bottle.
3. Add 10 mg of leucomalachite green.
4. Prepare fresh daily.

Reagent 2:

1. Prepare a 3% solution of hydrogen peroxide.

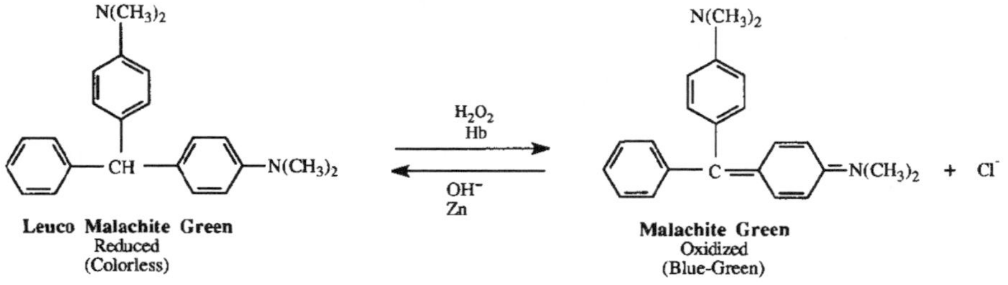

Figure 4.2

Method of Use

1. Elute a small sample of unknown stain onto a cotton-tipped swab or filter paper moistened with distilled water.
2. Add 1 to 2 drops of Reagent 1 (leucomalachite green).
3. Observe for any color changes. Color changes at this step would indicate the possible presence of oxidative contaminants.
4. Add 1 to 2 drops of Reagent 2 (3% hydrogen peroxide).
5. Observe for deep blue-green color formation (positive reaction) within 10 s.

Interpretation

The development of a deep blue-green color within 10 s after reagent addition is considered a positive leucomalachite green screening test (Figure 4.2). With the two-stage method, a color change which occurs prior to the addition of the hydrogen peroxide may indicate a "false positive" due to the presence of oxidative contaminants. The sensitivity of the leucomalachite test is approximately 1 part in 100,000.[4]

Phenolphthalein Test

Reagent Preparation

Stock Phenolphthalein Reagent:

1. Using a round bottom boiling flask, combine:
   2.0 g of phenolphthalein
   20 g of potassium hydroxide (or sodium hydroxide)
   20 g of powdered zinc
   100 ml of distilled water

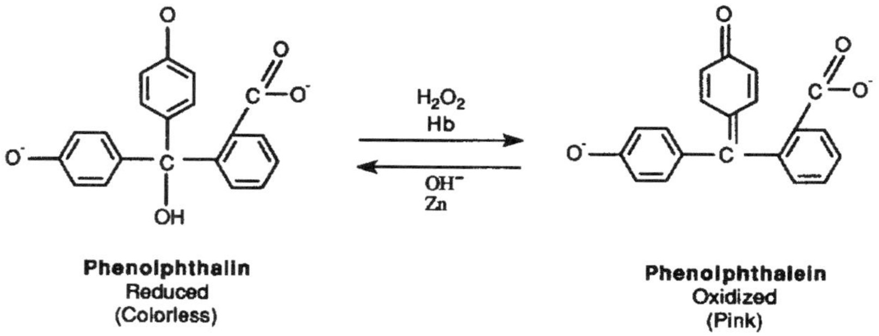

Phenolphthalin
Reduced
(Colorless)

Phenolphthalein
Oxidized
(Pink)

Figure 4.3

2. Reflux until the phenolphthalein solution has been reduced to phenolphthalein and the solution becomes colorless (2 to 4 h).
3. Add an excess of powdered zinc to the stock solution prior to storage. Store refrigerated in an amber bottle.

Working Phenolphthalein Solution:

1. In an amber reagent bottle, combine
   20 ml of phenolphthalein stock solution
   80 ml of absolute ethanol
2. Store refrigerated.

A solution of 3% hydrogen peroxide should be stored separately in a dropper bottle.

Method of Use

Apply 1 to 2 drops of the working phenolphthalein reagent to the swabs or filter paper containing the unknown samples. Observe for color reaction developing within 30 s of the addition of phenolphthalein reagent only. Add 1 to 2 drops of 3% hydrogen peroxide solution. The rapid development of a bright pink color is a positive test (Figure 4.3). The sensitivity of the phenolphthalein test is approximately 1 part in 5 million.

Luminol Test

Luminol is a well-known chemiluminescent compound and is used as a presumptive, catalytic test for the presence of blood utilizing the peroxidase-like activity of heme for the production of light as an end product rather than a true color reaction.

Reagent Preparation

A mixture of 0.5 g of luminol (3-aminophthalhydrazide) and 25 g of sodium carbonate is prepared and stored. A mixture of 3.5 g of sodium perborate in 500 ml of distilled water is prepared fresh as needed. At the time of use the luminol/sodium carbonate mixture and sodium perborate solution are mixed together for the working solution.

Method of Use

With the use of a spraying device, luminol reagent is applied on objects or areas containing traces of suspected bloodstains. A bluish white luminescence or light production on the suspected area is a positive test. The luminescence must be observed in the dark. Luminol reagent is best utilized for the detection of traces of blood that are not readily observable at crime scenes such as light tracking of blood on dark surfaces, cracks and crevices in floors, washed areas, and plumbing traps. The patterns of blood traces resolved by the luminol test may be as important as the detection of the blood itself. The patterns of luminescence can be photographed or videotaped for permanent documentation. Successful photography and videotaping have been accomplished with the attachment of night vision devices to the cameras. The luminol test is nondestructive and does not interfere with confirmatory or subsequent serological tests of the blood.

The sensitivity of the luminol test is approximately as high as 1 part in 5 million. Aged and decomposed blood reacts better with luminol than do fresher bloodstains. Sensitivity of the luminol test to trace quantities of fresher blood may be enhanced by prior spraying of the suspected area with 2% hydrochloric acid.

Sensitivity of Presumptive Tests for Blood

Screening tests for blood are so sensitive that a negative test can readily be interpreted as proof that no blood is present within detectable limits. This can, of course, mean that the stain has been effectively diluted past the point of detection — such as might be the case with cleanup attempts. The amount of dilution required in order to dilute a stain past the point of detection is substantial. For instance, a single drop of blood (50 µl) diluted in 4 gallons of water could still yield a positive screening test for blood with most methods commonly in use. In practical terms, this means that efforts to clean bloodstains must be extremely effective in order to remove or dilute the stains past the point of detection. Since most violent crimes cause much larger amounts of bloodshed, a large amount of diluting agent would be required to eliminate the detection of blood by screening tests.

Detection of Traces of Blood

The extreme sensitivity of screening tests makes it easy to imagine that blood-stains which are not visible to the naked eye could still be detected by the screening test. From a practical standpoint, dilutions of freshly collected, packed red blood cells prepared in distilled water no longer show visible indications of the presence of blood after dilution of 1:32,768 (i.e., there was no visible difference between the diluted red cells and a comparison tube of distilled water). By using the phenolphthalein screening test, though, blood can be detected in a dilution of 1:1,048,576. This represents a 32-fold increase between the screening test's ability to detect blood and the ability of the human eye to visualize blood.

How Much Unknown Needs to Be Tested?

Negative screening tests from stains which visually appear to be blood can leave the forensic scientist wondering if enough of the unknown stain was eluted onto the test substrate to give a valid result. Forensic scientists are frugal, to say the least, with the stains available for study. The less of a stain which must be eluted and tested to obtain valid results, the more stain will remain for subsequent definitive testing. To this end, a study was undertaken basically to answer the question "How much is enough?"

Doubling dilutions of freshly collected, packed red blood cells were prepared in distilled water. Then, 10, 25, and 50 µl of each dilution was tested using the phenolphthalein one-step; phenolphthalein three-step; leucomalachite green; and Hemastix® screening tests for blood. The 10 µl aliquot would closely simulate the situation where only very tiny amounts of a questioned stain can be tested. A 25 µl aliquot would simulate situations where elution of a questioned stain is minimal but not extremely limited.

No significant increase in sensitivity was seen with the addition of an increased amount of blood dilutions with the phenolphthalein or leucomalachite green tests. In situations where it is necessary to use only very small amounts of eluate, the phenolphthalein and leucomalachite green screening tests will be just as effective as they are in situations where large amounts of stains are available for testing.

The Hemastix® screening test did demonstrate an increase in sensitivity between the addition of 10 and 25 µl of known blood dilutions. Similar increases in sensitivity were not seen when the aliquot was increased from 25 to 50 µl. These results would indicate that the sensitivity of the Hemastix® might be altered in situations where only very small amounts of unknown can be tested. In other words, if the stain is very small and appears to be diluted, more stain will need to tested in order to achieve the expected sensitivity using Hemastix®. In most routine situations, though, even very small amounts of eluate will give essentially the same degree of sensitivity with the Hemastix® screening test.

Hemastix® Screening Test

Dilution	Amount tested		
	10 µl	25 µl	50 µl
1:128	3+		
1:256	3+		
1:512	3+		
1:1024	3+		
1:2048	3+		
1:4096	3+		
1:8192	2+	2+	
1:16,384	2+	2+	2+
1:32,768	1+	2+	2+
1:65,536	Trace	2+	2+
1:131,072	—	2+	2+
1:262, 144	—	2+	1+
1:524,288	—	1+	1+
1:1,048,576	—	Trace	Trace
1:2,097,152	—	Trace	Trace
1:4,194,304	—	—	—
1:8,388,608	—	—	—
1:16,777,216	—	—	—

False Positives

Substances other than blood may contain oxidants which can cause a positive reaction with the presumptive tests for blood in current usage. Since the reaction is driven by the presence of an oxidant, a positive color reaction is not actually a false positive. The use of the term *false positive* implies only that a positive reaction has occurred, **and** that the positive reaction has been caused by a substance other than blood.

In regards to body fluids other than blood causing a positive screening test for blood, suffice it to say that these tests do not definitely identify the body fluid as being or containing blood. They are only reliable to the point that they identify the presence of peroxidase or peroxidase-like activity. Perhaps it is also worthy of mention to note that body fluids from animals other than humans may cause identical reactions with the screening tests for blood. Other, more definitive tests must be conducted to identify the fluid causing the positive reaction and to determine the species of origin for the body fluid.

From a forensic standpoint, there is much more concern for reactions which are caused by a substance which is not a body fluid at all. Typical sources of such "false positives" are plant peroxidases and chemical oxidants. Plant peroxidases and chemical oxidants have the potential to be present in many areas where screening tests are applied at crime scenes or upon items of evidence. There are many and varied references to such false positive presumptive test reactions. A research project conducted in our laboratory sought to identify plant or chemical substances which might be more commonly encountered would cause a false positive screening test for blood. The results of this research project are provided in hopes that they will aid the practicing forensic scientist and that they will provide the basis for a prudent and cautious interpretation of these test reactions.

Positive and negative controls should be utilized during the performance of all presumptive tests. A positive test with a control of known human blood ensures that the reagents are working properly and the correct color reaction is being produced. A negative test reaction should be obtained with a sample taken from an unstained or nonbloody area of the surface being tested.

Results of Study

Table 4.1   Household Chemicals (Phenolphthalein Three Step and Hemastix®)

Item	Phenolphthalein (Three Step)	Hemastix®
Ajax Dish Detergent	–	–
Antimicrobial soap	–	–
Carpet Fresh	–	–
Clorox Bleach	wk+/–	+++
Clorox Cleanup with Bleach	wk+	n.t.
Clorox 2	wk+	n.t.
Cologne (Escape)	–	–
Comet	–	–
Conditioner	–	–
Disinfectant spray	–	–
Dispatch Hospital Cleaner	wk+/–	+++
Duster Plus	–	–
Enzymatic lab detergent	–	–
Fab Detergent	–	–
Furniture polish	–	–
Hairspray	–	–
Hyponex Plant Food	–	–
Jewelry cleaner	–	–
Lotion	–	–
Nail polish	–	–
Nail polish remover	–	–
Pine Sol	–	–
Shampoo	–	–
Shaving gel	–	–
Shout	–	–
Suede cleaner	–	–
Toothpaste	–	–
Windex	–	–
Woolite Rug Cleaner	–	–

Phenolphthalein (three step): + = strong pink color; wk+ = weak color reaction; – = no color change; n.t. = not tested. Hemastix® based on manufacturer's guidelines.

**Table 4.2   Household Products
(Phenolphthalein Three Step and Hemastix®)**

Item	Phenolphthalein (Three Step)	Hemastix®
Basil	−	−
BBQ sauce	−	−
Cinnamon	−	−
Cornmeal	−	−
Cream of tartar	−	−
Cumin seed	−	−
Dill weed	−	−
Dried parsley	−	−
Dry mustard	−	−
Flour	−	−
Garlic salt	−	−
Ground ginger	−	−
Ground oregano	−	−
Ground turmeric	−	−
Hot sauce	−	−
Instant coffee	−	−
Italian seasoning	−	−
Ketchup	−	−
Lemon pepper	−	−
Mrs. Butterworth	−	−
Nestle Quik	−	−
Onion salt	−	−
Oregano	−	−
Pancake mix	−	−
Paprika	−	−
Pepper	−	−
Red pepper	−	−
Sugar	−	−
Sugar ginger	−	−
Sweet 'n Low	−	−
Vegetable oil	−	−
White pepper	−	−
Whole oregano	−	−

Phenolphthalein (three step): + = strong pink color; − = no color change. Hemastix® based on manufacturer's guidelines.

Table 4.3   Chemicals (Phenolphthalein Three Step and Hemastix®)

Item	Phenolphthalein (Three Step)	Hemastix®
1-(2 Pyridylazo)-2 naphthol	+	−
1-Butaneboric acid	−	−
5-Amino-2,3,dihydro-phthal-azinidione	−	−
Acetic acid	−	−
Agarose	−	−
Aldehyde	−	−
Aluminum sulfate	−	−
Amido black	−	+++
Anthracene	−	−
β-estradiol	−	−
Boiling chips	−	−
Borax	−	−
Boric acid	−	−
Brij solution	−	−
Brilliant green	−	−
Bromphenol blue	−	−
Bromthymol blue	−	−
Calcium lactate	−	−
Citric acid monohydrate	−	−
Citric acid trisodium salt	−	−
Chloral hydride	−	−
Cobalt acetate	−	++
Cobalt chloride	−	+++
Copper sulfate	−	+++
Copper wire	−	−
Coumadin sodium	−	−
Crystal violet	−	−
Eosin	−	−
Ethylene-diaminetetraacetic acid	−	−
Ferrous sulfate	+	+++
Formaldehyde	−	−
Furacin	+	−
Glucose	−	−
Glycine	−	−
HEPES	−	−
Indigo carmine	−	+++
Iron wire	−	Trace
Lead acetate	−	++
Lead nitrate	−	+
Leucomalachite green	−	−
Magnesium	−	−
Magnesium perchlorate	−	−
Mercuric iodide	−	−
Methylene	−	+++
Naphthol	−	−
Nicotinic acid	−	−

Table 4.3 (continued)   Chemicals (Phenolphthalein Three Step and Hemastix®)

Item	Phenolphthalein (Three Step)	Hemastix®
Ninhydrin	−	−
Nuclear fast red	−	−
Orcein	−	−
Oxalic acid	−	−
p-Dimethylaminobenaldehyde	−	−
Phenazine methosulfate	−	−
Picric acid	−	−
Polyethylene glycol	−	−
Polyoxethylene sorbitan	−	−
Potassium bisulfate	−	++
Potassium carbonate	−	−
Potassium cyanide	−	−
Potassium dichromate	−	+++
Potassium ferracyanide	+	+++
Potassium oxalate	−	−
Potassium permanganate	−	+++
Potassium phosphate	−	−
Potassium sodium tartrate	−	−
Progesterone	−	−
Quinacrine	−	−
Salt	−	−
Silver acetate	−	++
Sodium bicarbonate	−	−
Sodium carbonate	−	−
Sodium hydrosulfate	−	+
Sodium hydroxide	−	−
Sodium metabisulfate	−	++
Sodium nitroferricyanide	−	−
Sodium perborate	−	−
Sodium periodate	+	+++
Sodium phosphate	−	−
Sodium phosphate dibasic	−	−
Sodium phosphate tribasic	−	−
Sodium sulfate	−	−
Soluable starch	−	−
Spermine tetrahydrochloride	−	−
Starch, hydrolyzed	−	−
Testosterone	−	−
Tin	−	−
Trifluoracetic acid sodium salt	−	−
Triton X-100	−	−
Trypan blue	−	−
Urea	−	−
Zinc metal	−	−

Phenolphthalein (three step): + = strong pink color; − = no color change. Hemastix® based on manufacturer's guidelines.

Table 4.4 Fruits and Vegetables — Phenolphthalein Three Step, Hemastix®, and Leucomalachite Green (LMG)

Item	Phenolphthalein (Three Step)	Hemastix®	LMG
Aloe vera	+	−	−
Apples			
Inside	−	++	−
Stem	−	++	−
Beet			
Inside	−	−	−
Stem	−	−	−
Black grapes	can't read	+	−
Butternut squash	−	−	−
Carrots	−	+	−
Carrot sticks	−	+	−
Carrot stem area	wk+	+	−
Cocktail sauce	−	−	−
Dried cherries	−	−	−
Garlic			
Inside	−	+	−
Root	−	+	−
Green onions			
Leaf	−	+	−
Stalk	−	++	−
Inside	−	++	−
Jalapeno			
Inside	−	+	−
Stem	−	+++	−
Lemon	−	−	−
Lettuce	−	+	−
Lime	−	−	−
Mold from lime	−	−	−
Nectarine			
Inside	−	+	−
Stem	−	++	−
Onion	−	−	−
Oranges			
Inside	−	+	−
Stem	−	++	−
Peach			
Inside	−	+	−
Stem	−	Trace	−
Pear	−	−	−
Plum			
Inside	−	−	−
Stem	−	−	−
Potato (red)	wk+	+++	−
Radish			
Stem	−	++	−
Inside	wk+	++	−

Table 4.4 (continued)   Fruits and Vegetables — Phenolphthalein Three Step, Hemastix®, and Leucomalachite Green (LMG)

Item	Phenolphthalein (Three Step)	Hemastix®	LMG
Red cabbage	–	–	–
Roma tomato			
Stem	can't read	+	–
Inside	can't read	+	–
Rutabaga	–	Trace	–
Strawberries			
Stem	wk+	–	–
Interior	can't read	–	–
Sweet Potato			
Outside	–	+	–
Inside	–	+	–
Turnip			
Inside	wk+	+	–
Stem	–	+	–
Yellow squash			
Skin	wk+	–	–
Stem	wk+	++	–
Inside	–	++	–

Phenolphthalein (three step): + = strong pink color; wk+ = weak color reaction; – = no color change; LMG: – = no color change. Hemastix® based on manufacturer's guidelines.

Table 4.5   Phenolphthalein (One Step)

Item	Phenolphthalein (One Step)
Household Chemicals	
Ajax Dish Detergent	–
Antimicrobial soap	–
Carpet Fresh	–
Clorox	–
Cologne (Escape)	–
Comet	–
Conditioner	–
Disinfectant spray	–
Dispatch Hospital Cleaner	–
Duster Plus	–
Enzymatic detergent	–
Fab Detergent	–
Furniture polish	–
Hairspray	–
Hyponex Plant Food	–
Jewelry cleaner	–
Lotion	–
Nail polish	–

Table 4.5 (continued)   **Phenolphthalein (One Step)**

Item	Phenolphthalein (One Step)
Household Chemicals (continued)	
Nail polish remover	−
Pine Sol	−
Shampoo	−
Shaving gel	−
Shout	−
Suede cleaner	−
Toothpaste	−
Windex	−
Woolite Rug Cleaner	−
Household Products	
Basil	−
BBQ sauce	−
Cinnamon	−
Cornmeal	−
Cream of tartar	−
Cumin seed	−
Dill weed	−
Dried parsley	−
Dry mustard	−
Flour	−
Garlic salt	−
Ground ginger	−
Ground oregano	−
Ground turmeric	+
Hot sauce	−
Instant coffee	−
Italian seasoning	−
Ketchup	−
Lemon pepper	−
Mrs. Butterworth	−
Nestle Quik	−
Onion salt	−
Oregano	−
Pancake mix	−
Paprika	−
Pepper	−
Red pepper	−
Sugar	−
Sugar ginger	−
Sweet 'n Low	−
Vegetable oil	−
White pepper	−
Whole oregano	−

Table 4.5 (continued)   Phenolphthalein (One Step)

Item	Phenolphthalein (One Step)
Chemicals	
1-(2 Pyridylazo)-2 naphthol	+
1-Butaneboric acid	−
5-Amino-2,3,dihydro-phthal-azinidione	−
Acetic acid	−
Agarose	−
Aldehyde	−
Aluminum sulfate	−
Amido black	−
Anthracene	−
B-estradiol	−
Boiling chips	−
Borax	−
Boric acid	−
Brij solution	−
Brilliant green	−
Bromphenol blue	−
Bromthymol blue	−
Calcium lactate	−
Citric acid monohydrate	−
Citric acid trisodium salt	−
Cobalt acetate	−
Cobalt chloride	−
Copper sulfate	−
Copper wire	−
Coumadin sodium	−
Crystal violet	−
Dihydrochloride	−
Eosin	−
Ethylene-diaminetetraacetic acid	−
Ferrous sulfate	+
Formaldehyde	−
Furacin	+
Glucose	−
Glycine	−
Hepes	−
Indigo carmine	−
Iron wire	−
Lead acetate	−
Lead nitrate	−
Leucomalachite green	−
Magnesium	−
Magnesium perchlorate	−
Mercuric iodide	−
Methylene	−
Naphthol	−

Table 4.5 (continued)   **Phenolphthalein (One Step)**

Item	Phenolphthalein (One Step)
Chemicals (continued)	
Nicotinic acid	−
Ninhydrin	−
Nuclear fast red	−
Orcein	−
Oxalic acid	−
p-Dimethylaminobenaldehyde	−
Phenazine methosulfate	−
Picric acid	−
Polyethylene glycol	−
Polyoxethylene sorbitan	−
Potassium bisulfate	−
Potassium carbonate	−
Potassium cyanide	−
Potassium dichromate	−
Potassium ferricyanide	+
Potassium oxalate	−
Potassium permanganate	−
Potassium phosphate	−
Potassium sodium tartrate	−
Progesterone	−
Quinacrine	−
Salt	−
Silver acetate	−
Sodium bicarbonate	−
Sodium carbonate	−
Sodium hydrosulfate	−
Sodium hydroxide	−
Sodium metabisulfate	−
Sodium nitroferricyanide	−
Sodium perborate	−
Sodium periodate	+
Sodium phosphate	−
Sodium phosphate dibasic	−
Sodium phosphate tribasic	−
Sodium sulfate	−
Soluable starch	−
Spermine tetrahydrochloride	−
Starch hydrolyzed	−
Testosterone	−
Tin	−
Trifluoracetic acid sodium	−
Triton X-100	−
Trypan blue	−
Urea	−
Zinc metal	−

Table 4.5 (continued)   Phenolphthalein (One Step)

Item	Phenolphthalein (One Step)
Fruits and Vegetables	
Apples	
Inside	–
Stem	–
Beet	
Inside	–
Stem	–
Black grapes	can't read
Butternut squash	–
Carrots	–
Carrot sticks	–
Carrot stem area	–
Cocktail sauce	–
Dried cherries	–
Garlic	
Inside	–
Root	–
Green onions	
Leaf	–
Stalk	wk+
Inside	–
Jalapeno	
Inside	–
Stem	–
Lemon	–
Lettuce	–
Mold from lime	–
Monkey grass leaves	–
Nectarine	
Inside	–
Stem	–
Onion	–
Oranges	
Inside	–
Stem	–
Peach	
Inside	–
Stem	–
Pear	–
Plum	
Inside	–
Stem	wk+
Potato	–
Radish	
Stem	–
Inside	can't read

Table 4.5 (continued)   Phenolphthalein (One Step)

Item	Phenolphthalein (One Step)
Fruits and Vegetables (continued)	
Red cabbage	−
Roma tomato	
Stem	can't read
Inside	can't read
Rutabaga	
Seeds of monkey grass	−
Strawberries	
Stem	wk+
Interior	can't read
Sweet potato	
Outside	−
Inside	−
Turnip	
Inside	+
Stem	wk+
Yellow squash	
Skin	wk+
Stem	wk+
Inside	−

Phenolphthalein (one step): + = strong pink color; wk+ = weak color reaction; − = no color change.

Heat Deactivation of Plant Peroxidases

Although plant peroxidases may cause a positive reaction with the screening tests for blood, exposure to temperatures of 100°C for a period of 7 min has been reported as effective means of deactivating plant peroxidases.[3] Studies conducted in our laboratory show that this statement is true for the phenolphthalein screening test for blood, but that the Hemastix® test method will require longer periods of heat exposure in order to inactivate the plant peroxidases to the point that they are no longer detectable by the Hemastix® reagent.

	Reaction after 100°C for 7 min	Reaction after 100°C for 17 min	Reaction after 100°C for 27 min
Green onion	+	+	−
Plum (interior)	+	+	−
Radish	+	+	−
Butternut squash	+	+	−

Will Heat Deactivation Adversely Affect Detection of Dilute Bloodstains?

For the practicing forensic scientist, this means that items of evidence which might have been exposed to plant materials, such as a suspect's shoes which might have been exposed to grass stains, might need to be exposed to temperatures of 100°C for a period of 7 min in order for one to feel confident that any positive screening test reaction is "valid." While such extreme measures are not always necessary, our studies have shown that exposure to such extreme heat will not adversely affect the reaction of bloodstains. As a matter of reassurance, the upper limits of sensitivity using the phenolphthalein screening test is identical whether the bloodstain dilution has been heated to 100°C for 7 min or merely tested in its unadulterated form.

References

1. Gaensslen, R. E., *Sourcebook in Forensic Serology, Immunology, and Biochemistry,* U.S. Dept. of Justice, National Institute of Justice, U.S. Govt. Printing Office, Washington, D.C., Aug. 1983, pp. 101, 105, 111.

2. Occupational Safety and Health Standards for General Industry with Amendments as of Sept. 5, 1989, OSHA 1910.1010, U.S. Dept. of Labor, Subpt. Z, Toxic and Hazardous Substances: Benzidine, Sect. 1010 (c)(2) and 1011 (b)(11), Commerce Clearing House, Chicago, 1989.

3. Saferstein, R., Ed., *Forensic Science Handbook,* Vol. 1, p. 273, Prentice-Hall, Englewood Cliffs, NJ, 1982.

4. Eckert, W. G. and James, S. H., *Interpretation of Bloodstain Evidence at Crime Scenes,* CRC Press, Boca Raton, FL, 1993.

5. *FBI Laboratory Serology Unit Protocol Manual,* U.S. Dept. of Justice, Federal Bureau of Investigation, May 1989, pp. 2–3, 2–4, 2–8, 2–9.

Approach to Case Evaluation and Report Writing

5

PAUL ERWIN KISH

Contents

0-8493-8108-8/99/$0.00+$.50
© 1999 by CRC Press LLC

Approaching Bloodstain Pattern Cases

The manner in which an individual sets out to solve a problem will often determine whether or not the problem will be resolved. This is also true with establishing the geometric significance of bloodstain patterns. In order to be successful, the bloodstain pattern analyst should approach every case as a new problem to be solved, with a "new" set of facts and circumstances to be considered.

Bloodstain analysts should:

- Be open-minded, without prejudice and possess a desire to learn;
- Be objective and not be swayed by the opinions and/or theories offered by the individual who has retained their services;
- Never render opinions beyond what the evidence will allow no matter the amount of pressure being placed upon them by their superiors, the individual who requested their assistance, or by any attorney.

One must remember bloodstain pattern interpretation is merely a forensic *tool* which may be used to better understand what may or may not have occurred during a bloodshedding event. As with any forensic *tool*, individuals in control of it must have a solid foundation and background within their respective discipline prior to applying their knowledge to a situation which may inevitably deprive another human being of liberty and/or life.

The stages of a bloodstain pattern analysis from the initial request for assistance through the generation of a bloodstain pattern report will be discussed within this chapter. These stages are meant to serve as an organized methodology for those who are asked to interpret the geometric significance of bloodstain patterns. These stages are in no way an alternative for the scientific method but rather are meant to be used as a method for organizing data specific to bloodstain pattern interpretation.

The people requesting bloodstain pattern interpretations are generally law enforcement agents, district attorneys, criminal defense attorneys, civil litigation attorneys, insurance company representatives, etc. A recent trend has been for criminal and civil defense attorneys to employ outside bloodstain pattern experts to reconstruct their clients' cases prior to the prosecution.

The bloodstain pattern analyst should realize that regardless of who is requesting an analysis of the bloodstain patterns, the person requesting the analysis will have his or her own theory of the case, as well as a predisposition to one side. The analyst must maintain a totally objective thought process beginning with the first conversation with the individual requesting services.

Prior to the commencement of the examination of evidence, photographs, or the crime scene, one must determine whether or not the request is within the realm of knowledge and expertise of the bloodstain pattern analyst. Routinely, we are asked questions which are ultimately referred to a forensic pathologist or a serologist. The bloodstain pattern analyst should not render opinions outside of the bloodstain pattern interpretation discipline, unless the analyst has a previously acquired expertise in an additional discipline.

The following should be requested prior to the reconstruction of a bloodstain pattern case:

1. *Brief* background information
2. Examination of the actual crime scene
3. Examination of physical evidence
4. Photographs of the crime scene
5. Photographs of the physical evidence
6. Photographs of the autopsy
7. Autopsy report(s)
8. Serology report(s)
9. Crime scene diagram(s)
10. Crime scene investigator's notes and/or reports
11. Responding officer's notes
12. Emergency medical technician's (EMT) notes and/or depositions
13. Additional forensic reports, such as:
    - Fingerprint (bloody prints)
    - Shoe print (bloody prints)
    - Firearms (blood on/in weapon)

Obviously, every case will not have each of the items listed above. However, if the information provided to is too scant, vague, or of poor quality, there is absolutely nothing wrong with the bloodstain analyst discontinuing his or her investigation by stating insufficient information exists to render a meaningful opinion in this matter.

Once this information has been received, a sequence for extracting the pertinent information needs to be established. Oftentimes the bloodstain analyst is only retained after all other investigative leads have been exhausted.

Sequence for Approaching Bloodstain Pattern Cases

Obtaining a *Brief* Background of the Case

Background information should be collected at the initial contact when the request is made for a bloodstain pattern analysis.

- Name of victim(s)
- Name of suspect(s)
- Time of incident (if established)
- Date of incident (if established)
- Geographical location of the incident
- Who contacted you
- When you were first contacted
- Determine why the individual contacting you believes a bloodstain pattern analysis is necessary in the case.

In certain circumstances the analyst can establish early on whether or not the case is worthy of an examination. For instance, many attorneys have the misconception that if their clients have no bloodstaining on their person they could not have been involved in the bloodshedding event. The absence of evidence is very rarely of any significance for a bloodstain pattern analyst who has been trained to interpret what is present and not to speculate on why something is not present.[1]

The analyst should limit the amount of superfluous information the contact person volunteers. Routinely, attorneys will attempt to provide an entire life history of their case and/or client. Generally, this type of information will have little if any bearing on the bloodstain evidence or the analyst's participation. In order to maintain a completely objective mind-set when reviewing a case, contact persons should be requested to refrain from reiterating any type of scenario in regard to what they believe occurred.

The attorney retaining a bloodstain expert should be somewhat skeptical of bloodstain analysts who ask for the attorney's opinion as to what the attorney believes occurred prior to conducting their own independent examination of the case.

Examination of the Crime Scene

The basics to examining a crime scene for bloodstain pattern evidence is the subject of a chapter in and of itself. Hence, in this chapter we will only discuss various crime scene issues which apply directly to the analyst's approach as it would pertain to the bloodstain patterns.

The bloodstain analyst will be dealing with essentially three types of crime scenes:

1. *Pristine Crime Scene* — A crime scene where no scene processing has commenced prior to the arrival of the bloodstain analyst on the scene.
2. *Recent Crime Scene* — A crime scene that has been previously processed for physical evidence but remains in control of law enforcement.
3. *Old Crime Scene* — A crime scene which has previously been released from the custody of law enforcement.

A primary concern of a bloodstain pattern analyst with any crime scene, whether visited by the analyst or not, is whether the bloodstain patterns identified are a direct result of the incident or, rather, the result of interventions made by EMTs, law enforcement, or by others trying to be of assistance.

The examination of the crime scene, whether pristine, recent, or old, should be viewed as the single greatest opportunity the bloodstain pattern analyst will have to obtain information. Regardless of the age of the scene, whenever possible the bloodstain pattern analyst should visit the crime scene. The actual crime scene frequently holds a wealth of useful information for the analyst.

The earlier the bloodstain pattern analyst can be brought to the crime scene, the better, although more often than not the bloodstain pattern analyst works on what we would refer to as a recent crime scene. With the recent scene, the analyst will have to initially differentiate between bloodstain patterns which were the direct result of the incident and bloodstain patterns which were artifactually created by EMT intervention, body removal, and scene-processing efforts made by earlier investigators. To assist with these determinations, the analyst should utilize a set of scene photographs taken at the time the scene was originally processed. If the bloodstain pattern analyst should ever question whether a bloodstain pattern is artifactual or not, *always document* the pattern and treat it as if it were authentic until further information is obtained to either include or exclude it as being created as a direct result of the incident. Cases have been reviewed personally in which the bloodstain patterns located at a crime scene actually resulted from a previous altercation within the same dwelling.

The true value of examining an old crime scene may not be fully understood until the bloodstain pattern analyst discovers a key piece of information from visiting an old crime scene. You will only have to find one piece of essential evidence from one old crime scene visit to make your past and future efforts worthwhile. Once again, the bloodstain analyst should utilize the original crime scene photographs when examining old crime scenes.

Initial Review of Crime Scene and Evidence Photographs

An initial review of the crime scene and evidence photographs should be one of the first tasks. This review is not meant for actual interpretation of the bloodstain patterns but rather for acquainting oneself with the crime scene, victim location, layout of the scene, bloodstain locations, physical evidence, etc. One may assimilate this review with the initial walk-through completed prior to processing the actual crime scene. It is important to obtain some idea of the task ahead, and the best method for accomplishing this is to first make a preliminary review of the scene and evidence photographs. Remember this is an initial review. Creating a hypothesis or case theory would be premature at this point.

Examination of Autopsy/Hospital Photographs

When examining the autopsy and/or hospital photographs, the bloodstain analyst should concentrate on extracting data about the:

- Injuries of the victim(s)
- Injuries of the suspect(s)
- Sources of bleeding
- Locations of wounds
- Type of wounds
- Clothes being worn by victim(s)
- Clothes being worn by the suspect(s)
- Types of medical interventions.

Examination of Autopsy Protocols and/or Hospital Records

From the autopsy protocols and/or hospital records, the bloodstain analyst should extract the following information:

- Injuries resulting in blood loss
- Damage to any major artery and/or vein
- Whether or not blood was located within nasal passages, mouth, or anywhere within the air passages which may result in the blood being forcefully expelled from the victim
- Height and weight of the victim(s)
- Type of injuries, such as:
    Gunshot wounds
    Stab wounds
    Blunt force trauma
    Lacerations
- Location of all injuries

Autopsy protocols and/or hospital records will indicate the location and type of blood sources which, in turn, will be useful in determining the type of mechanism(s) which could have created the bloodstain patterns at the scene. The hypothesis of a bloodstain pattern being the result of arterial spurting would be supported by identifying information within the autopsy report about a severed artery. Likewise, to support a hypothesis of a pattern being the result of blood being expirated from the injured party, it must be established that blood was present in the nose and/or mouth. A victim's height and weight may assist in locating a model for reconstruction efforts if needed. The type and location of an injury will be useful in supporting hypotheses concerning the mechanism of bloodstaining, as well as the location of the victim when the incident occurred. For example, if a bloodstain pattern whose size, shape, and distribution is consistent with a high-velocity impact spatter pattern and the pathology report indicates only an entrance gunshot wound, then one may deduce that the pattern was the result of high-velocity back spatter from an exit wound rather than forward spatter.

A background in human anatomy can be of great assistance when extracting information from autopsy and hospital reports. If the bloodstain analyst is unclear about any of the information or terminology contained in any report, the analyst needs to contact the person who wrote the report for clarifications.

Examination of Crime Scene Diagram(s)

Scene diagrams are useful in obtaining the size relationship within the scene as compared with the scene photographs. Scene diagrams also assist in establishing the location of physical evidence within the crime scene. It is helpful to utilize the scene diagrams when attempting to establish the location in which scene photographs were taken, especially if the bloodstain analyst was unable to attend the crime scene.

Examination of Crime Scene and Evidence Photographs

All scene photographs should be numbered and/or lettered prior to commencing with an examination. The photographs then need to be organized in a manner which will allow for easy retrieval. Organize them first by overall type of photograph and then organize each type by natural divisions within the scene.

An example of organizing photographs by general type:

I. Areas with bloodstaining
II. Areas without bloodstaining
III. Evidence photographs
IV. Autopsy photographs
V. Photographs of defendant(s)
VI. Additional photographs

An example of categorizing scene photographs within a particular type :

Residence:

I. Areas with bloodstaining
   A. Northwest bedroom
      1. North wall
         a. Window

   2. South wall
   3. East wall
   4. West wall
      a. Entry door
   5. Ceiling
   6. Furniture
      a. Dresser
         (1) Front, top, rear, left side, right side, bottom

An example for categorizing photographs of bloodstains on a body:

I. Areas with bloodstaining
    A. Deceased (Jane Doe)
       1. Head
          a. Face (ears, nose, mouth)
          b. Scalp
          c. Hair
       2. Arms
          a. Left anterior/left posterior
          b. Right anterior/right posterior
       3. Hands
          a. Left palm/left back
          b. Right palm/right back
       4. Torso
          a. Anterior
          b. Posterior
       5. Legs
          a. Left anterior/left posterior
          b. Right anterior/right posterior

   The categorizing of the scene photographs for analysis is the same as dividing the actual scene into specific areas for analysis. These divisions of photographs often apply to how the final report on the case will be organized. Obviously, the analyst will need to modify the photographic categories to fit each individual crime scene. The greatest degree of modification will be necessary in cases involving vehicles, outside crime scenes, and cases involving multiple victims.

   The bloodstain pattern analyst needs to extract only the facts about the bloodstain patterns from each photograph. These facts may include the following information about the bloodstain: size, shape, distribution, location within the scene, directionality, overall stain pattern appearances, relationship of one stain pattern to another and other physical evidence. Note any variables which may be evident within the scene photographs, such as the following:

- Excessive dirt and grime
- Movement of evidence between scene photographs
- Surface texture issues
- Photographic perspective concerns
- Overall quality of the photographs

When extracting information from scene photographs, note the number and/or letter previously assigned to the photograph, as well as the category the photograph was taken from. Information extracted from photographs may read as follows:

Photograph A — Northeast Bedroom — North Wall

- Spatters of 1 to 3 mm in diameter
- Upward directionalities
- Spatter pattern located between 0 and 27 in. from the floor
- Contact stain located between 4 and 9 in. from floor, center of pattern located 97 in. from East wall and 56 in. from the West wall
- Apparent hair within contact stain pattern
- Equally distributed with no void areas

Note the only pieces of information being extracted from the photographs are visible facts about the bloodstain patterns. No theories or conclusions are drawn at this time. At this stage the analyst should only be collecting data for later synthesis.

Examination of Physical Evidence

It is advantageous to categorize the physical evidence by where it was collected prior to its examination.

I.   Evidence collected from scene
II. Evidence collected from victim(s)
III. Evidence collected from suspect(s)

Examine all of the evidence collected from one location prior to moving to the articles of evidence in the next category. Note the size, shape, distribution, configuration, location, establish the side in which the bloodstaining originated, directionality, and overall appearance of the bloodstain patterns. Refer to the articles of evidence by their previously assigned item numbers wherever possible. Photograph all of the significant bloodstain patterns identified on each article of physical evidence. These photographs may be your only source of visual evidence, if the bloodstain pattern(s) are consumed during serological testing. These photographs of the bloodstain patterns on the physical evidence should be utilized when discussing the significance of the patterns within the analyst's final report. The bloodstain pattern analyst should make the report as visually orientated as possible. When presenting testimony in regard to the bloodstain patterns on garments, the analyst should utilize the actual garment when explaining the significance of the bloodstain patterns to the jury.

The bloodstain pattern analyst should utilize the scene photographs to verify the bloodstain patterns on the deceased's clothes. The removal and transport of the deceased from the crime scene to the morgue will result in the bloodstain patterns on the decreased's clothes being altered, destroyed, or new bloodstain patterns being inadvertently created. It is highly recommended that if an apparently significant bloodstain pattern is identified on the clothing of the deceased at the crime scene the pattern should be photographed excessively from various angles and with various lighting configurations; then the article of clothing containing the bloodstain pattern should be removed from the deceased at the scene to prevent it from being destroyed or altered.

Serology Reports

The bloodstain pattern analyst must work in conjunction with the forensic serologist. The analyst needs to be aware of whether or not the pattern the analyst has identified in fact is the blood of one of the parties involved in the incident. Bloodstain analysts should insist upon serological testing of any pattern to which they are attaching significance within a particular case, prior to issuing their final report. The pattern may only be referred to as an "apparent" bloodstain pattern until serological testing confirms it, in fact, is blood.

In order to assist in evaluating serological findings, the analyst should chart whose blood was found where and on what item. When dealing with multiple victims, multiple suspects, and multiple articles of physical evidence, a serology chart will be of assistance in synthesizing the data from the written matter with the bloodstain patterns you observed. A serology chart for the bloodstain pattern analysis would look similar to the following:

Serology Chart

Sample #	Location of Evidence	Victim's Blood	Suspect's Blood	Mixture of Blood of Victim and Suspect	Third Party's Blood	Inconclusive
S-1	NE Bedroom (Wall)	XXX				
S-2	Suspect's (Blue Pants)			XXX		

By charting the serological findings in a simple manner, as seen in this example, you will be better able to attach significance to a particular blood-stain pattern in regard to whose blood it is, as well as where it was located.

Crime Scene Investigator's Notes and Reports

Extract any and all information in regard to investigator's crime scene observations, the actions they took, any contact the victim and suspect had, climate conditions at the crime scene, and eyewitness statements. Establish whether or not there are any variables that may have a direct or indirect effect on the interpretation of the bloodstain patterns. Examples of such variables could be

- The suspect was actively treating the victim
- Police or EMTs came into contact with both the victim and the suspect
- The removal of the victim from the original location
- Overall poor handling of the bloodstain evidence

Responding Officer's Notes

The notes of the officers who first responded are often useful in devising a time line. Their notes will often inform the reader of how people were moved, as well as the original location of the victim and the suspect upon their initial arrival.

EMT's Notes and/or Depositions

EMTs can be a valuable source of information to the bloodstain pattern analyst. The EMT's medical interventions and actions taken while at the scene often account for many of the variables the bloodstain pattern analyst must consider when conducting the case evaluation. The saving of a life obviously takes precedent over all other situations, but in doing so the bloodstain patterns may in fact be jeopardized. It is critical that the bloodstain pattern analyst establish whether a particular bloodstain pattern is the result of the actual incident or of EMT intervention.

The following is a list of questions the bloodstain analyst should have answered by the EMTs who intervened:

- Who was assisting the injured party upon your arrival?
- Did you observe any bloodstaining on the person lending assistance to the injured party?
- With multiple injured parties, who treated who? Did the same EMT ever come in contact with both parties?
- How did you move or alter the position of the injured party(s)?
- What types of medical interventions were utilized?
- Was there any blood in air passages of the victim?
- Was the victim mobile upon your arrival?
- Did you alter the location of any piece of physical evidence (e.g., move the firearm)?

These questions, as well as any others asked of an EMT, should be designed to determine whether the bloodstain patterns were from the actual incident or as a result of the EMT's intervention.

Additional Forensic Reports

This category refers to the extracting of information from any other forensic reports which may assist in the reconstruction of the bloodstain patterns in a particular case — for example, the blood found within a firearm by a firearms examiner, the bloody shoe print reported upon by a shoe print expert, etc.

Synthesis of the Data

The data collected from the photographs, scene examination, physical evidence, and the reports and notes on the case must now be synthesized. Review your notes and establish correlations between what was observed at the scene and in the scene photographs with the information extracted from the written matter. While assimilating information, the analyst must consider all of the variables that surround the facts of the case.

An example of a data synthesis would be:

Data Synthesis for Bloodstain Pattern (A)

EMT's Notes:	• The injured party was inhaling and exhaling blood when we arrived.
Pathology Report:	• Blood present in, and extruding from, the nose and mouth

Scene Photographs:
- Spatters of blood less than 1 to 2 mm in diameter
- Located on the North wall of the master bedroom
- The North wall was adjacent to where the victim was discovered
- Some of the spatters had air bubbles within them

Formulation and Testing of Hypotheses

Based upon the synthesis of the scene data, hypotheses can be formulated. Simply stated, the analyst is formulating an educated guess related to the synthesized data based upon past experiences and the content of the previously extracted data. After the formulation of each hypothesis for each bloodstain pattern, all need to be tested. The testing may include one or all of the following: review of the scene photographs, review of the written matter, actual experimentation, review of the literature, review of past experiments, and personal experience.

If we continue with the last example:

Data Synthesis for Bloodstain Pattern (A)

EMT's Notes:
- The injured party was inhaling and exhaling blood when we arrived.

Pathology Report:
- Blood present in, and extruding from, the nose and mouth

Scene Photographs:
- Spatters of blood less than 1 to 2 mm in diameter
- Located on the North wall of the master bedroom
- The North wall was adjacent to where the victim was discovered
- Some of the spatters had air bubbles within them

Hypothesis for Bloodstain Pattern (A)

The bloodstain pattern located on the wall adjacent to where the victim was located is consistent with being an expirated bloodstain pattern which originated from the mouth and/or nose of the victim, while the victim was in the vicinity of the master bedroom's North wall.

Testing of Hypothesis of Bloodstain Pattern (A)

1. A review of the literature indicates that blood in the air passages, air bubbles within the blood, and a spatter size of less than 1 to 2 mm are factors indicative of an expirated bloodstain pattern.
2. All possible variables have been accounted for and excluded as possibly creating the pattern.

3. Experimentation with models expiring blood indicates the observed pattern to be of similar size, shape, and configuration with an expired bloodstain pattern observed at this crime scene.
4. The EMT's observations and autopsy findings support the previously stated hypothesis.

Formulating a Scenario

The development of a scenario and/or theory of the case should always be the last stage in any bloodstain pattern analysis. There is no guarantee the bloodstain pattern analyst will be able to derive a single scenario from the data. On numerous occasions the analyst will have more than one scenario which may equally fit the same set of facts. Likewise, the analyst may not be able to exclude enough possible scenarios to render a meaningful opinion as to what actually occurred at a particular scene. Remember not every question derived from the bloodstain patterns will have a definitive answer.

Factors to Consider When Analyzing a Bloodstain Pattern Case

- Never form any type of opinion until all data have been collected and synthesized.
- If you are unable to maintain a completely objective mind-set on the case, refer the case to another bloodstain analyst.
- If you cannot substantiate your opinion, you do not have an opinion to render.
- How successful the analyst will be is dependent upon how well the analyst can collect, organize, and synthesize large amounts of data.
- Notes should be brief and concise statements of fact, not opinion.

The Bloodstain Pattern Report

"Once your opinion is in writing you own it and everything about it, good, bad, or indifferent."

The purpose of the bloodstain pattern report is to convey the findings of the bloodstain analyst to the attorneys, to the court, and ultimately to the jury. Opinions within the bloodstain report must be capable of being scientifically substantiated. The report should be concise and worded in a manner that will allow it to be understood by those completely unfamiliar with the discipline.

The bloodstain pattern report should be a completely objective and unbiased work product of the bloodstain pattern analyst.

Report Phrasing

The interpretation portion of the bloodstain pattern interpretation discipline is where many people fail to realize that how something is said is equal in importance to what is said. In other words, the way the observations and opinions are phrased can dictate how well testimony will proceed. The wording used within a report must be firm but not excessively firm. Bloodstain pattern analysts must be selective about just how definitive or nondefinitive they are with their conclusions. Opposing counsel will and should zero in on any report which is excessively definitive or excessively inconclusive in nature. Phrases commonly used within bloodstain reports are:

Apparent bloodstains ...
Stain patterns ...
Consistent with ...
Indicative of ...
Would suggest ...
Appeared to be ...
Based upon current information ...
In the condition received ...
At the time of examination ...

These phrases are generally used when rendering an opinion and/or theory which may need room for further interpretation with the discovery of additional facts. However, when discussing facts that were extracted from the case, like the diameter of a stain, the analyst cannot write, "the diameter of the stain *appeared to be* 3 mm." When a definitive measurement is actually taken it must be reported in a definitive manner, "the diameter of the bloodstain is 3 mm." The opposing counsel should attack the bloodstain analyst whenever the analyst has "hedged" a definitive fact like a measurement.

When utilizing a "qualifying" phrase within a report, one must be aware that certain adverbs and phrases attach a degree of probability to an opinion which the analyst may not have intended or even been aware of, such as:

More likely ...
Likely ...
More ...
Tends to be ...

Once again, opposing counsel should rigorously cross-examine bloodstain experts who attach a degree of probability to their opinions, especially if they have not stated a foundation for such opinion.

Sections within a Bloodstain Pattern Report

Introduction of the Report

This could also be referred to as the "getting acquainted" section of the report. The Introduction should include the following information:

- Who contacted you and when.
- The location of the crime scene.
- A list of items received for examination.
- The chain-of-custody information in regard to the physical evidence received.
- Any administrative issues.

An optional addition to the report located between the Introduction and the Body is what may be referred to as a Definitions Section. Essentially, bloodstain analysts define the key bloodstain terms they will be utilizing throughout their report.

Body of the Report

The Body of the report should include the overall observations made by the analyst in regard to the bloodstain patterns. This is the foundation for all of the analyst's conclusions. The manner in which this section is approached is often dependent upon the issues surrounding the case. If the report deals specifically with the clothes of the suspect, then categories should be made dealing with the observations made of each item of clothing. Oftentimes, there will be several bloodstain patterns on a multitude of mediums and locations within the report, including the suspect, suspect's clothing, victim, victim's clothing, articles of physical evidence, and multiple rooms within the scene. Each pertinent issue must be presented and discussed independently. The opportunity to draw them together will present itself within the Conclusions portion of the report.

Within the Body of the report the following sequence, or a modification thereof, should be followed when addressing issues relating to a bloodstain pattern case:

a. Crime Scene
b. Physical Evidence (other than clothing) Collected at the Crime Scene
c. Victim's Clothes (including footwear)
d. Victim's Body

    e. Suspect's Clothes (including footwear)
    f. Suspect's Body
    g. Special Issues
       1. Reconstruction with Models
       2. Chemical Enhancement Techniques
       3. Experiments Conducted

The crime scene should be presented in a systematic manner. The bloodstain pattern location within the scene should be specified in great detail. The observations made by the bloodstain analyst should be depicted in a clear and concise manner. Scene photographs and diagrams should be utilized within the report to allow the reader to visualize what has been written. Jurors will be hard-pressed to believe what they are told if they cannot read the report and identify the particular stain pattern within the scene photographs. The analyst should refer to the scene photographs by whatever method the photographer had previously labeled them.

Physical evidence should be discussed in an obvious sequence, i.e., sequential evidence numbers or by the location in which it was collected. The bloodstain pattern analyst should indicate the type of examination conducted on each item of evidence, such as microscopic analysis, visual analysis with high-intensity illumination, or by utilizing a chemical enhancing technique. It is not out of the ordinary for the analyst to remove small portions of unstained fabric from an evidence garment for the purpose of conducting experiments. However, if done, the analyst should be able to account for all of the samples removed, due to the fact that bloodstain experiments are generally nondestructive in nature. Analysts should report, in detail, on any experiments they conducted on the samples they removed from the evidence garment. Any sample taken from an article of evidence must be documented in regard to its size and the location from which it was removed from the garment, as well as the purpose for taking a sample.

Special issues are areas which are not routinely addressed in every case and/or report. These issues would include the use of models, experiments conducted for specific case questions, chemical enhancement procedures, etc. These procedures and/or techniques are generally employed to resolve specific questions surrounding the bloodstain patterns within a case.

The examination of clothing evidence on a laboratory bench is one thing, but it does not allow for a three-dimensional perspective. Hence, it is often very useful to employ a model of the same anatomical size as the original wearer of the clothes to model the evidence clothing. Naturally, some form of protection, such as a body suit, should be worn by the model under the evidence clothing. A model can be positioned in the exact fashion that best represents the position the original wearer of the clothes claims to have been in when the garments were bloodstained. If a model is utilized in a reconstruction and discussed in a report, it is recommended that photographs of the model wearing the evidence garments be included in the report. This will tend to prevent any confusion about the analyst's opinion for the attorneys, as well as for the jurors.

The bloodstain analyst will routinely have to develop and conduct experiments in order to answer specific questions about a case. If any of the opinions and/or conclusions are supported by experimentation, the experiments must be discussed within the report. Once again, it is helpful to provide photographs and/or a videotape of the experiments. Bloodstain experiments are routinely conducted to verify opinions based on previous knowledge or to answer specific case questions including the following:

- Drying time of blood
- Volume of blood
- The side in which a bloodstain pattern originated, on a garment
- Sequencing of bloodstain patterns

When blood-enhancing reagents such as luminol are used, the results should be discussed in their own separate section within the Body of the report. The blood enhanced patterns *should not* be discussed at the same time as the nonenhanced patterns are discussed. It can be very confusing to read a report in which the analyst is discussing visible bloodstain patterns in one sentence and, in the very next sentence, enhanced bloodstain patterns are discussed. The utilization of blood-enhancing techniques should be treated as actual experiments. The procedure, methodology, how variables were controlled, as well as the results, should be discussed within the report. The results should be photographed if any significance is to be attached to the blood enhancements. The bloodstain pattern analyst is obligated to make the reader aware that blood-enhancing techniques are *only* presumptive indicators of blood and that confirmatory testing is necessary.

Conclusions of the Report

The Conclusions portion of the report is a summary of the findings and should be listed in a sequential order, point by point. Conclusions should be clear, concise, and, above all, should be substantiated by the information included in the Body of the report. To formulate the conclusions, information may be drawn upon from multiple areas within the Body of the report. Conclusions will often represent the hypotheses that the analyst was able to prove. Generally, due to the concise nature of the analyst's conclusions, this portion of the report will be relatively brief as compared with the Introduction and the Body of the report.

The Finished Report

When writing or reading a bloodstain report, the following should be remembered:

- The purpose of the report is to inform, not to convict or to exonerate.
- Bloodstain pattern interpretation is only a forensic *tool* and should be used accordingly.
- The report should reflect the objective and unbiased opinion of the bloodstain pattern analyst.
- The report should be limited only to opinions which fall within the discipline of bloodstain pattern interpretation and the degree of the analyst's expertise.
- Written reports must be grammatically sound.
- The reports should be short and to the point. The excessively wordy or drawn out report will only facilitate a lengthy cross-examination.

Reference

1. Kish, P. E. and MacDonell, H. L., Absence of evidence is not evidence of absence, *Journal of Forensic Identification,* Vol. 46, No. 2, March/April, 1996.

Legal and Ethical Aspects of Bloodstain Pattern Evidence

6

CAROL HENDERSON

Contents

Introduction

The importance of expert testimony continues to increase, not only in the frequency of its use, but also in the new techniques which find their way into the courtroom. Data from the laboratory or crime scene has no real meaning in law until presented to the judge or jury. Lawyers must rely on expert testimony as a vehicle for communicating this data.

This chapter is designed to aid the expert and attorney in the following matters:

1. The evidentiary foundation required for the admissibility of the evidence;
2. The rights and obligations regarding discovery of scientific evidence;
3. An outline of attorneys' goals and methods of direct and cross-examination of the expert; and
4. Ethical considerations in the selection and use of experts.

Legal Issues

Admissibility

The issue of admissibility of an expert's evidence is decided by a judge applying one of the two tests for admissibility. The oldest of these tests is the *Frye* test or "general acceptance" test of admissibility. This test is drawn from the often-quoted language of *Frye v. United States*,[1] which dealt with the admissibility of the precursor of the polygraph:

> Just when a scientific principle or discovery crosses the line between the experimental and demonstrable stages is difficult to define. Somewhere in this twilight zone the evidential force of the principle must be recognized, and while courts will go a long way in admitting expert testimony deduced from a well-recognized scientific principle or discovery, the thing from which the deduction is made must be sufficiently established to have gained general acceptance in the particular field in which it belongs.[2]

The court held that the systolic blood pressure test had not yet gained recognition in the physiological and psychological communities; therefore, the evidence was inadmissible.

The *Frye* test became the polestar to guide the admissibility of scientific evidence for many years;[3] however, it was not without its critics.[4] The test has been criticized as unworkable.[5] The problem of identifying the relevant field into which a particular scientific technique falls caused additional criticism.[6] Arguably, the field in which bloodstain pattern analysis belongs is the

---

[1]   *Frye v. United States*, 293 F.1013 (D.C. Cir. 1923).
[2]   *Id.* at 1014.
[3]   Paul C. Giannelli, *The Admissibility of Novel Scientific Evidence: Frye v. United States, A Half Century Later*, 80 Colum. L. Rev., 1197, 1205 (1980).
[4]   *Id.* at 1223–1225.
[5]   *Id.* at 1250.
[6]   Andre A. Moenssens, James E. Starrs, Carol E. Henderson, Fred E. Inbau, *Scientific Evidence in Civil and Criminal Cases*, 9 (4th ed., 1995), Foundation Press, Westbury, N.Y.

field of crime scene investigation and reconstruction; however, it also employs principles from the fields of physics, chemistry, biology, and mathematics.[7]

The majority of courts, applying *Frye* to bloodstain pattern analysis (or "blood splatter" evidence, as some have wrongly called it), have held that the evidence meets the general acceptance standard.[8] Not every jurisdiction has held such evidence to be admissible under the *Frye* standard. For example, in *People v. Owens*,[9] an Illinois appellate court held that a police officer's testimony regarding the analysis of bloodstain evidence found at a murder scene was improperly admitted for failure to lay a foundation establishing that the technique was based on a well-recognized scientific principle or that it had gained general acceptance in the scientific community.

Some courts and commentators observed that the *Frye* test was superseded by Rule 702 when the Federal Rules of Evidence were enacted in 1975.[10] Federal Rule of Evidence 702 provides:

> If scientific, technical, or other specialized knowledge will assist the trier of fact to understand the evidence or to determine a fact in issue, a witness qualified as an expert by knowledge, skill, experience, training, or education, may testify thereto in the form of an opinion or otherwise.[11]

Therefore, scientific evidence, to be admissible pursuant to Federal Rule of Evidence 702, needs to be helpful, relevant, and reliable.

Bloodstain pattern interpretation evidence was admitted pursuant to this new test of admissibility. For example, in *United States v. Mustafa*, the prosecution introduced expert testimony which analyzed the trail of blood and patterns found near the victim at the scene of a rape–murder.[12] The appellate court, in affirming the lower court's decision, held that bloodstain pattern interpretation need not be generally accepted by the scientific community; rather, the testimony need only explain the evidence to the jury.[13] The court noted that the analysis was "grounded in established laws of physics and common sense"; thus, it was reliable, relevant, and the expert's testimony would assist the jury.[14]

---

[7]   *Lewis v. State*, 737 S.W.2d 857 (Tex. Ct. App. 1987), *rev'd on other grounds*.

[8]   *See* Danny R. Vielleux, Annotation, *Admissibility, In Criminal Prosecution, of Expert Opinion Evidence as to "Blood Splatter" Interpretation*, 9 A.L.R. 5th 369 §6[a] (1993); *see, e.g., Robinson v. State*, 574 So.2d 910 (Ala. Crim. App. 1990); *People v. Knox*, 459 N.E.2d 1077 (Ill. App. Ct. 1984).

[9]   *People v. Owens*, 508 N.E.2d 1088 (Ill. App. Ct. 1987).

[10]   Moenssens et al., *supra* note 6, at 12.

[11]   Fed. R. Evid. 702.

[12]   22 M.J. 165 (C.M.A.), *cert. denied*, 479 U.S. 953 (1986) (Mil. R. Evid. 702 is similar to Fed. R. Evid. 702).

[13]   *Id.* at 168.

[14]   *Id.*

After 1975, the issue in federal court then became whether or not the Federal Rules of Evidence's "assist the trier of fact standard," seemingly more liberal than *Frye,* superseded the *Frye* "general acceptance" test. The answer was made clear in 1993 when the United States Supreme Court decided *Daubert v. Merrell Dow Pharmaceuticals, Inc.*[15] In that case, the Supreme Court mandated that proof that establishes the scientific reliability of expert opinion evidence be produced before it may be admitted into evidence.

The *Daubert* opinion states that the courts must assume a "gatekeeping" role regarding the admission of scientific evidence.[16] The Supreme Court construed Federal Rule of Evidence 702 as requiring the trial court to make a twofold inquiry: (1) whether the expert testimony will assist the trier of fact and (2) whether it amounts to "scientific knowledge." A proposition amounts to "scientific knowledge" if it is derived by the scientific method. Therefore, the judge's inquiry needs to focus on how the expert's conclusions or opinions were reached. The Court identified factors which judges should consider in applying their definition of scientific knowledge. The Court stated that the list is not a definitive checklist.[17] These factors include:

1. Whether the proposition is testable.
2. Whether the proposition has been tested.
3. Whether the proposition has been subjected to peer review and publication.
4. Whether the methodology or technique has a known error rate.
5. Whether there are standards for using the methodology.
6. Whether the methodology is generally accepted.

The Court emphasized that this new test is a flexible one, wherein not one factor is determinative.

The Court recognized that general acceptance of a theory or technique is still relevant in two respects: "[F]irst, when the proposition is generally accepted ... it qualifies for judicial notice under Federal Rule of Evidence 201.[18] Second, general acceptance of the methodology can be persuasive circumstantial evidence that the methodology is sound."[19]

When the *Daubert* case was remanded to the Ninth Circuit to apply the factors, the Ninth Circuit judges added an additional factor to their analysis — the technique or method could not have been developed solely for the litigation.[20] If the proffered expert testimony is not based on independent research, the party proffering it must come forward with other objective,

---

[15] 113 S.Ct. 2786 (1993), *on remand* 43 F.3d 1311 (9th Cir. 1995).
[16] *Id.* 113 S.Ct. at 2798.
[17] *Id.* at 2796.

verifiable evidence that the testimony is based on scientifically valid principles. One means of showing this is by proof that research and analysis supporting proffered conclusions have been subjected to normal scientific
scrutiny through peer review and publication.

While the Court based its analysis in *Daubert* on the statutory construction of the language of the Federal Rules of Evidence, it is important to note
their decision has implications beyond federal practice. "[B]y mid-1993, 35
states had adopted evidence codes patterned directly after the [federal] rules.
Daubert is mandatory authority in federal court and will be highly persuasive
authority in the other jurisdictions with statutes similar to ... [Federal Rules
of Evidence] 702."[21]

The *Daubert* ruling has had a great impact in states that have evidence
codes based upon the Federal Rules of Evidence as well as those states who
followed *Frye* in the absence of specific evidence rules or statutes similar to
the federal rules. At the writing of this chapter, the majority of states have
decided to follow the *Daubert* analysis while a minority of states have continued to follow the *Frye* analysis.[22]

Bloodstain pattern analysis testimony that is otherwise admissible may
still be excluded if its probative value is outweighed by prejudice or if it

---

[18] Fed. R. Evid. 201 (1995) provides:

Judicial Notice of Adjudicative Facts

(a) **Scope of rule.** This rule governs only judicial notice of adjudicative facts.
(b) **Kinds of facts.** A judicially noticed fact must be one not subject to reasonable dispute
    in that it is either (1) generally known within the territorial jurisdiction of the trial
    court or (2) capable of accurate and ready determination by resort to sources whose
    accuracy cannot reasonably be questioned.
(c) **When discretionary.** A court may take judicial notice, whether requested or not.
(d) **When mandatory.** A court shall take judicial notice if requested by a party and
    supplied with the necessary information.
(e) **Opportunity to be heard.** A party is entitled upon timely request to an opportunity
    to be heard as to the propriety of taking judicial notice and the tenor of the matter
    noticed. In the absence of prior notification, the request may be made after judicial
    notice has been taken.
(f) **Time of taking notice.** Judicial notice may be taken at any stage of the proceeding.
(g) **Instructing jury.** In a civil action or proceeding, the court shall instruct the jury to
    accept as conclusive any fact judicially noticed. In a criminal case, the court shall
    instruct the jury that it may, but is not required to, accept as conclusive any fact
    judicially noticed.

[19] Edward Imwinkelreid, *The Daubert Decision: Frye is Dead, Long Live the Federal Rules
    of Evidence*, 29 Trial, Sept. 1993, at 60.
[20] *Daubert v. Merrell Dow Pharmaceuticals, Inc.*, 43 F.3d 1311 (9th Cir. 1995).
[21] Imwinkelried, *supra* note 19, at 64.
[22] Heather G. Hamilton, *The Movement from Frye to Daubert: Where Do the States
    Stand?*, 38 Jurimetrics J. 201 (1998).

confuses the jury.[23] For example, in *State v. Johnson*, the appellate court reversed the defendant's murder convictions and remanded the case for a new trial, concluding that the limited probative value of the prosecution's expert's testimony was outweighed by the risk of the danger of undue prejudice.[24] Although conceding that the testimony was not irrelevant, the court found that it was largely corroborative of other, essentially unchallenged testimony indicating the manner of death. The court noted that the prosecution's expert's lengthy presentation which exposed the jury to numerous crime scene photos, as well as 42 slides depicting bloodstain pattern exemplars, could not help but focus the jury's attention on the gruesome details of the conditions of the victims' bodies, rather than on the defendant's guilt.[25]

Since *Daubert* makes general acceptance by the scientific community just one factor in the court's analysis, generally accepted techniques are now vulnerable to challenge. Lawyers proffering experts now have to elicit detailed testimony regarding the scientific methodology used, such as the tests conducted, the standards used, and the error rate. These new requirements even apply to well-accepted forensic techniques.

The admissibility of scientific evidence is a question of law which the judge decides. The only time judges' decisions regarding admissibility will be overturned on appeal is if they abuse their discretion. A judge has broad discretion.[26] The U.S. Supreme Court in *General Electric Company v. Joiner* adopted the abuse of discretion standard for reviewing a trial court's admissibility decision under *Daubert v. Merrell Dow Pharmaceuticals, Inc.*[27]

Weight of the Evidence

Once a judge decides to admit an expert's testimony, the jury must then decide what weight to give the expert's testimony. Studies have shown that jurors accord great weight to expert testimony. For example, a recent poll taken by the *National Law Journal* and Lexis/Nexis found that jurors not only find experts generally credible, but the experts often influenced the outcome of the case.[28] Overall,

---

[23] *See* Fed. R. Evid. 403 (1996) which states:

Exclusion of Relevant Evidence on Grounds of Prejudice,
Confusion, or Waste of Time

Although relevant, evidence may be excluded if its probative value is substantially outweighed by the danger of unfair prejudice, confusion of the issues, or misleading the jury, or by considerations of undue delay, waste of time, or needless presentation of cumulative evidence.

[24] 576 A.2d 834 (1990).
[25] *Id.* at 853.
[26] Frank E. Haddad, *Admissibility of Expert Testimony*, in 1 Forensic Sciences, 1–1, 1–17, Cyril Wecht, Ed. (1993), Matthew Bender, New York.
[27] *General Electric Company v. Joiner*, 118 S. Ct. 512 (1997).

71% of the jurors said the experts made a difference in the verdict.[29] In criminal cases, 95% of the jurors thought the expert very believable or somewhat believable. In spite of this inherent credibility, in most states, the judge will instruct the jurors that an expert's opinion is only reliable when given on a subject which the jurors believe him or her to be an expert and the jurors may choose to believe or disbelieve all or any part of an expert's testimony. For example, Florida's Standard Jury Instruction in Criminal Cases 2.04(a) states:

> Expert witnesses are like other witnesses, with one exception — the law permits an expert witness to give his opinion. However, an expert's opinion is only reliable when given on a subject about which you believe him to be an expert. Like other witnesses, you may believe or disbelieve all or any part of an expert's testimony.[30]

Determining the weight to accord evidence is a fact question for the jury or for the judge in a bench trial. In order to determine the weight to accord scientific evidence, jurors will weigh factors such as acceptance of the scientific principles or theories, the basis of the expert's opinion, and the credibility of the expert. The weight accorded an expert's testimony hinges in large part upon the credibility of the expert. One way in which jurors judge an expert's credibility is by the expert's qualifications.

Qualifications of Experts

Once the court decides whether expert testimony is admissible, it must then determine whether the proffered expert is qualified to render an opinion. At this point, the court will examine the expert's qualifications. According to the rules of evidence, a witness may qualify as an expert on the basis of knowledge, skill, training, experience, or education.[31]

In making this evaluation, the court may consider the expert's educational background, work experience, publications, awards, teaching or training positions, licenses or certifications, speaking or other professional engagements, prior expert witness testimony, and membership in professional associations and positions held in those associations.

In the field of bloodstain pattern interpretation, there is no universal agreement regarding adequate qualifications for one to be an expert. Herbert MacDonell, the "father" of bloodstain interpretation, is of the view that such experts should possess a bachelor of arts degree in either a science or criminal

---

[28] Joan Cheever & Joanne Naiman, *The View from the Jury Box*, Nat'l. L. J., Feb. 22, 1993, at S4. The survey found that experts were thought believable by 89% of the criminal and civil jurors.

[29] *Id.*

[30] Fla. Std. Jury Inst. in Crim. Cases (1993).

[31] Fed. R. Evid. 702 (1996).

justice.[32] This view has been criticized by those who recognize that some individuals may lack formal education but are nonetheless qualified through skill, experience, and training.[33] A study of 1500 jurors revealed that jurors are most impressed by the amount and type of training an expert has received and they expect such an expert to belong to a professional association.[34]

Professor MacDonell is also of the view that experts in this field should be members of one or more of the professional associations dedicated to the forensic sciences, such as the American Academy of Forensic Sciences, the International Association for Identification (I.A.I.), and the International Association of Bloodstain Pattern Analysts.[35]

Board certification, available in some of the forensic sciences,[36] has recently begun in the area of bloodstain pattern identification. The International Association for Identification is now offering board certification of bloodstain pattern examiners. The I.A.I. requires a basic 40-hour course that adheres to certain guidelines; 3 years of practice following the 40-hour course; a minimum of 240 hours of training in associated fields of study (e.g., photography, crime scene investigation, medical-legal death investigation, etc.); and an examination.[37]

Just as experts in the field differ as to adequate expert qualifications, so do the courts.[38] One 40-hour course, three prior qualifications as an expert, and field experience has been held by one court to constitute sufficient qualifications.[39]

Courts have found proffered experts of varied backgrounds qualified to testify as experts in the area of bloodstain pattern interpretation. Chemists,[40] forensic scientists,[41] serologists,[42] and pathologists[43] have all been

---

[32]   Herbert L. MacDonell, *Bloodstain Pattern Interpretation,* in 3 Forensic Sciences, 37-1, 37-68, Cyril Wecht, Ed. (1993), Matthew Bender, New York.

[33]   Norman H. Reeves, *The Police As a Bloodstain Pattern Analyst,* 2 (1994) (unpublished manuscript).

[34]   Sgt. Charles Illsley, U.S. Department of Justice, *Juries, Fingerprints, and the Expert Fingerprint Witness,* 26 (1987).

[35]   MacDonell, *supra* note 31, at 37-69.

[36]   Board certification presently exists in the following areas of forensic science: forensic anthropology, crime scene reconstruction, criminalistics, document examination, forensic odontology, forensic pathology, forensic psychiatry, forensic toxicology.

[37]   Telephone conversations with Judith L. Bunker, Secretary, I.A.I. Bloodstain Pattern Identification Certification Board (Mar. 19 and Mar. 24, 1998). The first examination offered at 1998 I.A.I. meeting.

[38]   *See,* e.g., *Robinson v. State,* 574 So.2d 910, 917 (Ala. Crim. App. 1990) (qualifying investigator from coroner's office as an expert who had attended a workshop on crime scene reconstruction, testified as to blood pattern interpretation five times in the past 5 years, and attended two 40-hour courses on the subject); *State v. Raudenbaugh,* 864 P.2d 596, 601–602 (Idaho 1993) (admitting expert testimony because witness was a forensic pathologist, had taken a 1-week course in blood spatter, and had investigated numerous crime scenes).

[39]   *Cheshire v. State,* 568 So.2d 908, 913 (Fla. 1990).

found qualified. Courts have also accepted testimony from investigators[44] and law enforcement agents.[45]

A few words of caution regarding qualifications. An expert should be wary of joining professional associations which routinely provide board certification without rigorous testing or evaluation or which allow promotion to fellowship status without significant contribution to the scientific field and the professional association. Membership in professional associations which are not perceived as credible will harm an expert's expertise and may even result in a judge finding the expert not qualified to render an opinion. Furthermore, in some states, if an expert misrepresents association with or academic standing at a postsecondary educational institution or makes a false oral or written statement regarding an academic degree or title, the expert may be prosecuted for fraud.[46] The sanctions for such violations include incarceration, fines, and suspension or revocation of the person's license or certification to practice his or her occupation or profession. If the expert makes a false statement under oath with regard to a material matter, the expert may be prosecuted for perjury. Falsifying records is also a crime.

---

[40] *See Clayton v. State*, 840 P.2d 18, 28–29, (Okla. Crim. App. 1992) (holding that the witness with college degrees in chemistry was qualified).

[41] *See State v. Rodgers*, 812 P.2d 1208, 1212 (Idaho 1991).

[42] *See State v. Moore*, 458 N.W.2d 90, 96 (Minn. 1990) (holding that serologist who had interpreted over 30 bloodstain patterns was sufficiently qualified to give expert testimony).

[43] *See State v. Satterfield*, 592 P.2d 135, 140–141 (Kan. 1979); *Whittington v. State*, 523 So.2d 966 (Miss. 1988).

[44] *See United States v. Mustafa*, 22 M.J. 165, 166–167 (C.M.A.), *cert. denied*, 479 U.S. 953 (1986) (admitting expert testimony by a special agent of the Army Criminal Investigation Command).

[45] See *State v. Howard*, 626 So.2d 459, 464 (La. Ct. App. 1993) (holding that police officer with over 15 years of experience in blood spatter interpretation was sufficiently qualified to give expert testimony). In *People v. Smith*, 633 N.E.2d 69 (Ill. App. Ct. 1994), the Illinois court affirmed the lower court's decision to qualify a crime scene processor as an expert in blood pattern interpretation. *Id.* at 71. The witness had been a detective for the Decatur police department for 25 years, 20 of which had been spent investigating crime scenes. Additionally, as part of his training as a crime scene processor for the police department, the witness was instructed in blood pattern interpretation. The defense, however, contested the qualifications of the witness, arguing that general police training was not enough. But because the witness only testified as to the characteristics of the blood patterns, and did not attempt to reconstruct the crime, the court held that the witness was sufficiently qualified. *Id.* at 73.

Similarly, in a Florida case, *Morris v. State*, 561 So.2d 646 (Fla. Dist. Ct. App. 1990), the court affirmed the trial court's decision to admit blood spatter analysis by a homicide detective. Although the court stated that the trial court had erred in admitting this witness's testimony on blood spatter, the court nevertheless upheld the trial court's decision. The court reasoned that, because the detective's testimony was cumulative to the testimony given by a forensic serologist and a medical examiner, the error by the trial court was harmless.

[46] *See* Fla. Stat. §§ 817.566; 817.567 (1997).

Burden of Proof

In criminal cases, the burden of proof, i.e., the burden of producing evidence of the elements of the crime and the burden of persuading the jury of the elements of the crime, is on the prosecution. The prosecutor must produce evidence and persuade the jury beyond a reasonable doubt that the elements of the crime are met. Thus, the bloodstain pattern expert may assist the prosecutor in producing evidence and persuading the jury of the identity of the perpetrator or the victim.

The standard of proof of "beyond a reasonable doubt" does not mean beyond any doubt. A reasonable doubt is not a speculative, imaginary, or possible doubt. If the jury, after carefully considering, comparing, and weighing all the evidence, does not have an abiding conviction of guilt, or if, having a conviction, it is one which is not stable but wavers and vacillates, then there is a reasonable doubt.

The standard of proof in a civil case is by a preponderance of the evidence. This is a much less stringent standard of proof than beyond a reasonable doubt. You meet a preponderance of the evidence by the greater weight of the evidence or evidence which is more credible and convincing.

Chain of Custody

To lay a complete foundation for scientific evidence, lawyers need to establish four things: (1) proving the chain of custody for any physical sample from the time of seizure until it is introduced in court; (2) teaching the trier of fact about the scientific area; (3) describing when and how the analysis was done; and (4) interpreting the evidence for the trier of fact.

During trial, one who offers real evidence, such as a bloodstain found at a crime scene, must account for the custody of the evidence. Custody of the evidence must be documented from the crime scene to the moment in which it is offered in evidence. With the small samples common with blood evidence, chain of custody becomes an important issue. In order to lay the appropriate foundation for admissibility of real evidence, the attorney needs to demonstrate to the court, through witnesses' testimony, that the path of the evidence from the crime scene to the trial is well documented. Many experts mistakenly believe that once the evidence is safely at the laboratory, the chain of custody is no longer a problem. Not only must the experts establish the chain of custody of the evidence in the laboratory, they must also establish the chain of custody from the laboratory to the courthouse on the day of trial.

It is important to ensure that the laboratory has good documentation since chain of custody is a fertile area for lawyers to explore in discovery and during cross-examination. Opposing counsel will scrutinize the collection, preservation, and handling of blood evidence to probe the possibility of contamination or sample misidentification.

Discovery

Discovery is a pretrial process used in both criminal and civil cases to obtain facts and information about the case from the opposing party to assist in preparation for trial. The general policies underlying discovery are to prevent surprise at trial; to narrow the issues to be tried; and to speed the administration of justice by encouraging settlement (plea bargaining) of those cases where both sides know the strengths or weaknesses of the evidence.

> The discovery of scientific information is, in one sense, merely a part of the total discovery of a party's case and the same general purposes apply. However, special considerations arise with regard to expert discovery. The major reason given for expert discovery in both criminal and civil actions is the need for the opposing attorney to adequately prepare himself for cross-examination. The cross-examining lawyer often needs to have a very technical knowledge of the particular scientific field to put the expert's conclusions to a meaningful test. This is different from the cross-examination of a direct evidence witness (e.g., eyewitness), where the lawyer may draw from his own knowledge of the common fallibilities of sense perception and memory.[47]

Tools of discovery include depositions, interrogatories, and production of documents and reports. The process by which discovery is conducted is set forth in the civil and criminal rules of procedure. For example, Rule 16(a)(1)(D) of the Federal Rules of Criminal Procedure sets forth the prosecutor's discovery obligation to the defense, if requested, regarding scientific evidence:

> **(D) Reports of Examinations and Tests.** Upon request of a defendant the government shall permit the defendant to inspect and copy or photograph any results or reports of physical or mental examinations, and of scientific tests or experiments, or copies thereof, which are within the possession, custody, or control of the government, the existence of which is known, or by the exercise of due diligence may become known, to the attorney for the government, and which are material to the preparation of the defense or are intended for use by the government as evidence in chief at the trial.[48]

The defense then has a reciprocal obligation to turn over its results or reports of tests or experiments.[49]

The prosecution must also disclose material exculpatory evidence, i.e., evidence material to a defendant's guilt or punishment which tends to justify,

---

[47] Moenssens et al., *supra* note 6, at 32.
[48] Fed. R. Crim. P. 16(a)(1)(D) (1996).
[49] Fed. R. Crim. P. 16(b)(1)(B) (1996).

excuse, or clear the defendant from alleged fault or guilt.[50] The United States Supreme Court held that a defendant is denied due process if the government suppresses exculpatory information, material to a defendant's guilt or punishment, which the government knew.[51] Therefore, if the prosecution expert's analysis shows that the accused did not do the crime or is guilty of a lesser crime, the prosecution must disclose this information to the defense.[52] This requirement applies in criminal cases in federal court and in state court.

Another federal criminal discovery obligation is set forth in the Jencks Act.[53] The Jencks Act requires the government to produce, upon the defendant's request, any statements by a government witness which relate to that witness's testimony. Statements include written statements signed or adopted or approved by the witness; a contemporaneously recorded verbatim recital of a witness's oral statement; or a witness's statement to a grand jury. Therefore, if the prosecutors or investigators wrote down, verbatim, the expert's conversation during an interview, or wrote down what the expert said and read it back to him or let him read it, they have created Jencks material.

In a civil case, discovery of experts and their opinions may be obtained by interrogatories. The interrogatories require the party to disclose each person that the party expects to call as an expert at trial. Furthermore, the party must state the subject matter and substance of the facts and opinions to which the expert is expected to testify as well as a summary of the grounds for each opinion.[54] Any person expected to be called as an expert witness at trial may be deposed. An expert who has been retained or specially employed by a party in anticipation of, or preparation for, trial who is not expected to be called as a trial witness, may only be discoverable upon a showing of exceptional circumstances.

A deposition is another method of pretrial discovery which consists of a statement of a witness under oath. It is taken in question-and-answer form with opportunity given to the adversary to be present and cross-examine. This is reported and transcribed stenographically or it may be videotaped in some instances.

The opposition's objectives in taking an expert's deposition include to gather additional information; to attempt to impeach the expert; to lock the expert into a position or story which will be difficult to maintain at trial; to

---

50 *Brady v. Maryland,* 373 U.S. 83 (1963).

51 *Id.*

52 *See,* e.g., *Ex Parte Mowbray,* 943 S.W.2d (Tex. Crim. App. 1996) in which the prosecution's knowing failure to disclose blood pattern analyst's report supporting defense theory that deceased committed suicide was held to warrant a new trial.

53 18 USCA § 3500 (1997).

54 *E.g.,* Fla. R. Civ. P. 1.280 (1995).

assess the expert's demeanor as a witness; to demonstrate to the expert's proponent the extent of knowledge and expertise the opposition possesses.

Florida, Iowa, Indiana, Nebraska, and Missouri allow for discovery depositions of experts in criminal cases.[55] Depositions of experts in civil cases are universally allowed.

A federal civil procedure discovery rule requires a party to identify experts who are retained or specially employed and who may be used at trial.[56] The party proffering the expert must provide a written report containing a complete statement of all opinions to be expressed and the basis and reasons therefore; the data or other information considered by the witness in forming the opinions; any exhibits to be used as a summary of or support for the opinions; the qualifications of the witness, including a list of all publications authored by the witness within the preceding 10 years; the compensation to be paid for the study and testimony; and a listing of any other cases in which the witness has testified as an expert at trial or by deposition within the preceding 4 years.[57] Federal Rule of Civil Procedure 26 permits each district court, by local rule or order, to "opt out" of the rule's requirements. The majority of the 94 district courts have adopted Rule 26(a)(2); however, it is best to check with the local district court to determine the local discovery requirements.

The court's power in the discovery process is far-reaching. One court has held it was not an abuse of discretion for a trial court to order the plaintiff's expert to identify the accountant who prepared his tax return, as it might lead to information regarding the amount of income he derived from testifying for the plaintiffs which may be relevant to show bias.[58] The appellate court also upheld the lower court's decision to preclude the expert's testimony as a sanction for refusing to identify the accountant. Sanctions for discovery violations range from contempt to mistrial.

The process of discovery is a continuing obligation. Both parties must disclose discoverable information through the trial. Not all information is discoverable. Some information may be privileged. Privileges are governed by rules, statutes, or case law. Privileges were developed to encourage communications between parties in special relationships, e.g., doctor–patient, attorney–client. By protecting these communications from disclosure, communication between the parties is encouraged and the relationship is fostered.

A communication is protected by the attorney–client privilege if it is between privileged persons, in confidence, for the purpose of seeking or

---

[55] Moenssens et al., *supra* note 6, at 53.
[56] Fed. R. Civ. P. 26(a)(2)(A)–(C) (1995).
[57] Fed. R. Civ. P. 26(a)(2)(b)(1995).
[58] *Plitt v. Griggs*, 585 So.2d 1317 (Ala. 1991).

obtaining legal assistance.[59] A communication is confidential if not intended to be disclosed to third persons other than those to whom disclosure is in furtherance of the rendition of professional legal services to the client and

---

[59]   The attorney–client privilege may be a common law privilege (existing in case law only) in your jurisdiction or it may be codified. *See*, e.g., Fla. Stat. § 90.502 (1997) which provides:
(1) For purposes of this section
   (a) A "lawyer" is a person authorized, or reasonably believed by the client to be authorized, to practice law in any state or nation.
   (b) A "client" is any person, public officer, corporation, association, or other organization or entity, either public or private, who consults a lawyer with the purpose of obtaining legal services or who is rendered legal services by a lawyer.
   (c) A communication between lawyer and client is "confidential" if it is not intended to be disclosed to third persons other than:
      1. Those to whom disclosure is in furtherance of the rendition of legal services to the client.
      2. Those reasonably necessary for the transmission of the communication.
(2) A client has a privilege to refuse to disclose, and to prevent any other person from disclosing, the contents of confidential communications when such other person learned of the communications because they were made in the rendition of legal services to the client.
(3) The privilege may be claimed by:
   (a) The client.
   (b) A guardian or conservator of the client.
   (c) The personal representative of a deceased client.
   (d) A successor, assignee, trustee in dissolution, or any similar representative of an organization, corporation, or association or other entity, either public or private, whether or not in existence.
   (e) The lawyer, but only on behalf of the client. The lawyer's authority to claim the privilege is presumed in the absence of contrary evidence.
(4) There is no lawyer–client privilege under this section when:
   (a) The services of the lawyer were sought or obtained to enable or aid anyone to commit or plan to commit what the client knew was a crime or fraud.
   (b) A communication is relevant to an issue between parties who claim through the same deceased client.
   (c) A communication is relevant to an issue of breach of duty by the lawyer to his client or by the client to his lawyer, arising from the lawyer–client relationship.
   (d) A communication is relevant to an issue concerning the intention or competence of a client executing an attested document to which the lawyer is an attesting witness, or concerning the execution or attestation of the document.
   (e) A communication is relevant to a matter of common interest between two or more clients, or their successors in interest, if the communication was made by any of them to a lawyer retained or consulted in common when offered in a civil action between the clients or their successors in interest.
(5) Communications made by a person who seeks or receives services from the Department of Revenue under the child support enforcement program to the attorney representing the department shall be confidential and privileged as provided for in this section. Such communications shall not be disclosed to anyone other than the agency except as provided for in this section. Such disclosures shall be protected as if there were an attorney–client relationship between the attorney for the agency and the person who seeks services from the department.

those reasonably necessary for the transmission of the communication.[60] Thus, expert witnesses may be included within the lawyer–client privilege.

Work product includes written statements, private memoranda, and personal recollections prepared or formed by an attorney which reflect the attorney's efforts at investigating and preparing a case, assembling information, determining relevant facts, preparing legal theories, planning strategy, and recording mental impressions.[61] Therefore, if any attorney discusses trial strategy with the expert or writes letters or memos to the expert regarding trial strategy, it may be work product. Note that the inadvertent production of a work product–protected document will constitute a waiver of the privilege.

Direct and Cross-Examination of the Expert

Attorneys' Goals and Methods of Direct Examination

The direct examination is the unfolding of the evidence told from each side's perspective. The attorney should ask the expert witness short, direct, concise questions to elicit the following information:

Who are you? (e.g., your qualifications)
What did you do? (protocol)
Why did you do that? (did you consider alternative analyses,
   methodology, additional factors, underlying assumptions,
   and contrary theories)
What did you find? (basis of opinion)
What does that mean to you? (your opinion)

The expert should educate the members of the jury and help them understand why and how the expert reached the opinion. The expert cannot do an adequate job of educating the jury unless there has been extensive preparation. An expert should insist on a conference with the attorney prior to trial.

When testifying, experts must be wary of exceeding the scope of their expertise, or their testimony may be stricken from the record or the entire case may be overturned on appeal. A Florida case involving a medical examiner

---

[60] E.g., *Id.* at (1)(c)1.

[61] *Hickman v. Taylor*, 329 U.S. 495 (1946). For an example of the privilege contained in state discovery rules, *see* Fla. R. Crim. P. 3.220(g) (1997) which provides:

   (1) *Work Product.* Disclosure shall not be required of legal research or of records, correspondence, reports, or memoranda to the extent that they contain the opinions, theories, or conclusions of the prosecuting or defense attorney or members of their legal staffs.

illustrates this point. The medical examiner testified that a sneaker found at the crime scene was responsible for marks on the decedent's body. Her testimony was based on only one experiment with a colleague during which she slapped his back with the sneaker and concluded it left marks like those on the decedent. The court overturned the conviction since the testimony was improperly admitted, as the medical examiner was not an expert in shoe pattern analysis.[62]

Demonstrative Evidence

The modern world is increasingly oriented toward visual stimuli. "It has been estimated that upon graduation, the average high school student has completed 11,000 hours of classroom education while viewing over 15,000 hours of television."[63] Studies have shown that people retain 87% of the information presented to them visually, but only 10% of what they hear.[64] Therefore, in order to communicate effectively to judges and jurors, experts must give considerable thought to the types of exhibits they wish to use at trial. Real evidence is evidence furnished by things themselves, as distinguished from a description of them through a witness's testimony.[65] The suspected murder weapon would be real evidence in a homicide case. Demonstrative evidence illustrates, demonstrates, or helps explain oral testimony.[66] Examples of demonstrative evidence include models, diagrams, charts, and computer animations and simulations.[67]

Demonstrative evidence can be used to highlight salient points of an expert's testimony; increase the jurors' comprehension; illustrate information difficult to comprehend; permit the jury to digest large amounts of data;

---

[62] *State v. Gilliam*, 514 So.2d 1098 (Fla. 1987) (medical examiner was not an expert in shoe pattern analysis; therefore, it was error to allow her to testify that defendant's sneaker left marks on decedent); *see also, Behn v. State*, 621 So.2d 534 (Fla. Dist. Ct. App. 1993) (accident reconstructionist testified regarding extent of injuries that would have been suffered had truck's brakes been fully operative; beyond competence since he was not an expert in medicine, physiology, or biomechanics); *Kelvin v. State*, 610 So.2d 1359 (Fla. Dist. Ct. App. 1992) (held error to allow evidence technician to testify to trajectory of bullets depicted by dowels stuck into purported bullet holes in sofa at crime scene; technician not a reconstructionist and had no training in ballistics); *Wright v. State*, 348 So.2d 26 (Fla. Dist. Ct. App. 1977), *cert. denied*, 353 So.2d 679 (Fla. 1977) (medical examiner, offered as expert in forensic pathology, testified that injuries had been inflicted upon deceased by accused prior to death by suffocation. Court held this evidence of premeditation was beyond the competence of the medical examiner to give).

[63] Robert F. Seltzer, *Demonstrative Exhibits: A Key to Effective Jury Presentations*, 387 P.L.I./*Lit* 371 (1990).

[64] *Id.*

[65] *Black's Law Dictionary*, 1264 (6th ed., 1990).

[66] *Id.* at 432.

[67] For an introduction to frequently used demonstrative evidence and the legal concerns in utilizing such evidence *see* Ch. 2, Demonstrative Evidence, in Moenssens et al., *supra* note 6. There is an extensive bibliography of resources at the end of the chapter.

recreate or reconstruct critical events in an evidentiary chain; and add dramatic effect to oral testimony.[68]

To be admitted, demonstrative evidence must illustrate or explain a relevant issue in the case. The admissibility of such evidence is within the court's discretion and the judge's decision will only be overturned if the court abused its discretion. In determining the admissibility of such evidence, the court must weigh the probative value against any prejudicial effect the evidence might cause. Studies have shown that jurors and judges are impressed by visual aids.[69] In fact, in a study of judges and their impressions of fingerprint experts, the judges noted that a lack of visual aids was one of the three major obstacles to jurors' understanding of expert testimony.[70] More than 75% of the judges surveyed felt an expert should make a charted enlargement even for nonjury trials.[71]

Another study has found that jurors perceive an expert who demonstrates something, like a chart or diagram, in front of the jury to be more credible than an expert who does not leave the witness stand.[72]

Attorneys' Goals and Methods of Cross-Examination

The cross-examination can be the most frightening and intimidating part of the trial for the novice expert witness. The opposing lawyer's cross-examination will generally emphasize these points: what the expert is not; what the expert did, or did not, do; what the expert does not know.

The scope of the cross-examination is limited to the subject matter of the direct examination and matters affecting the credibility of the witness.[73] However, the court does have discretion to permit inquiry into additional matters.[74] The attorney will ask leading questions in order to control the witness.[75]

Wide latitude is often granted attorneys on the cross-examination of experts to test their opinions on matters that are not common knowledge. Cross-examination of an expert is allowed for the purpose of explaining, modifying, or discrediting the expert's testimony. The jury has a right to

---

[68] Mark A. Dombroff, *Dombroff on Demonstrative Evidence*, 4 (1983), Wiley & Sons, New York.

[69] Illsley, *supra* note 33, at 49.

[70] Telephone conversation with Charles Illsley.

[71] *Id.*

[72] Richard Tanton, *Jury Preconceptions and Their Effect on Expert Scientific Testimony*, 24, J. Forensic Sci., 681 (1979).

[73] Fed. R. Evid. 611(b) (1997).

[74] *Id.*

[75] Leading questions are those which usually limit the answer to a "yes" or "no," or those which suggest to the witness the answer desired.

know the extent of the witness's expert knowledge and experience. The expert's credentials and past record are relevant areas of inquiry.

There are many methods of cross-examination. Nine methods will be discussed here. The first method is to attack the field of expertise. In order to diminish an expert's credibility, an attorney wants to demonstrate that the field of expertise is art, not science.

The second method of cross-examination is exposing bias — "Isn't it true you only work for the prosecution? Isn't it true you've never testified for the defense?" Through this line of cross-examination, the attorney is trying to make the jury believe the expert favors one side over the other. Another area where attorneys attempt to demonstrate bias is by inquiring into the amount of money an expert earns as an expert witness as well as the number of times certain firms retain the expert. Some courts have allowed the opposing counsel to inquire into an expert's income records for the previous 2 years as well as inquire into the amount of referrals the expert receives from the law firm that retained him.[76]

The third method of cross-examination is attacking the chain of custody. The attorney will explore the laboratory's record keeping, evidence storage, and documentation. Some courts have held that a case must be dismissed if crucial evidence, such as fingerprint evidence, has been lost or misplaced.[77] In order to avoid such disastrous results, some laboratories have developed evidence-tracking devices not unlike the bar-coding system used at grocery stores.[78]

The fourth method of cross-examination is inquiring into laboratory protocol. Each laboratory should have documented training and protocols for each area of forensic science. If no protocol exists, the lawyer may cross-examine by intimating sloppy laboratory procedure. If protocol does exist and it was not followed, the attorney will establish this fact on cross-examination and will not ask the expert for an explanation. Rather, the attorney will argue to the jury in closing to disbelieve an expert who does not follow established procedures, thus casting doubt on the credibility of the analysis as well as the expert.

The fifth method of cross-examination is attacking the expert's factual basis for his or her opinion. Most experts would concede that their opinions are only as good as the factual and theoretical bases upon which they are founded. When attorneys utilize this method of cross-examination, they will inquire into such matters as the fact that the expert was not at the crime scene, did not lift the latent print or take the suspect's prints.

---

[76] *See, e.g., Trower v. Jones*, 520 N.E.2d 297 (Ill. 1988).

[77] *See, e.g., Scoggins v. State*, 802 P.2d 631 (N.M. 1990).

[78] John Donnelly, *Death Goes High Tech: Body Toe Tags Get Bar Codes*, Miami Herald, Oct. 4, 1993, at A1.

Attacking the instruments used by the expert to do the analysis is the sixth method of cross-examination. Lawyers will explore areas such as how data is entered, whether the equipment is calibrated, how is it maintained, and whether it is state of the art or a dinosaur-like relic.

The seventh method of cross-examination is an inquiry into proficiency testing. An expert's laboratory should participate in such testing on a periodic basis. During discovery, lawyers may inquire into the laboratory's and expert's results on such tests in order to unearth material to use in a cross-examination.

Laboratory accreditation and experts' board certification is also a relevant area of inquiry on cross-examination. If a laboratory has been put on probation by an accrediting body, such an action may reflect adversely on the expert. Attorneys may cross-examine an expert if board certification exists in the expert's area of expertise and the expert is not certified, or the expert was certified and had the certification revoked or not renewed.

The eighth method of cross-examination is attacking an expert's qualifications. This may occur during a motion in limine when one side is asking the court to rule on the admissibility of the field and the expert's expertise, or during the *voir dire* of an expert. The ninth method of cross-examination is impeachment with a learned treatise. When using this method of cross-examination, the attorney will ask the expert if he or she recognizes a text as the leading authority in the field. Note that some courts will not accept a person as an expert unless the person is familiar with the leading texts and journals in their field of expertise.[79] Once the expert admits that fact, the attorney is free to utilize that authority to contradict the expert's analysis and/or opinion, thus impeaching the expert's credibility.

When preparing for cross-examination of an expert, diligent attorneys will read all of the expert's publications and will locate deposition testimony, transcripts of trial testimony, and reported decisions of cases in which the expert testified. All of these items may reveal potential impeachment material, such as a change in theory, or a contrary opinion on a similar factual basis.

The key to reducing an expert's vulnerability on cross-examination is preparation on the part of both expert and attorney. This means the expert must do his "homework" and help the attorney become familiar with the area of expertise, credentials, and potential areas of weakness. If the attorney knows these things in advance of trial, he or she can present the expert in a most favorable light and minimize or even eliminate the possibility of an uncomfortable cross-examination experience.

Another way of reducing vulnerability on cross-examination is to maintain control. The adverse attorney is attempting to control the expert on cross-examination. That is why the attorney asks only leading questions. If

---

[79] *See,* e.g., Trial transcript at 522–523, December 10, 1991, *United States v. Parks,* Case No. CR 91-358-JSL (C.D. Cal.).

the expert maintains a calm, thoughtful demeanor, and does not lose his or her temper or composure in spite of the lawyer's tactics, the expert's credibility will be enhanced.

Advice to the Expert — Guidelines for Deposition and Trial Testimony

In order to enhance the effectiveness of your testimony at deposition, trial, or hearing, we have prepared guidelines based upon our experience with many witnesses in different cases. Consider the following suggestions:[80]

1. Tell the truth.
2. Prepare yourself by review of the facts.
3. Remember that most questions can be answered:
   "Yes"
   "No"
   "I don't know"
   "I don't remember"
   "I don't understand" or
   By stating a single fact.
4. If "yes" or "no" will do, that should be your answer.
5. Limit your answer to the narrow question asked. Then stop talking.
6. Never volunteer information or answers.
7. Do not assume you must have an answer for every question.
8. Be cautious of repeated questions about the same point.
9. Do not lose your temper.
10. Speak slowly, clearly, and naturally.
11. Your posture should be forward, upright, and alert.
12. Do not nod or gesture in lieu of an answer.
13. Don't be afraid to ask for clarification of unclear questions.
14. Do not be afraid of the examining attorneys.
15. Be accurate about all fact conditions, damages, and injuries.
16. Restrict your answers to facts personally known to you.
17. State basic facts, not opinions or estimates, unless they are asked for.
18. Be cautious of questions that include the word "absolutely" or "positively."
19. Remember, "absolute" means forever, without exception.
20. Be cautious about time, space, and distance estimates.
21. Do not guess if you do not know the answer.
22. Do not fence, argue, or second-guess the examining counsel.
23. Admit that you discussed your testimony previously if you did.

[80] Reprinted with permission. © Feder, Morris, Tamblyn & Goldstein, P.C., July 1989.

24. Do not memorize a story.
25. Avoid such phrases as "I think," "I guess," "I believe," or "I assume."
26. Maintain a relaxed but alert attitude at all times.
27. Do not answer too quickly — take a breath before answering each question.
28. Do not look to counsel for assistance.
29. Make sure you understand the question before answering.
30. Do not answer if you are told not to do so.
31. Never joke during a deposition or testimony.
32. Do not exaggerate, underestimate, or minimize.
33. Dress conservatively in clean clothes.
34. Be serious before, after, and during testimony.
35. If you make a mistake, correct it as soon as possible.
36. Remain silent if attorneys object during the examination.
37. Listen carefully to dialogue between attorneys.
38. Avoid mannerisms that signal nervousness.
39. Do not use technical language without translating it for your lay hearers.
40. Speak simply.
41. Do not discuss the case in the hallways or restrooms.
42. Do not converse with opposing parties, attorneys, or jurors.
43. Tell the truth.

Ethical Issues

Expert's Ethics

An expert witness has certain ethical obligations. They may be spelled out in an employee handbook, in the code of a professional association, or even by state statute.[81]

For example, members of the American Academy of Forensic Sciences (AAFS) are prohibited from making misrepresentations of their education or of the data upon which their professional opinions are based.[82] If an AAFS

---

[81] E.g., National Association of Medical Examiners Bylaws, Article Ten, Ethics (1992), which provides that members of N.A.M.E. shall conform to the published ethics of the American Medical Association. The National Society of Professional Engineers Code of Ethics (1990) sets forth fundamental canons, rules of practice, and professional obligations; The American Board of Criminalistics has promulgated rules of professional conduct which must be complied with by applicants and diplomates; Bylaws, Article IV.5 (1992).

[82] The American Academy of Forensic Sciences Bylaws Code of Ethics and Conduct, Art. II, Section 1 (1997).

member is found to have violated the code, an ethics committee may impose sanctions, such as censure, suspension, or expulsion from the organization.[83]

Some courts have sanctioned experts for their unethical behavior. In *Schmidt v. Ford Motor Co.*,[84] the court banned the plaintiff's accident reconstruction expert from testifying in federal court in Colorado because he had conveyed intentionally misleading information in depositions and informal conversations with the defense expert. The expert also concealed his knowledge from the defendant that one of the plaintiffs had tampered with the evidence.

Attorneys' Ethics in Dealing with Experts

Attorneys' ethical obligations are contained in each state's Rules of Professional Conduct or Code of Professional Responsibility. While no specific rule deals directly with attorneys and expert witnesses, some of the American Bar Association Model Rules of Professional Conduct are applicable. The Model Rules have been adopted in a majority of states.[85] Some of the model rules which impact upon an attorney's use of expert witnesses are the following:

> Rule 3.3 (Candor Toward the Tribunal) requires the attorney to investigate the background of expert witnesses to avoid putting on perjurious testimony regarding their credentials.

> Rule 3.8 (Special Responsibilities of a Prosecutor) specifies that the prosecutor's role as a "minister of justice" requires him to make timely disclosure of evidence or information that will negate evidence of guilt or mitigate guilt. Therefore, if fraud is uncovered relating to the expert's acts or knowledge it must be disclosed.

> Rule 5.3 (Responsibilities Regarding Nonlawyer Assistants) applies to experts as well as paralegals, and extends to situations where the lawyer is in essence ratifying the unethical conduct of the expert.

> Rule 8.3 (Reporting Professional Misconduct) requires the prosecutor to report unethical conduct of other attorneys. Therefore, if the opposing party's counsel knowingly uses an expert discovered to be a fraud, counsel is obligated to report the other lawyer to the grievance committee. If counsel doesn't report, counsel is in violation of the rule.

---

[83] *Id.* at Art. II, Section 2.
[84] 112 F.R.D. 216 (D. Colo. 1986).
[85] By 1997, 40 states and the District of Columbia and the Virgin Islands had adopted the Model Rules.

Rule 8.4(c) (Misconduct) states that it is professional misconduct to violate the Model Rules, commit a criminal act that reflects adversely on a lawyer's honesty, trustworthiness or fitness; engage in conduct involving dishonesty, fraud, deceit or misrepresentation; or engage in conduct that is prejudicial to the administration of justice.

Additionally, an attorney shall not fabricate evidence, counsel or assist a witness to testify falsely, offer an inducement to a witness that is prohibited by law, make frivolous discovery requests, or intentionally fail to comply with a legally proper discovery request.[86] A lawyer shall not make false statements of material fact or law to a third person, such as an expert witness.[87]

Model Rules 1.1 (Competence) and 1.3 (Diligence) require an attorney to seek out expert services, if needed by the client. Failure by a defense counsel in a criminal case to obtain the services of expert witnesses may later be deemed by courts to have resulted in the ineffective assistance of counsel.[88]

A lawyer may not promise an expert a fee contingent on the outcome of the case,[89] nor may an attorney share fees with an expert.[90] An attorney has been held to have an ethical obligation to pay an expert's fees unless he gives an express disclaimer of responsibility.[91]

Attorneys have been sanctioned by the bar for abusing an expert witness on cross-examination. A prosecutor was suspended from the practice of law for 30 days for improperly eliciting irrelevant testimony from the defense's expert witness, a psychiatrist. The prosecutor insulted the witness, ignored the court's rulings on defense objections which were sustained, and inserted his personal opinions on psychiatry and the insanity defense into his questioning.[92]

It should also be noted that Rule 11, Federal Rules of Civil Procedure, provides for sanctions to punish an attorney who knowingly files a false and misleading pleading. Courts have held that failure to disclose a contrary expert opinion alone is an insufficient basis for imposing Rule 11 sanctions.[93] In *Coffey v. Healthtrust, Inc.*[94] the defendant moved for Rule 11 sanctions against a plaintiff's attorney claiming that, when the lawyer filed an economic

---

[86] Model Rules of Professional Conduct, Rule 3.4 (1995).

[87] Model Rules of Professional Conduct, Rule 4.1 (1995).

[88] *Profitt v. United States*, 582 F.2d 854 (4th Cir. 1978), *cert. denied* 447 U.S. 910 (1980); *Moore v. State*, 827 S.W.2d 213 (Mo. 1992) — counsel ineffective for failing to request serological test.

[89] *Dupree v. Malpractice Research, Inc.*, 445 N.W.2d 498 (Mich. Ct. App. 1989).

[90] Sharing fees with nonlawyers violates ABA Model Rule 5.4(1), Model Rules of Professional Conduct (1993).

[91] *Copp v. Breskin*, 782 P.2d 1104 (Wash. Ct. App. 1989) — the court cited ABA Model Rules of Professional Conduct, 1.8(e) and 4.4 as authority.

[92] *The Florida Bar v. Schaub*, 618 So.2d 202 (Fla. 1993).

[93] *Schering Corp. v. Vitarine Pharmaceuticals, Inc.*, 889 F.2d 490 (3d Cir. 1989).

[94] 1 F.3d 1101 (10th Cir. 1993).

study, expert's affidavit, and accompanying brief supporting plaintiff's position that the hospital did not have competitors in its geographic market, the study's authors had told him that the expert's use of the study to support plaintiff's position would be misguided. The Tenth Circuit reversed, noting that while the attorney lied at the Rule 11 hearing regarding whether the study's authors talked with him, it may be a disciplinary matter but not a subject for Rule 11 sanctions. The court reasoned that an attorney must be allowed to reasonably rely on an expert's opinion as the basis of the client's position without fear of punishment for the expert's errors in judgment. Furthermore, the court found that the attorney's reliance on the expert's opinion had been reasonable because (1) the expert had sworn to his position in his affidavit, (2) the trial court had accepted the witness's expert status, and (3) the expert had held his position even when confronted with the contradictory conclusions of the study's authors. The court noted that opposing counsel had the opportunity and the duty to expose weaknesses in evidence.

The American Bar Association Standards Relating to the Administration of Criminal Justice also set forth standards for prosecutors and defense counsel to follow when working with expert witnesses in criminal trials. The standards provide that the attorney should respect the expert's independence, not dictate the formation of the expert's opinion, and that paying excessive or contingent fees is unprofessional conduct.[95]

Expert Witness Malpractice

In recent years, the law has been developing a new cause of action designed to hold expert witnesses, like doctors and lawyers, responsible for their negligent professional behavior. The law of expert witness negligence has developed largely in response to a recent recognition that such negligence is not uncommon.[96] Here are a few recent examples:

1. *A hospital and a national drug laboratory misdiagnosed toxins in a baby's blood, leading a jury to send the baby's mother to prison for murder.* The experts and the laboratory settled a civil suit on the eve of trial for undisclosed sums.[97]

---

[95] American Bar Association Standards Relating to the Administration of Criminal Justice, Standards 3-3.3, 4-4.4 (3d ed. 1992).

[96] Philip Hilts, *Misconduct in Science Is Not Rare, a Survey Finds*, The New York Times [Natl. ed.] Nov. 12, 1993, at A-13; James E. Starrs, *In the Land of Agog: An Allegory for the Expert Witness*, 30 J. For. Sci. 289 (1985) — Professor Starrs cites numerous instances of erroneous expert testimony. *See also*, Moenssens, *Novel Scientific Evidence in Criminal Cases: Some Words of Caution*, 84 J. Crim. L. & Criminology 801 (1993) — this article contains numerous recent instances of expert incompetence, negligence, and intentional fraud.

[97] Don DeBenedictis, *Off-Target Opinions*, ABA Journal, November 1994 at 76.

2. A police serologist falsified evidence against an accused rapist, sending the man to a West Virginia prison for five years. When the extent of the supposed expert's misdeeds in two states became clear, the state exonerated the man and agreed to pay him $1 million.[98]

3. A jury awarded a Los Angeles aircraft parts maker $42 million after litigation support experts damaged the company's civil rights suit against General Motors Corp.[99]

4. Martin Frias was convicted of murdering his girlfriend and spent three years in prison as a result of the negligence of the coroner.[100] Mr. Frias was eventually granted a new trial. He was acquitted after a forensic pathologist reexamined the case and determined that the coroner's ruling that the death was a homicide and not a suicide was erroneous.

Erroneous conclusions have been reported even with well-accepted scientific techniques, such as fingerprint identification. Federal and state officials reviewed 159 criminal cases in North Carolina after local authorities discovered what they determined to be questionable fingerprint identifications.[101] The review was prompted by a fingerprint misidentification that resulted in the dismissal of two murder charges by the district attorney's office.

Even if an expert is not negligent in rendering an opinion, the expert's opinion is only as good as the underlying basis for the opinion. That basis may depend on other experts' opinions. Whether engaged as a consulting or testifying expert, in a civil or criminal matter, an expert should be aware of the ethical responsibilities and potential liabilities in that role.

At present, the law does little to regulate the quality of expert testimony.[102] Solutions offered by the scientific and legal communities to curb expert abuses include capping expert witness fees,[103] prescreening experts, using only court-appointed experts, adherence to a strict code of ethics,[104] peer review,[105] and a science court.[106] Additionally, it has been suggested that

---

[98] *In the Matter of an Investigation of the West Virginia State Police Crime Laboratory, Serology Division,* Civil Action No. 93-MISC-402, Report by The Hon. James O. Holliday, Senior Judge. [Hereinafter Report].

[99] On remand of *Mattco Forge Inc. v. Arthur Young & Co.,* 5 Cal. App. 4th 392, 6 Cal. Rptr. 2d 781 (1992).

[100] Frank E. James, *Local Coroners' Lack of Forensic Training Raises Issue of Fitness,* Wall St. J., Dec. 16, 1988, at 1, Col. 1. In this article Mr. James recounts many instances of coroners' incompetence.

[101] Barry Bowden and Mike Barrett, *Fingerprint Errors Raise Questions on Local Convictions,* Fayetteville Times, Jan. 15, 1988, at 1A.

[102] Joseph Peterson & John Murdock, *Forensic Science Ethics: Developing an Integrated System of Support and Enforcement,* 34 J. For. Sci., 749 (1989).

[103] Florida Senate Bill 380 (1990), proposed capping expert fees at $250 an hour.

[104] National Forensic Center Summarized Code of Professional and Ethical Conduct (1992).

[105] Thomas S. Burack, *Of Reliable Science: Scientific Peer Review, Federal Regulatory Agencies and the Courts,* 7 Va. J. Nat. Resources L. 27 (1987).

fraudulent experts be prosecuted,[107] and that the principal safeguard against errant expert testimony is the opportunity for opposing counsel to cross-examine.[108] The reality is that most lawyers do a woefully inadequate job in cross-examining experts.[109] One reason for this is improper preparation. Another may be that lawyers are often reluctant to incur the risks involved in challenging experts in their own fields. Many lawyers do not even avail themselves of the assistance of experts in preparing for cross-examination and are therefore unable to challenge statements made by experts effectively. Finally, the vast majority of civil and criminal cases are settled or plea-bargained prior to trial so that the expert may never be subjected to rigorous questioning during the adversary process.

To date, none of the solutions offered to curb expert abuses has succeeded in accomplishing its goal. Arguably, attempts at monitoring expert testimony may serve to deter some expert negligence and also result in experts being held personally accountable. However, such steps do not necessarily provide for compensation to individuals harmed by an expert's negligence.

In view of the inadequacy or unavailability of the solutions to expert negligence and/or intentional professional misconduct, and that professional sanctions against an expert do not make whole a person injured as a result of such misconduct, tort actions for damages against experts and their employers are being resorted to more and more frequently. In the West Virginia serologist's case, a civil action for damages filed against the State resulted in a $1 million settlement.[110]

Of the solutions offered to curb expert abuses, only an expert witness malpractice cause of action will protect and compensate injured individuals, as well as deter future misconduct. It will ensure "quality control" of expert opinions by encouraging experts to be careful and accurate. The four elements of the expert witness malpractice action are (1) the existence of a duty owed to the plaintiff arising out of the relationship between the expert and

---

[106] See *Twenty-Five Year Retrospective on the Science Court: A Symposium*, 4 RISK-Issues in Health & Safety 95–188 (1993), containing a series of articles by advocates and detractors of the science court, including one by its "inventor." See Arthur Kantrowitz, *Elitism vs. Checks and Balances in Communicating Scientific Information to the Public*, 4 RISK-Issues in Health & Safety 101 (Spring 1993).

[107] Report, *supra* note 90.

[108] *Trower v. Jones*, 121 Ill.2d 211, 117 Ill.Dec. 136, 520 N.E.2d 297 (1988); *Sears v. Rutishauser*, 102 Ill.2d 402, 80 Ill.Dec. 758, 466 N.E.2d 210 (1984).

[109] Kevin M. Dowd, Book Review, Anderson & Winfree, *Expert Witnesses: Criminologists in the Courtroom*, [1987], 14 N. Eng. L. on Crim. & Civ. Confinement, 169, 171 (1988).

[110] Report, *supra* at note 90, at 2. The Report discloses that the filing of the civil law suit by the released Woodall resulted in the preliminary discovery that the serologist's errors and other misconduct were a matter of common practice, and induced the state insurance carrier to recommend settlement for the policy's limit. This settlement then led to the mandate by the state supreme court to investigate all the past cases wherein the serologist gave expert testimony.

the plaintiff; (2) a negligent act or omission by the expert in breach of that duty; (3) causation; and (4) damages.[111]

The premise of the expert witness malpractice cause of action is that, first of all, expert witnesses owe a duty to their clients. However, the duty does not end there. Expert witnesses also owe a duty to any foreseeable plaintiff who may be affected by the expert's conduct and who is likely to suffer damages due to a negligently rendered opinion. These duties, based upon their professional knowledge and skills, are similar to those duties owed by a doctor to a patient and a lawyer to a client.

The standard of care for a forensic scientist is that of the reasonably prudent practitioner in the relevant scientific field. Standards of professional practice and ethical codes as promulgated by the discipline may be used to help define the duty of care. Most disciplines within the forensic sciences have adopted such standards of conduct. In order for a plaintiff to prevail, it must be determined that the expert did not adhere to the standard of a reasonably prudent expert in rendering an opinion, in conducting an examination, or in giving testimony. Ordinarily, an independent evaluation by a disinterested expert skilled in the same field will be required to determine whether or not an expert deviated from the required standard of care.

A crucial element of the tort of malpractice is causation. Causation tests whether the defendant's actions were in fact connected by physical events to the plaintiff's injury, and whether the connection was close enough to allow compensation to the injured party. As stated by Richard S. Frank, a past president of the AAFS, "[t]he impact of the forensic scientist's conclusions affords no room for error, because such an error may be the direct cause of an injustice."[112] In some cases, it will be readily apparent that an expert's testimony alone "caused" the wrong. This is especially true when the expert evidence is the only determinative evidence presented in the litigation. Many studies have demonstrated that, despite jury instructions to the contrary, jurors give expert testimony greater weight than other evidence.[113] Thus, it is clear that financial injury to a potential plaintiff or conviction and incarceration of a potentially innocent individual who is prosecuted on the basis of an expert's opinion evidence[114] are reasonably foreseeable consequences of negligence, incompetence, or intentional misconduct by an expert.

Where a claim of expert witness malpractice is proved to have occurred in civil litigation, the measure of direct damages could include the difference between a full verdict of proved loss and the reduced verdict resulting from

---

[111] W. Page Keeton et al., *Prosser and Keeton on the Law of Torts* § 30, at 164–165 (5th ed., 1984), West, St. Paul, MN.

[112] Richard S. Frank, *The Essential Commitment For a Forensic Scientist*, 32 J. For. Sci., 5 (1987).

[113] Kurt Ludwig & Gary Fontaine, *Effects of Witnesses' Expertness and Manner of Delivery of Testimony on Verdicts of Simulated Jurors*, 42 Psychol. Rep., 955 (1978).

the expert's testimony; the difference between a full settlement and the reduced settlement that resulted from the expert's misconduct; and/or the cost in experts' investigators', and attorneys' fees for responding to the expert's testimony and in proving the misconduct.

Expert witness malpractice causes of action are gaining momentum. Courts in New Jersey,[115] Texas,[116] California,[117] and Missouri[118] are among the growing number of jurisdictions that have allowed plaintiffs to sue experts for their malpractice. Only one jurisdiction, Washington,[119] has clearly granted immunity to expert witnesses, stating that experts ought to be accorded absolute immunity and should be shielded through the testimonial privilege. Such limitations are rare, however, and the general recognition that such actions will be recognized by courts has induced defendants in malpractice suits to agree to settlements in many cases.

While no courts shield erring expert witnesses from perjury charges for willful deceptions or from damage actions where the expert's conduct involved intentional or grossly negligent conduct, a few courts have shielded experts from civil liability for damages in ordinary negligence cases. The courts have arrived at this result in one of two ways: (1) by holding that negligent mistakes or inaccuracies do not constitute perjury or (2) by holding that testimony and reports provided to courts are privileged.[120] Some courts hold that the expert witness who gives opinion evidence is the court's witness, and therefore enjoys immunity against all post-trial damage claims whether sued by a party or nonparty to the action. Two cases addressing such issues arose in California and Missouri. In *Mattco Forge, Inc. v. Arthur Young & Co.*,[121] the court held that the litigation privilege in the California Civil Code does not protect a negligent expert witness from liability to the party who hired the witness. In so holding, the court stated "applying the privilege does not encourage witnesses to testify truthfully; indeed by shielding a negligent expert witness from liability, it has the opposite effect."[122] The case went to

---

[114] Courts have awarded plaintiffs damages of a certain amount per month for illegal confinement due to legal malpractice, rejecting the argument that estimating the value of a person's loss of liberty is speculative. E.g., *Geddie v. St. Paul Fire and Marine Ins. Co.*, 354 So.2d 718 (La. Ct. App. 1978). See also, *Holliday v. Jones*, 264 Cal.Rptr. 448 (Ct. App. 1989), awarding damages for emotional distress as a result of wrongful incarceration due to professional malpractice.

[115] *Levine v. Wiss & Co.*, 478 A.2d 397, 399 (N.J. 1984).

[116] *James v. Brown*, 637 S.W.2d 914 (Tex. 1982).

[117] *Mattco Forge, Inc. v. Arthur Young & Co.*, 6 Cal. Rptr. 2d 781 (Cal. Ct. App. 1992).

[118] *Murphy v. A.A. Mathews*, 841 S.W.2d 671 (Mo. 1992).

[119] *Bruce v. Byrne-Stevens & Assoc. Engineers, Inc.*, 776 P.2d 666 (Wash. 1989).

[120] Michael J. Saks, *Prevalence and Impact of Ethical Problems in Forensic Science*, 34 J. For. Sci., 772 (1989) — containing a summary of some cases involving litigation against expert witnesses.

[121] *Supra* note 115.

trial and, in July 1994, the jury returned a verdict of $995,717 out-of-pocket expenses, $14,200,000 in compensatory damages and $27,680,000 in punitive damages against the expert witnesses for their negligence.[123] Also, in *Murphy v. A.A. Mathews*,[124] the Missouri Supreme Court held that witness immunity does not bar an action against a professional who agrees to provide litigation-related services for compensation if the professional is negligent in providing the agreed services. The court stressed, however, that its holding would not subject an adverse expert to malpractice liability because the expert owes no professional duty to the adversary. The court also stated that an expert retained by the court, independent of the litigants, would not be subject to malpractice liability. The *Matthews* holding is limited to pretrial, litigation support activities.

Witness immunity is an exception to the general rules of liability. The rule is traditionally limited to defamation cases and is extremely narrow in scope. Immunity is not meant to bar a suit against a professional who negligently performs services. The complaint is not with the testimony provided in court, it is with the out-of-court work product which was negligently produced. By testifying, the expert is merely publishing his or her negligence in court. Therefore, no absolute immunity should be afforded experts; they are neither judges nor their adjuncts, but merely third-party participants in litigation. The courts, the legal profession, and the forensic disciplines recognize that the trend is toward permitting claims for damages resulting from negligent testimony by experts.

Conclusion

Some concern may be voiced over whether or not the growing recognition of a cause of action for expert malpractice will have a chilling effect on the willingness of persons to serve as forensic experts in litigation. The emergence of such a cause of action may in fact result in the disappearance of some experts who are habitually negligent or incompetent, but this is of course a salutary by-product of the legal trend. Even if the existence of a cause of action for expert malpractice has an effect on the availability of a number of

---

[122] *Id.* at 788. The court stated, however, that the California litigation privilege would still shield experts that are court appointed, and would also shield expert witnesses from suit by opposing parties. *Id.* at 789.

[123] The Expert Witn. J., 1 (July 1994). The case has been reversed and remanded since the trial court erred in ruling that Mattco Forge was not required to establish that absent Arthur Young & Co.'s negligence, Mattco would have prevailed in the underlying case. *Mattco Forge, Inc. v. Arthur Young & Co.*, 60 Cal. Rptr. 2d 780 (Cal. Ct. App. 1997).

[124] 841 S.W.2d 671 (Mo. 1992).

experts, or results in an increase in the fees charged for their services, these results are not so compelling as to justify a public policy against recognizing a cause of action for expert witness malpractice. The very existence of the cause of action will ensure that experts are held accountable for their opinions. The full and accurate development of evidence in civil and criminal litigation is not served by protecting the negligent, incompetent, or dishonest expert witness. The justice system as a whole benefits when such causes of action are permitted. The forensic sciences themselves will enjoy greater respect and admiration when it is known their practitioners are accountable for misdeeds and that the professions favor eliminating the unworthy among them.

To be more effective, an expert should be aware of the legal and ethical responsibilities in that role. The expert should understand the test for admissibility for expert evidence, the rules of discovery and procedure, and any other statutory responsibilities. The expert should also be aware of the potential liability for malpractice as an expert witness.

Bloodstain Pattern Interpretation: A Post-Conviction Analysis

MARIE ELENA SACCOCCIO

Contents

Introduction

This chapter is dedicated to post-conviction attorneys dealing with issues concerning bloodstain pattern interpretation. While the emphasis is on post-conviction cases, the law is the law. As such, this chapter should prove useful to trial attorneys dealing with issues of admissibility, expert qualifications, via a motion in limine, or during examination of the expert at trial. The coverage will overlap and complement Chapter 6, Legal and Ethical Aspects of Bloodstain Pattern Evidence. While this is not presumed to be the authoritative source on each jurisdiction, this chapter provides an overview of issues to be evaluated and addressed at the post-conviction stage. Since there is a dearth of precedent on specific issues you may encounter in each jurisdiction, it will be beneficial to look to other jurisdictions for a case on point. Further, a list of appellate opinions dealing with bloodstain pattern evidence and presumptive blood tests is presented in Appendices 3 and 4 to aid in your inquiry.

0-8493-8108-8/99/$0.00+$.50
© 1999 by CRC Press LLC

A Bit of History

Any butcher is just as good an expert on that as this witness.

Commonwealth v. Sturtivant (1875)[1]

At the outset, despite the verbiage in some contemporary opinions, there is nothing new about appellate courts addressing admissibility or expert qualifications with respect to bloodstain pattern interpretation.

In 1857 the Supreme Judicial Court of Maine held that bloodstain pattern analysis was admissible and was a proper subject for expert testimony. The case was *State v. Knight*.[2] The expert proffered by the prosecution was Dr. Augustus Hayes, a scientist trained in the microscopic and chemical analysis of blood.[3]

The case was interesting and the theme, familiar. The crucial issue before the jury was whether Mary Knight committed suicide or was murdered by her husband, George.[4] To be sure, George's defense was that Mary had killed herself. And, in support of this, his mother, Lydia, testified that on the fateful night, she was awoken by Mary. Mary wanted to join her in bed and Lydia complied. Then Lydia heard an "outcry" and Mary's arms fell on her. Lydia saw no other person in the room, nor did she see the final act.[5]

The prosecution's case mirrored that presented in a contemporary homicide. Two doctors testified that Mary's death resulted from one mortal wound; i.e., her throat had been slashed and the slash was 5 in. long and 3 in. deep. She died instantly. She would not have been capable of any movement after such a wound so that the blood found on the window stool and on the floor were not caused by her.[6] Further, such a wound would have necessarily caused blood on Lydia, who was sleeping next to her. The evidence at trial was that Lydia had no blood on her that evening.[7]

Especially significant was blood found on the defendant's undershirt, worn on the night of the murder.[8] Dr. Hayes testified that the bloodstain on the undershirt was not caused by the defendant bleeding as the stain was deeper in color on the outer side of the undershirt than the side touching his body. The defendant's position at trial was that he had cut his arm and had bled on the undershirt at some other time.[9] Further, Dr. Hayes testified

---

[1]   *Commonwealth v. Sturtivant,* 117 Mass. 122, 126 (1875).
[2]   *State v. Knight,* 43 Me.11 (Me. 1857).
[3]   *Id.* at 19.
[4]   *Id.* at 20, 61.
[5]   *Id.* at 62.
[6]   *Id.* at 41, 98–99, and 130–131.
[7]   *Id.* at 28–29 and 41.
[8]   *Id.* at 24.
[9]   *Id.* at 24.

that the stain likewise did not result from the spurting of a vein "from without," except through the "interstices of some other fabric which had strained it of some of its original coloring matter."[10] L.D. Rice, a witness for the state, testified that on the day after the killing, he saw George wearing a shirt with a bloodstain on the sleeve.[11] The shirt, worn over the undershirt, was never found.

On appeal, the defendant objected to the testimony of Dr. Hayes, arguing that "the opinion of experts should be limited and confined to such matters as are of a scientific nature."[12] "Since his testimony on the bloodstains was easily observable to the jury, expert testimony on the subject should have been excluded."[13] In response, the appellate court held that the opinion of the witness was based on chemical experiment and observations aided by the microscope and resulted from scientific knowledge and experience.[14]

In *Commonwealth v. Sturtivant,* an opinion rendered in 1875, the Massachusetts Supreme Judicial Court addressed the admissibility of blood spatter interpretation and the qualifications of the "expert."[15] The witness, a chemist accustomed to chemical and microscopic examination of blood and bloodstains, testified for the prosecution as to directionality; i.e., "If the force of a stream of liquid, whatever it may be, and especially blood, be from below upward, the heaviest portion of the drop will stop at the further end of the stain; if from above downward, it will stop below."[16] Defense counsel objected to this testimony at trial, stating, "That is pure opinion as to a matter of mechanics, not chemistry. Any butcher is just as good an expert on that as this witness."[17]

On appeal, defense counsel argued that such testimony was inadmissible since the witness was allowed to opine as to directionality. This was incompetent evidence.[18] The witness was not qualified as an expert. Further, the "theory of the witness was incorrect in point of fact."[19]

In analogizing to the competency of lay witnesses to opine on identity of persons, things, animals or handwriting; size, color, weight of objects; time and distance; sounds and their direction; and footprints, the court held, "It is within the range of common knowledge to observe and understand those appearances, in marks or stains caused by other fluids, which indicate the

---

[10] *Id.* at 102.
[11] *Id.* at 128.
[12] *Id.* at 85.
[13] *Id.*
[14] *Id.* at 133.
[15] *Sturtivant,* 117 Mass. at 130, 138.
[16] *Id.* at 124, 126.
[17] *Id.*
[18] *Id.* at 130.
[19] *Id.* at 131.

direction from which they came, if impelled by force...."[20] "There is no question of science or learning necessarily involved in the understanding.... Blood is a fluid which coagulates and stiffens rapidly when exposed to the air and might, therefore, more decidedly give indications of its direction."[21] If the theory of the witness were incorrect in point of fact, such a position should have been explored in cross-examination of the expert.

Massachusetts was not alone in its reasoning. Likewise in 1875, in *Lindsay v. People of the State of New York,* the Supreme Court of New York held admissible the "expert" testimony as to bloodstain evidence obtained 6 months after the body was discovered, because such evidence tended to corroborate the testimony as to manner in which the body was taken from the murder scene to a loft.[22] The 6-month time lapse went to the weight of the evidence, not its admissibility.[23] Again, as in *Sturtivant,* the "expert," by training and experience, was a scientist who analyzed blood.[24]

Not every jurisdiction was as receptive to this type of evidence. In 1880 the Supreme Court of Mississippi held that the exclusion of expert testimony on bloodstain interpretation was correct.[25] The case was *Dillard v. State* and the defendant had proffered testimony of several physicians about the relative positions of the combatants, as indicated by the bloodstains. Their proffered opinion was that, based on the bloodstain patterns, the defendant was probably prostrate on the ground and the deceased on top of him when the bloodstains on the shirt were received.[26] The defense position at trial was that the deceased had first attacked the defendant, by hitting him with a piece of railing, the men fought, and when the cutting was done by the defendant he was lying on the ground with the victim on top of him. After the fight, the defendant called some neighbors and explained that he had stabbed someone and the circumstances of the fight. He summoned them to the body to help.[27] Also noted at the time were scratches and bruises on the defendant's face, evidencing the fight.[28]

On appeal, the defendant cited to *Knight* as precedent for the admissibility of expert testimony on bloodstain pattern analysis.[29] The appellate court failed to address it as persuasive legal authority. Paradoxically, in affirming the exclusion of such highly relevant evidence, the appellate court cited to *Sturtivant,* which had unequivocally approved the admission of bloodstain

---

[20] *Id*. at 134–135.
[21] *Id*. at 136–137.
[22] *Lindsay v. People of the State of New York,* 63 N.Y. 143, 155 (1875).
[23] *Id*.
[24] *Id*. at 147.
[25] *Dillard v. State,* 58 Miss. 368, 389 (1880).
[26] *Id*. at 380.
[27] *Id*. at 371.
[28] *Id*.
[29] *Id*. at 383.

pattern evidence via lay testimony.[30] Thankfully, though charged with murder, Dillard was only found guilty of manslaughter.[31]

In *Wilson v. United States*, a most interesting opinion rendered in 1895, the United States Supreme Court held that "… the existence of bloodstains at or near a place where violence has been inflicted is always relevant and admissible."[32] And, in so holding, the Supreme Court cited to *Sturtivant*.[33] The issue as to the competency or qualifications of the witness was never raised. The bloodstain evidence admitted was bloody bedclothes; bloody soak-through on a bed; a pillow sewed over blood spots; a bloody ax; charred pieces of cloth at a camping site, with some blood on the ground where the fire had been.[34] The victim's body was badly decomposed so that no cause of death could be determined, though a crushed skull was noted.[35] At trial Wilson called witnesses to show that the blood found on the bedclothes, and presumably the bed, had gotten there from the blood of a prairie chicken which they had killed, and also from the bleeding of sick horses.[36] What these men were doing in their bedclothes with a prairie chicken and a sick horse is beyond the scope of this chapter.

While bloodstain interpretation has certainly developed as a recognized scientific expertise, capable of quantification and grounded in established laws of physics and "common sense,"[37] echoes of *Sturtivant* are alive and well in more recent decisions. In *State v. Hall,* a 1980 decision rendered by the Supreme Court of Iowa, the court ignored the "general acceptance" requirement and approved the admission of blood spatter interpretation, reasoning that "[s]uch observations are largely based on common sense, and in fact, lie close to the ken of an average layman.… Such evidence need not wait an assessment of the scientific community, as it is inherently understandable and reliable."[38] Further, in *People v. Clark,* a 1993 opinion rendered by the Supreme Court of California, *en banc,* the court stated, "It is a matter of common knowledge, readily understood by the jury, that blood will be expelled from the human body if it is hit with sufficient force and that inferences can be drawn from the manner in which the expelled blood lands upon other objects."[39]

---

[30] *Id.* at 389.
[31] *Id.* at 370, 372.
[32] *Wilson v. United States*, 162 U.S. 613, 620 (1895).
[33] *Id.*
[34] *Id.* at 614.
[35] *Id.*
[36] *Id.* at 615.
[37] *United States v. Mustafa*, 22 M.J. 165 cert. *denied*, 479 U.S. 953 (CMA 1986).
[38] *State v. Hall*, 297 N.W.2d 80, 86 (Iowa 1980).
[39] *People v. Clark*, 857 P.2d 1099, 1142 (Cal. 1993) — In approving the admission of blood spatter interpretation, the Court held the *Kelly/Frye* "general acceptance" inapplicable because the methods employed are not new to science or law; i.e., the proffered evidence was not novel to trigger a *Frye* hearing, because such evidence predated *Kelly*, citing *People v. Carter*, 312 P.2d 665 (1957).

Despite these very liberal holdings on admissibility, it cannot be ignored that each court premised its reasoning on the inherent understandability, relevance, and reliability of such evidence. Further, most proponents therein would probably be qualified as experts today based on training and experience. Note, in *Sturtivant*, *Knight*, and *Lindsay*, the witnesses were scientists, accustomed to chemical and microscopic examination of bloodstains for the purpose of determining the origin of blood, i.e., whether it was human or animal.[40] To be sure, as scientists, their training also included mathematics and physics. In *Hall*, the "expert" turned out to be Herbert MacDonell, the "granddaddy" of bloodstain interpretation as we know it today.[41] In *Clark*, the court specifically found that the witness had (1) attended lectures and training seminars on blood dynamics in both California and Oregon; (2) read relevant literature; and (3) conducted relevant experiments.[42] Perhaps the only aberration is *Wilson*, but the qualifications of the witness were not raised in that appeal; i.e., the issue was simply not before the court.[43]

To the point, bloodstain interpretation has a history of admissibility spanning well over a century. The objections addressed by the court in *Knight*, *Sturtivant*, and *Lindsay* are the same considerations presented in post-conviction proceedings today. Starting from this vantage point will lend credibility and significance to post-conviction issues on this topic. It is neither novel, nor obscure.

The Post-Conviction Attorney's Role — So Daunting a Task

To be sure, in evaluating a case, post-conviction, one begins with the trial transcript, pleadings, and discovery provided. Of course, as a prosecutor, you just lie and wait; and if the issue is raised as to the competency of bloodstain evidence, or lack thereof, you respond. However, defense counsel's job is much more onerous. It is the defense counsel's job, and indeed her duty, to assess the bloodstain evidence as developed at trial. In its absence, the question then becomes should there have been such evidence? Both evaluations are equally important and determine the post-conviction path taken.

---

[40] *Knight*, 43 Me. at 19; *Sturtivant*, 117 Mass. at 24–26.
[41] *Hall*, 297 N.W.2d at 83; *Ex Parte Mowbray*, 943 S.W.2d 461 at 462 n.1 (Tex. Cr. App. 1996). (The prosecution sought agreement that MacDonell "is the expert or THE grand daddy of blood spatter").
[42] *Clark*, 857 P.2d at 1142.
[43] *Wilson*, 162 U.S. at 619. (Further, it appears that Wilson, who was sentenced to death by hanging, was not represented by counsel before the United States Supreme Court as "no appearance for plaintiff in error" was noted).

The Appeal

In a case in which bloodstain pattern evidence was admitted, the following questions should be helpful:

1. Is there precedent in that jurisdiction for its admission?
2. What is the appropriate standard of review?
3. Was the proponent a qualified expert by training or experience?
4. Was there the requisite foundation for the expert's testimony?
5. How was the defendant prejudiced by the admission of such evidence?

To breathe some life into this checklist and make it most useful for appellate counsel, the issues will be discussed below in the context of appellate opinions from various jurisdictions, whenever possible.

Admissibility

To be sure, as expressed above, bloodstain interpretation enjoys a history of admissibility spanning well over a century. This is true today not because it is perceived as "close to the ken of an average layman" as in *Sturtivant*, but rather because it is viewed as a scientific discipline, based on well-settled principles of chemistry and physics.[44] Not only has bloodstain evidence never been excluded from trial for lack of "general acceptance," its reliability is subject to judicial notice in some jurisdictions.[45] The shift from the *Frye* standard of admissibility to *Daubert* should not substantially alter its admissibility.[46] In fact, *Daubert* has a much more liberal thrust aimed at admitting scientific evidence not yet deemed "generally accepted."[47] In a jurisdiction adhering to *Frye*, the "general acceptance" in the scientific community can certainly be satisfied by beginning with the list of cases, affirming the admissibility, provided in Appendix 3. On the other hand, *Daubert*, the first United States Supreme Court case addressing the admissibility of scientific evidence, presents a different obstacle. Now the trial judge must, *inter alia*, make a preliminary determination that the "reasoning or methodology underlying

---

[44] *State v. Eason*, 687 A.2d 922, 925–926 (D.C.App.1996); *State v. Moore*, 458 N.W.2d 90, 97 and n.6 (Minn. 1990).

[45] *Moore*, 458 N.W.2d 90, 97 (Minn. 1990); *Knox*, 459 N.E.2d 1077, 1080 (Ill.App.3 Dist. 1984).

[46] *Frye v. United States*, 293 F.1013, 1014 (D.C. App. 1923) (employing "general acceptance" as prerequisite for admissibility of expert testimony); *Daubert v. Merrell Dow Pharmaceuticals, Inc.*, 113 S.Ct.2786, 2795 (1993) (rejecting *Frye* and adopting, *inter alia*, a "reliability" evaluation of "scientific, technical and specialized knowledge" that might be helpful to the jury," consistent with F.R.E. 702).

[47] *Daubert*, 113 S.Ct. at 2794.

the testimony is scientifically valid."[48] However, the absence of *Frye*'s "general acceptance" in the relevant scientific community is no longer an impediment to admissibility, and "general acceptance" continues to be the significant and often the only issue.[49] As such, in jurisdictions holding bloodstain interpretation admissible under *Frye*, it should now be admissible under *Daubert*.[50]

Standards of Review

In addition, for the purposes of appellate/post-conviction analysis, some mention of the standard of review is critical as the standard has varied within the federal circuits and among state courts. The purpose of this presentation is twofold: first, it serves to stress the importance of the standard of review in assessing your case, as well as secondary authority in sister states; second, it serves to demonstrate the lack of judicial uniformity in what boils down to essentially an overall reliability assessment of scientific knowledge, despite the different tests employed.

In *Daubert*, the United States Supreme Court was silent on the issue. Previously, the Supreme Court had stated that the trial judge had broad discretion as to the admissibility of expert testimony and the decision would be sustained unless "manifestly erroneous."[51] Whether considering *Frye* or *Daubert*, or some hybrid species peculiar to a particular jurisdiction, there is distressing variance in the standards of review utilized by appellate courts.

For example, when employing *Daubert*, the First, Second, Eighth Circuits, and the District of Columbia has applied the "manifestly erroneous" standard when reviewing the admissibility of scientific evidence.[52] The Ninth and Eleventh Circuits have reviewed the trial court's decision for an "abuse of

---

[48] *Id.* at 2796.

[49] *Commonwealth v. Lanigan*, 641 N.E.2d 1342, 1348–1349 (Mass. 1994); *but see, Commonwealth v. Sands*, 675 N.E.2d 370, 371 (1997) (reaffirms *Lanigan* but states it has adopted *Daubert*, in part, with "general acceptance" the overruling factor); *State v. Porter*, 694 A.2d 1262, 1278 (Conn. 1997).

[50] ABA Section on Science and Technology, Scientific Evidence Review, Monograph No. 2, at 8, Professor Stephen Salsberg, *Daubert: Framework of the Issues.* ("Thus, while *Frye* no longer governs, the concept of general acceptance may retain importance. I suspect that a trial judge will have a difficult time excluding as unreliable evidence which is generally accepted . . . if it is met, reliability will be presumed; and if it is not, the burden of demonstrating reliability or unreliability must be born by the proponent or opponent of the evidence").

[51] *Salem v. United States Lines Co.*, 370 U.S. 31, 35 (1962).

[52] *Bogosian v. Mercedes-Benz of North America, Inc.*, 104 F.3d 472, 476 (1st Cir. 1997); *McCulloch v. H.B. Fuller Co.*, 61 F.3d 1038, 1042 (2nd Civ. 1995); *Wintz by and through Wintz v. Northrop Corp.*, 110 F.3d 508, 512 (8th Cir. 1997); *Raynor v. Merrell Pharmaceuticals, Inc.*, 104 F.3d 1371, 1374 (D.C. Cir. 1997).

discretion."[53] The Third Circuit has taken a "hard look" to ensure that the district court's exercise of discretion was sound and that it correctly applied the several *Daubert* factors.[54] The Seventh Circuit has afforded *de novo* review of whether or not the trial court properly followed the framework of *Daubert*.[55] And, the Tenth Circuit has reviewed the application and relevance of *Daubert* as a matter of law, thus requiring *de novo* review; however, the trial court's ultimate decision as to admissibility has been reviewed for an "abuse of discretion."[56] Finally, some four years after *Daubert,* the U.S. Supreme Court decided that an appellate court, in reviewing a trial court's decision to admit or exclude expert testimony, should apply the abuse of discretion standard. The case is *General Electric Company v. Joiner* and was decided December 15, 1997.

State courts employing differing standards for the admissibility of scientific evidence likewise apply different standards of review on appeal. For example, Florida, which recently reaffirmed its adherence to *Frye*, affords *de novo* review on appeal.[57] Massachusetts, in rejecting *Frye* and following *Daubert*, like Florida, affords *de novo* review."[58] North Carolina, a jurisdiction not adhering to *Frye* or *Daubert*, apparently presents two different tests depending on whether the proffered evidence is deemed "experimental" or "scientific, technical or specialized knowledge." In a case in which "experimental" evidence is proffered, e.g., actual testing forming the basis for the experts opinion or a demonstration for the jury, admissibility is based on relevance and substantial similarity of the experimental evidence to the circumstances in controversy.[59] And, appellate courts review such admissibility as a question of law, i.e., *de novo*.[60] However, the admissibility of "scientific, technical, or specialized knowledge" is controlled by North Carolina Rule of Evidence 702, a corollary to Fed. R. Evid. 702, and the standard of review is abuse of discretion.[61] Similarly, in Nebraska, a jurisdiction not employing *Frye* or *Daubert*, but rather a four-prong test provided by statute, the appellate court reviews the trial court's decision for clear error.[62]

[53] *United States v. Amador-Galvan,* 9 F.3d 1414, 1417 (9th Cir. 1993); *Joiner v. General Electric Co.,* 78 F.3d 524, 529 (11th Cir. 1996).

[54] *In re Paoli R.R. Yard PCB Litigation,* 35 F.3d 717, 733 (3rd Civ. 1994).

[55] *Bradley v. Brown,* 42 F.2d 434, 437–438 (7th Cir. 1994) — citing *Cella v.United States,* 998 F.2d 418, 422 (7th Cir. 1993).

[56] *Compton v. Subaru of America, Inc.,* 82 F.3d 1513, 1517 (10th Cir. 1996).

[57] *Hadden v. State,* 690 So.2d 573, 578–579 (Fla. 1997) (reaffirming its rejection of *Daubert* and specifically noting the trial courts ruling on the admissibility of expert testimony is a matter of law subject to *de novo* review).

[58] *Commonwealth v. Vao Sok,* 425 Mass. 787 (1997).

[59] *State v. Clifton,* 481 S.E.2d 393, 397 (N.C. App. 1997).

[60] *Id.*

[61] *State v. East,* 481 S.E.2d 652, 662–663 (N.C. 1997).

[62] *State v. Thieszen,* 560 N.W.2d 800, 809 (Neb. 1997).

To be sure, as always, *de novo* review is the most advantageous standard at the appellate/post-conviction stage, and there is precedent for its utilization under both *Frye* and *Daubert*. Despite a different standard employed in a particular jurisdiction, appellate counsel may want to argue for *de novo* review so as to ensure against inconsistency and nonuniformity in decisions on admissibility.[63] If, indeed, as is the case, all admissibility tests focus on the reliability of the proffered scientific knowledge, the abuse of discretion standard makes no sense because the reviewing court is thereby obligated to uphold any determination of the trial court "that falls within a broad range of permissible conclusions."[64] In other words, such a standard affords the trial court discretion to admit unreliable evidence so long as the discretion is not abused or manifestly erroneous. If, indeed, there is something called "scientific knowledge," judicial determinations of admissibility should be uniform. Either the foundation of the evidence is scientifically valid or it is not. However, this is not to posit that there should be no inquiry into the actual application of methodologies employed or the qualifications of a particular expert. These are separate and distinct issues.

To further support *de novo* standard of review, it can be argued that the admission or exclusion of the bloodstain evidence was a violation of due process, rendering the proceeding fundamentally unfair.[65] It is axiomatic that the United States Constitution guarantees criminal defendants "a meaningful opportunity to offer a complete defense."[66] In fact, there are times when the exclusion of evidence, legally inadmissible under state law, violates the Due Process Clause of the Fourteenth Amendment. Such was the ruling of the United States Supreme Court in *Green v. Georgia*[67] and *Chambers v. Mississippi*.[68] As such, the issue of the admissibility or inadmissibility of the expert evidence should be presented as constitutionally based, citing to the Federal Constitution and its cognate provision in the particular jurisdiction. And, constitutional issues are issues of law. As the Supreme Court has repeatedly held, " '[j]udicial review of issues of law is straightforward. The standard is always *de novo*.' There are no exceptions."[69]

---

[63] *See,* Jay P. Kesan, *An Autopsy of Scientific Evidence in a Post-Daubert World,* 84 Georg. L.R. 1985, 2037–2038 (1996); *Commonwealth v. Vao Sok,* 425 Mass. 787 (1997) and cases cited therein.

[64] *Cooter v. Gell v. Hartmaxx Corp.,* 496 U.S. 384, 400 (1990).

[65] *State v. Myers,* 391 S.E.2d 551 (S.C. 1990). (In reversing and remanding for retrial, the Supreme Court of South Carolina held that the exclusion of the defendant's expert impacted on the *fairness of the trial*. The interpretation of blood spatters was outside the knowledge of ordinary jurors. Depriving the jury of blood stain analysis interfered with the jury's ability to evaluate the evidence).

[66] *California v. Trombetta,* 104 S.Ct. 2528, 2532 (1984).

[67] *Green v. Georgia,* 442 U.S. 95, 97 (1978).

[68] Chambers v. Mississippi, 410 U.S. 298–303 (1972).

[69] *Pierce v. Underwood,* 487 U.S. 552, 558 (1988).

Expert Qualifications

> An expert, as the word imports, is one having had experience. No clearly
> defined rule is to be found in the books what constitutes an expert. Much
> depends upon the nature of the question in regard to which an opinion is
> asked.
>
> *Oil Co. v. Gilson* (1869)[70]

> The ground, upon which one is called as an expert, is, that the subject in
> controversy depends on science or peculiar skill, knowledge, or experience
> … and this must often depend upon circumstances of so peculiar a nature
> and character, that it is difficult to lay down any general rule to guide the
> decision of the judge in such a case.
>
> *Lincoln & wife v. Inhabitants of Barre* (1850)[71]

Despite the passage of well over a century since the above-quoted opinions, there remains no clearly defined rule. One would presume, *ab initio*,
that "experts" presenting the worst qualifications would probably be excluded
pretrial, via a motion in limine, or during trial, on *voir dire* as to qualifications. However, from a survey of the case law on the issue, this presumption
is questionable.[72]

To date, in cases in which appellate courts have addressed the qualifications of bloodstain pattern experts, there seems to be little uniformity, or for
that matter, comprehension of what the expertise demands. As such, the
courts have deemed qualified coroners, pathologists, medical examiners,
crime scene investigators, serologists, firearms examiners, police officers,
forensic science investigators, and a witness who stated no particular qualifications at all.[73] To exacerbate the problem further, the majority of courts
overwhelmingly review the trial court's decision as to qualifications for abuse
of discretion, and, in the minority of jurisdictions, the appellate court reviews
for clear error. To the point, this is a difficult road on appeal. The following
cases provide ample support for this statement.

In *State v. Thieszen*, a 1997 opinion, the Supreme Court of Nebraska
addressed the issue of the qualifications of an expert in a first-degree murder
case.[74] The expert did hold a master's degree in science and had major hours

---

[70] *Oil v. Gilson*, 63 Pa. St. 146, 150 (1869).
[71] *Lincoln & wife v. Inhabitants of Barre*, 59 Mass. 590, 591 (1850).
[72] *See* Danny R. Vieulleux, Annotation, *Admissibility, In Criminal Prosecution, of Expert
Opinion Evidence as to "Blood Splatter" Interpretation*, 9 A.L.R. 5th 369 sections 6[a],
and 13–16 and (Supp. 1997).
[73] *Id.*
[74] *State v. Thieszen*, 560 N.W.2d 800, 808–809 (Neb. 1997).

in physics, mathematics, and biology; his education included training in the physics of flowing fluids, viscosity, absorbtivity, but no training in the interpretation of forensic evidence, in general, or bloodstain analysis, specifically.[75] He was certified, but as a science teacher in Nebraska.[76] While he had never before testified about the flow of fluids, he had previously examined and evaluated photographs of crime scenes in his consulting business.[77] Affirming the conviction, the court explained, "There is no exact standard for determining when one qualifies as an expert and a trial court's factual finding that a witness qualifies as an expert will be upheld on appeal unless clearly erroneous."[78]

In *State v. Knox*, the Appellate Court of Illinois approved the qualifications of a police officer who had testified as a blood spatter expert.[79] While the expert had attended a school in "blood flight splashings and patterns" at Elmira College and a "blood flight" workshop at the St. Louis Medical Examiner's Office, the primary objection was that he had no training at all in physics.[80] Dismissing the substance of the objection, the court held that the expert's testimony was not of such a "complex nature" to require a foundation in physics.[81] In finding no abuse of discretion, the court stated, "The degree and manner of knowledge and experience required of an alleged expert is directly related to the complexity of the subject matter,"[82] a recurring theme in other opinions. Note, despite the machinations of the appellate court in affirming the qualifications of the "expert," the "expert" did testify that the woman was stabbed while lying down in her bed. And, this was his opinion though there was blood on the sidewalk, in the doorway, and on the walls.[83] Upon arrival of the investigating police, the defendant asserted that his wife had attacked him with a knife. In the struggle to take the knife away, he stabbed her.[84] To be sure, the bloodstain evidence went to the heart of the defense and was more complex than perceived.

In *People v. Owens* 4 years later, the Appellate Court of Illinois again addressed the qualifications of a blood pattern expert, but this time held that it was an abuse of discretion to admit the testimony.[85] Again, the purported expert was a police officer. The officer had been employed by the Illinois State Police for more than 17 years and as a crime scene technician for

---

[75] *Id*. at 808.
[76] *Id*.
[77] *Id*. at 809.
[78] *Id*.
[79] *People v. Knox*, 459 N.E.2d 1077, 1081 (Ill. App. 3 Dist. 1984).
[80] *Id*.
[81] *Id*.
[82] *Id*.
[83] *Id*. at 1079.
[84] *Id*.
[85] *People v. Owens*, 508 N.E.2d 1088, 1094–1095 (Ill. App. 4 Dist. 1987).

approximately 7 years.[86] He explained that his responsibilities as a crime scene technician were to "process crime scenes for the physical evidence, do all the photography, the sketching, fingerprinting, collection of the evidence, packaging and receipt of the evidence [and] relaying the evidence to the crime lab for analysis."[87] However, the appellate court found that this did not provide a proper foundation for qualifying the police officer as a blood spatter analyst.[88] Although the officer did testify under cross-examination that he had studied "blood spatter technique" under "Professor McDonald [sic]," such testimony was not viewed as sufficient to satisfy the state's burden.[89] And this was because the police officer's testimony at trial was a full-scale crime reconstruction, and the evidence was "closely balanced" between the prosecution's theory and the defendant's self-defense claim.[90] As such, the error was not harmless, and a reversal was warranted.[91]

Likewise, in *State v. Philbrick*, the Supreme Court of Maine vacated a murder conviction based on the trial court's failure to rule on whether or not the police officer was qualified to testify as a bloodstain pattern expert.[92] Just as in *Owens*, the only basis the officer presented for his expert opinion was that he had attended a "short three-week training course at 'bloodspatter school.' "[93] At trial, the officer presented a full-scale demonstrative reconstruction of the positions of the bodies, and the sequence of the shots, based primarily on the bloodstains.[94] Such evidence went to the heart of the defense as the defendant asserted that the death resulted while he was defending himself against the sexual assault of the victim.[95] In the words of the appellate court, the officer's "in-court demonstration of the shooting incident and his 'expert' opinion testimony regarding the positions of the bodies when each shot was fired tainted the trial with reversible error."[96]

In 1994, the Appellate Court of Illinois, revisiting the issue of the requisite qualifications of a bloodstain expert, stated that " [i]ndicia of expertise is not a given level of academic qualification, but whether the expert has knowledge and experience beyond that of the average citizen which would assist the jury in evaluating the evidence."[97] *In vacuo*, this is a liberal holding, diverging from its own precedent on this issue. The case, *People v. Smith*, addressed the

---

[86] *Id*. at 1090.
[87] *Id*.
[88] *Id*. at 1094.
[89] *Id*. at 1094–1095.
[90] *Id*. at 1095.
[91] *Id*.
[92] *State v. Philbrick*, 436 A.2d 844, 861 (Me. 1981).
[93] *Id*.
[94] *Id*. at 858–859.
[95] *Id*. at 859.
[96] *Id*. at 861.
[97] *People v. Smith*, 633 N.E.2d 69 (Ill. App. 4 Dist. 1993).

qualifications of a crime scene technician whom the police department employed.[98] In affirming the trial court's decision to qualify the expert, the appellate court reasoned that, contrary to *Owens* which presented a full-scale crime reconstruction, determining direction of gunshots, location of body, and position of the body when shot, the technician in *Smith* merely distinguished high- and low-velocity blood markings.[99] As such, the court held any crime scene technician "with even a modicum of experience in processing crime scenes to be fully qualified to offer such limited testimony."[100]

In 1995 the Oklahoma Court of Criminal Appeals rendered a notable and instructive decision. The case was *Clayton v. State*.[101] The issue of the qualifications of the blood spatter expert was raised in a post-conviction proceeding, after appeal, as a violation of due process.[102] The collateral attack alleged, *inter alia*, that the "expert" had overstated his qualifications and, indeed, was not qualified.[103] In support of this allegation, the defense proffered three affidavits attacking the expert's qualifications to testify as a blood spatter expert in a different case. One affidavit, authored by Herbert Mac-Donell, stated that the "expert" received insufficient training to qualify him as a blood spatter expert; also proffered were two affidavits by a police sergeant and a captain asserting the same.[104] In addition, the defense submitted three letters written by the Oklahoma State Bureau of Investigations to the Attorney General's Office and the Tulsa District Attorney, disavowing the witness as a blood spatter expert.[105] Faced with this newly discovered evidence, the Oklahoma Court of Criminal Appeals held that the admission of the witness's testimony was error. However, unfortunately, the court further held that such error was harmless.[106]

Eason v. United States, a 1996 opinion rendered by the District of Columbia Court of Appeals, held that a detective had the requisite qualifications, based on knowledge and experience, to testify as to location of blood spatters, transfers, direction of drip, and location of the murder victim's body when shot.[107] Applying the "sliding-scale" approach, previously addressed in other case analyses, the court stated, "Witnesses testifying in court can be placed on a sliding scale. Lay witnesses generally testify solely on their personal observations or knowledge while, generally, expert witnesses testify based on

---

[98] *Id.* at 73.
[99] *Id.*
[100] *Id.*
[101] *Clayton v. State*, 892 P.2d 646 (Okl. Cr. 1995).
[102] *Id.* at 649, 652.
[103] *Id.* at 652.
[104] Id.
[105] *Id.*
[106] *Id.* at 653.
[107] *Eason v. United States*, 687 A.2d 922, 926 (D.C. App. 1996).

their experience and knowledge in a field. The more complex the subject matter the more closely we scrutinize the expertise of the witness testifying."[108]

Again there was a familiar theme. The objectionable expert in *Eason* was a police officer.[109] He had been on the force for 16 years, with 4 years experience as a homicide detective.[110] The homicide training included specific instruction and experiments regarding blood spatter.[111] He had worked with more-experienced detectives analyzing blood spatter and had analyzed it himself at innumerable crime scenes.[112] No mention was made of any prior testimony on the subject matter. The trial judge allowed the testimony on very narrow grounds, i.e., that the victim was kneeling when shot.[113] In finding no abuse of discretion, the appellate court reasoned that the witness did not engage in sophisticated blood spatter analysis involving more-complicated calculation or experiments.[114] The testimony only concerned the location of the spatter and transfers and the ultimate opinion of the position of the body.[115]

Eason bears a striking factual resemblance to *Knox*. The defendant, Anthony Eason, banged on his neighbor's door and blurted out that he had shot his fiancée after she had hit him in the head with a hammer.[116] He further asserted that after he had knocked the hammer out of her hand, she retrieved a gun.[117] Eason attempted to take the gun out of her hands and during the struggle the gun discharged. As in *Knox*, the position of the body went to the heart of the defense.[118] The police officer, qualified as an expert, testified that the victim was kneeling when shot.[119]

To further complicate the matter, the trial court qualified the pathologist to testify as to the bloodstain evidence, with no indication as to her qualifications on the subject other than she had performed 2000 autopsies.[120] She opined that the victim was kneeling when shot.[121] Based on her experience, presumably conducting autopsies, the appellate court ruled there was no abuse of discretion in allowing her testimony.[122]

[108] *Id.* at 924–925.
[109] *Id.* at 925.
[110] *Id.*
[111] *Id.*
[112] *Id.*
[113] *Id.*
[114] *Id.* at 925–926.
[115] *Id.* at 926.
[116] *Id.* at 924.
[117] *Id.*
[118] *Id.*
[119] *Id.* at 131.
[120] *Id.* at 926.
[121] *Id.*
[122] *Id.*

Evading any substantive discussion on qualifications, as is often the case, in *State v. East*, the Supreme Court of North Carolina ruled that the trial court did not abuse its discretion in qualifying a crime scene technician as a blood spatter expert.[123] *East* was a death penalty case, based on the gruesome murders of the defendant's elderly aunt and uncle.[124] The proffered expert had extensive experience in crime scene collection and processing. She held a bachelor's degree in criminology, during which she attended a crime-lab class, and a master's degree in criminal justice.[125] In its analysis the court explained that "[I]t is not necessary that an expert be experienced with the identical subject matter at issue or be a specialist, licensed, or even engaged in a specific profession.... It is enough that the expert witness 'because of his expertise is in a better position to have an opinion on the subject than is the trier of fact.' "[126] As such, based on the witness's education and experience, she was deemed qualified to testify as an expert on bloodstain pattern analysis.[127] This is not a surprising holding given the very liberal standard for expert qualification enunciated by the court.

Contrary to *East*, in *People v. Hogan*, the Supreme Court of California reversed the defendant's conviction of two first-degree murders.[128] As special circumstances warranting the death penalty, the prosecution alleged that the defendant was present during the killings.[129] The criminalist testified in detail that specific stains were "splatters" caused by blood propelled by impact, rather than mere contact with a bloody object. Further, he opined that the blood on the boots was not consistent with someone stepping in a pool of blood.[130] When the defendant was examined, there was no blood on his head or chest hair, but considerable bloodstains were found on his pants and boots, including the pant cuffs and the inside seams of his pants up to his knees.[131]

At trial, the criminalist admitted that he had no formal training or education on the subject, and that his opinion was essentially based on some diagrams he had once viewed which demonstrated patterns of blood dropped from various heights and angles. Further, he had performed no experiments to support his opinion, nor had he sought to verify it in any way.[132]

The appellate court found his qualifications to be "nonexistent."[133] Its reasoning was clear: while the criminalist was qualified to testify about

[123] *State v. East*, 481 S.E.2d 652, 662–663 (N.C. 1997).
[124] *Id*. at 657.
[125] *Id*. at 662.
[126] *Id*. at 662 (citations omitted).
[127] *Id*. at 663.
[128] *People v. Hogan*, 647 P.2d 93, 116 (Ca. 1982).
[129] *Id*. at 95.
[130] *Id*. at 114, 115.
[131] *Id*.
[132] *Id*. at 115.
[133] *Id*.

whether the stains were blood and about the blood type, the expert's qualification about such related subject matter was not sufficient to support the testimony on bloodstain pattern analysis.[134] The "mere observation of pre-existing stains without inquiry, analysis or experiment, does not invest the criminalist with expertise to decide whether the stains were deposited by 'spatters' or 'wipes.'"[135]

Unlike the above-cited cases, there are times in which the issue of the competency of the expert is rather frivolously raised. And a description of such a case is helpful in evaluating whether or not there is a genuine issue as to competency when evaluating any case, post-conviction.

In *State v. Ordway*, a 1997 opinion rendered by the Supreme Court of Kansas, the expert had been a forensic scientist in the biology unit of the Kansas Bureau of Investigation for more than 9 years; she had attended a 40-hour class on blood pattern technique, and later attended a 3-day refresher course.[136] Her primary duties on the job were in bloodstain pattern analysis. She had a graduate degree combining the administration of justice, investigation, and chemistry. She was nationally certified as a medical laboratory technician; she had been regional vice president of the International Association for Bloodstain Pattern Analysts; and she had been an assistant instructor in bloodstain pattern analysis.[137]

Clearly, the trial court did not abuse its discretion in qualifying this expert. She had an appropriate academic background in science; she had substantial, professional training in bloodstain analysis; she had on-the-job experience, and the high regard of her peers, evidenced both by her position in the relevant professional organization and her teaching appointment on the subject.

In sum, the various tests employed for evaluating qualifications of an expert are vague and grant seemingly unbridled discretion to the trial judge. The 19th century quotations from *Oil Co. v. Gilson*[138] and *Lincoln & wife v. Inhabitants of Barre*[139] could easily be implanted into contemporary opinions. While some jurisdictions employ a "sliding-scale" approach to qualifications, correlated with the perceived complexity of the bloodstain evidence,[140] others qualify the expert with just a modicum of experience, beyond the average

---

[134] *Id.*

[135] *Id.*

[136] *State v. Ordway*, 934 P.2d 94 (Kan. 1997) (Ordway asserted an insanity defense to charges of the first degree murders of his parents. When arrested, Ordway told the officer that he had killed his mother 3 days prior and had been living in the car with her ever since. When asked if he wanted to call his father, he said, "No, he won't answer.") .

[137] *Id.* at 110–111.

[138] 63 Pa. St. at 150.

[139] 59 Mass. at 591.

[140] *Eason v. United States*, 687 A.2d 922, 926 (D.C. App. 1996); *People v. Knox*, 459 N.E.2d 1077, 1081 (Ill. App. 3 Dist. 1984).

person.[141] To further exacerbate the problem, appellate review of the trial court's ruling is circumscribed by the abuse of discretion and clearly erroneous standards of review.

Despite this, there are some unifying principles. There seems to be "strict scrutiny" of the qualifications of police officers by the defense bar and the appellate courts. Presumably, this is because most officers lack academic credentials in the sciences to be testifying in matters dependent upon physics, chemistry, and mathematics. Moreover, it is significant that empirical studies have shown that "jurors rated police appearing as experts to be the most honest, understandable, confident, likeable, and believable, and that these experts were discredited less often than other witnesses."[142] This being the case, strict scrutiny is appropriate.

Likewise, when the testimony is perceived by the appellate courts as per se "complex," as in a full-scale crime reconstruction or in-court reenactment/demonstration, "strict scrutiny" is employed. To the point, when raising the issue of the qualifications of a purported bloodstain expert on appeal, whether that expert is a police officer, technician, or anyone else, one needs to convince the appellate court that the bloodstain evidence was, indeed, complex. This is a challenging task in that bloodstain evidence is deceptively simple. Unlike testimony of blood typing, DNA analysis, pathology, etc., we have all witnessed "spatter," "smears," "transfers," and "wipes" in our daily lives. Yet, we have never sought to verify our categorizations for accuracy, nor engaged in sophisticated mathematical calculations, aimed at reenactment, and dependent upon angles, trajectories, velocity, size, shape, and distance. Nor are we qualified to do so. It is the verification and interpretation of the categorizations, based on specialized training, knowledge, and experience, that is essential to a qualified expert in this field.

Even in a case in which the appellate court clearly acknowledges the error, it may deem that error harmless. As such, whenever raising the issue of the qualifications of an expert, it is essential to demonstrate to the appellate court that the inadmissible expert testimony was not cumulative of other admissible expert testimony, and that the testimony was somehow pivotal to the case. Further, be aware that the erroneous admission of bloodstain evidence can also prejudice the jury as it usually is the basis for the admission of gruesome and inflammatory photographs, perhaps otherwise inadmissible.

---

[141] *State v. East*, 481 S.E.2d 652, 662–663 (N.C. 1997); *People v. Smith*, 633 N.E.2d 69 (Ill. App. 4 Dist. 1993).

[142] Daniel W. Shuman, Anthony Champagne, and Elizabeth Whitaker, *Juror Assessments of the Believability of Expert Witnesses*, 36 Jurimetrics, Journal of Law, Science and Technology, No. 4, Summer, 1996, at 375.

Noticeably absent from the cases discussed is any mention of the trial testimony of a blood spatter expert delineating the proper qualifications of an expert in that field. To the point, few cases really present a scenario in which one expert at trial deems the qualifications of another blood spatter expert insufficient. Usually this problem is resolved at the pretrial stage, and the incompetent expert, who truly lacks qualifications, simply does not testify. This may very well account for the lack of clarity and uniformity, and the basic misunderstanding of the expertise in appellate opinions. Since on appeal the appellate court is confined to the record below, the only meaningful way of educating the appellate court is through a well-developed trial record. Where the battle has really taken place during discovery, and outside the record, there is very little substantive information on the expertise available to the appellate court.

The Collateral Attack

Post-conviction relief is especially onerous and circumscribed in scope. It is a collateral attack on the conviction, filed in the trial court. While it is neither a new trial, nor a new appeal, it affords a unique opportunity to expand the trial record beyond that presented in a direct appeal. Though an evidentiary hearing will not always be afforded, expert affidavits may be submitted in support of a Petition for Post-Conviction Relief. Thereafter, if a new trial is denied and the denial is appealed, the appellate record contains those affidavits. In the event an evidentiary hearing is granted, that transcript, and the experts' reports, if any, are before the appellate court.

To be sure, a collateral attack on the conviction is the optimum vehicle when defense counsel at trial failed to retain or present the necessary bloodstain expert. Of course, the legal claim would be ineffective assistance of counsel, citing to the Sixth Amendment to the United States Constitution, and its cognate provision in the state constitution. When this is the asserted claim, post-trial, then defense counsel at trial is alleged to have been ineffective. When this is the asserted claim, post-trial and post-appeal, then defense counsel at trial and appellate counsel for the defense have been ineffective.

While most collateral attacks dealing with bloodstain evidence are raised as ineffective assistance of counsel, bloodstain evidence can be the basis of a *Brady* violation, a claim of newly discovered evidence, expert perjury, or prosecutorial misconduct.

As in the previous sections of this chapter, the above post-conviction issues will be discussed in the context of actual cases. These cases were chosen because they are thorough and instructive on the legal avenues to explore, the procedural and substantive hurdles to be overcome, and the potential for bloodstain evidence to have a dramatic effect at this late stage.

Perjurious Expert Testimony — Newly Discovered Evidence

In *Clayton v. State*, [143] discussed previously on the issue of expert qualifications, the defendant/petitioner applied to the trial court for post-conviction relief and relief was denied. He had previously been convicted of first-degree murder and was sentenced to death. The judgment and sentence were affirmed on direct appeal.[144]

In applying for post-conviction relief, petitioner alleged that the prosecution's bloodstain expert had "overstated" his qualifications and that this evidence was newly discovered.[145] Also, because the expert's "lies" regarding his qualifications were revealed during the discovery phase of another case after Clayton's trial, but before his appeal, he also alleged ineffective assistance of appellate counsel.[146] The petitioner/defendant appended three affidavits attacking the prosecution expert's qualifications in the other case to his application for relief. Herbert MacDonell authored one affidavit, asserting that the prosecution's expert was not qualified to testify to bloodstain pattern interpretation. A police sergeant and police captain authored the other affidavits, and asserted the same. In addition, the petitioner submitted three letters from the General Counsel for the Oklahoma State Bureau of Investigation disavowing the government witness as a blood spatter expert.[147]

The Oklahoma Court of Criminal Appeals held that the trial court abused its discretion in not determining that the admission of the expert testimony was erroneous.[148] However, while acknowledging the "devastating impact of erroneous and incompetent expert testimony," the appellate court further held that the admission of the erroneous evidence was harmless in view of the overwhelming evidence, independent of the bloodstain testimony.[149]

Prosecutorial Misconduct — Denial of Due Process

Ex Parte Mowbray, rendered in 1996 by the Court of Criminal Appeals of Texas, *en banc,* is an intriguing state *habeas corpus* case, replete with accusations of perjury and prosecutorial misconduct.[150] The petitioner/defendant was convicted of the murder of her husband, sentenced to life, and fined

---

[143] 892 P.2d 646 at nn. 101–106, *supra,* and accompanying text.
[144] *Id.* at 651–652.
[145] *Id.* at 651–652.
[146] *Id.*
[147] *Id.* at 652.
[148] *Id.* at 649.
[149] *Id.* at 652–653.
[150] *Ex Parte Mowbray,* 943 S.W.2d 461 (Tex. Cr. App. 1996).

$10,000.00. The judgment and sentence were affirmed on appeal.[151] In her application for post-conviction relief, the petitioner asserted that the State's expert knowingly gave false and misleading testimony; that the state knowingly used false testimony; and that trial counsel for the defense was ineffective.[152]

The evidence at trial was that Susie Mowbray shot her husband while he was asleep in their bed.[153] They were alone in the bedroom and it was night.[154] The defense theory was that Mowbray and her husband were lying in bed with a pillow barrier between them. Mowbray saw her husband's elbow point upward. She reached to touch it and the gun went off.[155] Just as in *Knight,* was it suicide or was it homicide? Just as in *Knight,* the case turned on the blood spatter evidence.

At trial, Dusty Hesskew, a police sergeant, testified as bloodstain expert for the prosecution. In essence, he stated that he examined Susie Mowbray's nightgown and found "high velocity impact [blood] staining." Specifically, he counted 48 small stain areas around the stomach and chest of the night-gown, consistent with high-velocity spatter, i.e., a kind of mist. Thus, in his opinion Mowbray could not have been lying beside her husband at the time of his death. Luminol was employed to identify and measure the bloodstains, otherwise invisible to the naked eye.[156]

Pursuant to court order, Herbert MacDonell testified at the *habeas* hearing. MacDonell had previously been retained by the prosecution to review the photographs and physical evidence 7 months prior to trial. His examination revealed no bloodstains either visible to the naked eye or under a microscope. MacDonell's opinion was that it was unlikely that the nightgown was in close proximity to the gunshot wound at the time of the shooting. As such, it was more probable than not that the deceased died from a suicide rather than a homicide. At the request of the prosecution, MacDonell memorialized his findings in a written report, which he delivered to the prosecution 2 weeks prior to trial. And that report was then delivered to Mowbray's defense attorney. Very predictably, the prosecution did not call MacDonell to testify at trial. [157]

At the *habeas* hearing MacDonell was especially critical of Dusty Hesskew's exclusive use of luminol to identify the stains as blood and as a means to measure the pattern. MacDonell explained that luminol was merely a presumptive test in that it can react with various other substances and thus give a false positive result. He opined that the luminescence from a luminol

[151] *Mowbray v. State,* 788 S.W.2d 658 (Tex. App. Corpus Christi 1990).
[152] *Ex Parte Mowbray,* at 461.
[153] *Mowbray v. State,* 788 S.W.2d at 662.
[154] *Ex Parte Mowbray,* at 461.
[155] *Id.* at 462.
[156] *Id.* at 462–463.
[157] *Id.*

reaction cannot be accurately measured. He further stated that he had never heard of anyone trying to measure it, and that even if someone attempted to do so, the validity of the conclusion would be highly suspect. In MacDonell's opinion, Hesskew did not understand the chemistry of luminol testing.[158]

In response, Hesskew admitted that his testimony at trial absolutely depended on his erroneous assumption that someone had performed confirmatory testing on the invisible stains to ensure that they were, indeed, blood. He conceded that his trial testimony was scientifically invalid and that his ultimate opinions, that the victim died as a result of a homicide and that her account of the incident was impossible, had no scientific basis.[159]

Tom Bevel, a captain with the Oklahoma City Police Department, also testified at the hearing. He had previously testified as a bloodstain expert for the defense at trial. His opinion then was that the deceased could have died by suicide, and that it was impossible to measure high-velocity impact spatter in the manner utilized by Hesskew. Like Hesskew, Bevel did not conduct any confirmatory testing to determine if the stains were blood. However, he stated that Hesskew informed him that the Department of Public Safety laboratory had confirmed human blood on the nightgown. He relied on this assertion.[160] A chemist in the Texas Department of Public Safety crime laboratory also testified at the hearing and stated that prior to trial he had conducted two confirmatory tests for the presence of blood on the nightgown and that both tests were negative.[161]

The prosecutor conceded that the state's case "depended upon" the blood spatter evidence, and asserted that he did not call MacDonell to testify at trial because of the expense of securing his testimony.[162] Defense counsel, a board-certified criminal law specialist, testified that he did not call MacDonell to testify because he did not know how MacDonell would respond, and he feared MacDonell might alter his favorable opinion.[163]

Following the hearing, the *habeas* judge entered Findings of Fact and Conclusions of Law, and determined that Susie Mowbray was denied due process. Thus, the judge recommended that the appellate court set aside the conviction and grant a new trial. As a basis, the judge entered the following findings.

The rationale for suicide was "equally persuasive." The deceased had attempted suicide twice before and had shot himself on one of those occasions. Also, he had vowed to kill himself. The "linchpin" of the state's case

[158] *Id.* at 463.
[159] *Id.*
[160] *Id.*
[161] *Id.* at 463–464.
[162] *Id.* at 464.
[163] *Id.*

was the high-velocity impact spatter found on the nightgown. Hesskew "recanted" his trial testimony and admitted that his opinion was devoid of scientific validity. Bevel, too, disavowed his trial testimony.[164] The State's conduct with respect to Herbert MacDonell was, "at best, questionable trial strategy, and, at worst, intentional deception" of Mowbray's trial counsel. The State was aware of the extent of MacDonell's opinion 7 months prior to trial, and was under court order to disclose all *Brady* material then. Instead, on the eve of trial they provided the defense a scant report. To further exacerbate the situation, the state led defense counsel to believe that Mac-Donell would be a witness and available for cross-examination. The court found that defense counsel was not ineffective, but the prosecution was and this violated Mowbray's due process right to a fair trial.[165]

Citing to *Brady v. Maryland*, the appellate court noted that "the State has an affirmative duty to disclose favorable evidence under the Due Process Clause." Further, it held that the bloodstain evidence was favorable and material. Consistent with the *habeas* judge's recommendation, the appellate court set aside the verdict and remanded the case for a new trial.[166] On retrial, Susan Mowbray was acquitted.

Ineffective Assistance of Counsel — Federal Case

Smith v. Angelone presents another *habeas corpus* case, but this time in *federal* court. After the murder conviction and death sentence of Roy Bruce Smith were affirmed on direct appeal and he unsuccessfully sought state *habeas corpus* relief, he petitioned for federal *habeas corpus* relief.[167] Following an evidentiary hearing, the federal district court denied his petition, and the United States Court of Appeals for the Fourth Circuit affirmed the denial.[168] Smith then filed a petition for *certiorari* and a petition to stay his execution to the United States Supreme Court. In July of 1997, both requests were denied.[169] Roy Bruce Smith was executed soon after.[170]

Smith's murder conviction was based on the willful, deliberate, and pre-meditated killing of a uniformed police officer.[171] The death sentence was premised on the jury's finding that the crime was "vile" and/or that Smith presented a future danger.[172] In his petition for federal *habeas corpus* relief,

---

[164] *Id*. at 464–465.
[165] *Id*.
[166] *Id*. at 466.
[167] *Smith v. Angelone*, 111 F.3d 1126 (4th Cir. 1997).
[168] *Id*. at 1126–1127.
[169] *Smith v. Angelone, cert. denied*, 66 L.W. 3128 (July 17, 1997). (Justices Stevens and Ginsberg voted to grant the application for a stay of the execution).
[170] Telephone conversation with Stuart James, bloodstain expert for Smith.
[171] *Smith v. Angelone*, Findings of Fact and Conclusions of Law (E.D.Va. 1996) [hereinafter cited as Findings of Fact and Conclusions of Law].

Smith alleged, *inter alia*, that trial counsel was ineffective for failing to seek appointment of forensic experts.[173]

The facts underlying the conviction follow. After engaging in an ongoing argument with his wife, Smith drank "prodigious" amounts of beer and then returned to his home. He took two loaded pistols, a .357 magnum and a .44 magnum, as well as a loaded rifle out to his front steps. Smith shot the rifle into the air. The neighbors heard him state, "Wait 'til I start shooting people.... I hope somebody calls the police because I will shoot the first one that arrives and I hope they shoot me in return." He then reentered his house. Not surprisingly, the neighbors called the police. The police arrived at approximately 9:00 p.m. and secreted their vehicles as they had been forewarned that he was armed and dangerous. When Smith noticed a motion-sensitive light had been triggered in his backyard, he went outside to investigate. Sgt. Conner, the police officer who was later fatally shot, was alone in the backyard with Smith. Another officer heard Sgt. Conner say, "Drop the rifle, drop the rifle now." Then he heard gunfire, 8 to 12 sharp sounds, followed by a short pop and a succession of very sharp cracks. The officer ran to the scene and spotted Smith struggling with officers 20 to 25 feet from Sgt. Conner's body. Smith was subdued and his weapons were thrown on the grass.[174]

The government's theory at trial was that Smith shot Conner with the rifle and the pistols, wounding Conner's right leg, right forearm, and his back. Then Smith chased the wounded Conner down an alley and, at very close range, administered the coup de grace to the head with the .357 magnum. Five casings from Conner's 9 mm. pistol were found. The ejection pattern suggested that Conner was near the gate to Smith's property when he first shot. Two shots were in the alleyway, one of which hit Smith in the foot. One of Conner's shots resulted in a self-inflicted wound to his thigh. Conner's other bullets were never found. Empty casings from Smith's rifle were found in three locations. Two casings were found near his front stoop, presumably the rifle shots which triggered the neighbors call to the police. Nine casings were found in a grouping in the alleyway behind Smith's backyard. And one casing was found near the boundary between the alleyway and Smith's backyard. Smith denied ever traveling down the alleyway that evening or, in fact, shooting his .357 magnum. The government's only proof that Conner was shot by Smith's .357 magnum from inches away was the alleged "back spatter" on the gun. Not disclosed at trial and only educed at the *habeas* hearing was that Officer Goodman was in the alleyway near its southern end and was armed with a .357 revolver at the relevant time.[175] In essence, Smith's

---

[172] *Smith v. Angelone*, 111 F.3d at 1128.
[173] *Id.* at 1131.
[174] *Id.* at 1128–1129.

attorney for the *habeas corpus* petition alleged that had Smith's trial counsel presented forensic testimony, there would have been reasonable doubt in the guilt/innocence and sentencing phases at trial. In support, Smith presented the testimony of Steven D. Benjamin, an experienced capital defense lawyer, regarding the necessity of expert assistance in capital cases, employing *Strickland* analysis. Benjamin testified that defense counsel's representation is constitutionally deficient if he does not request expert assistance when there is a substantial issue that requires expert testimony for its resolution and the defendant's position cannot be fully presented in its absence.[176] The *habeas* judge accepted this standard as well grounded in reason and experience, also noting that such a standard parallels the circumstances in which courts have an obligation to provide expert assistance to indigent defendants.[177] Benjamin testified that defense counsel at trial knew that the government would rely on experts because there was no eyewitness to the shooting, and the government's theory of the case was that Smith used the .357 magnum to shoot Conner in the head, and Smith fired this shot from inches away.[178] Benjamin further testified that an element of the capital murder offense was that Smith knew the person he was shooting was a police officer in the performance of his duties. Conner was wearing a uniform, and this element would be satisfied if Smith saw the uniform. If Smith delivered the final shot to the head from inches away, no jury could have a reasonable doubt that Smith saw Conner's uniform. On the other hand, if Smith were 20 feet away, as he was when subdued, and Smith had merely fired into a dark alleyway, jurors may have doubted whether the prosecution had proved this element beyond a reasonable doubt.[179] Benjamin also testified that another element of the capital murder offense was that Smith killed Conner willfully, deliberately, and with premeditation. If Smith traveled down the alley and shot the wounded Conner in the head from inches away, no jury would have doubted that he had the requisite *mens rea*. However, if Smith merely fired a volley of bullets in Conner's direction from 20 feet away, reasonable jurors could have doubted whether Smith had the intent to kill, or was just acting recklessly.[180] Moreover, at the penalty phase the jury had to determine whether the crime was "vile" and/or whether Smith posed a danger in the future. These were the two aggravating circumstances triggering the death penalty. To be sure, the factual circumstances of the crime are crucial to the assessment of both aggravating factors. If Smith coldly shot the already wounded Conner in the head from inches away, no reasonable juror would doubt these aggravating factors.

---

[175] Findings of Fact and Conclusions of Law.
[176] *Id.*
[177] *Id.*
[178] *Id.*
[179] *Id.*
[180] *Id.*

Alternatively, if Smith shot at Conner from where he was subdued, some 20 feet away, during a shoot-out with an officer returning fire, reasonable jurors might have questioned whether the killing was "vile," and/or whether Smith would pose a threat in a structured prison setting.[181]

Based on Benjamin's testimony, the *habeas* judge ruled that Smith had satisfied the first prong of the *Strickland* test. Specifically, the judge found that "Defense counsel knew or should have known before trial that there were substantial issues that required the assistance of experts. Defense counsel knew or should have known before trial that the defendant's position could not be fully developed without professional assistance." Unfortunately, the court's analysis only began there. The assessment of prejudice awaited.[182]

At trial, the prosecution presented a parade of forensic experts. The most damaging was Dr. Francis Field, the medical examiner. She opined that there was powder residue in Conner's head wound, indicating a close gunshot wound, within 3 feet with a pistol, and within 6 feet with a rifle. She further stated that blood found on Smith's .357 magnum was consistent with "blow back" blood spatter from a gun fired 4 to 6 inches away from the officer's head. Julien Mason, a firearms identification expert, testified that there were bullet abrasions on Smith's fence that were consistent with the bullets of a .357 magnum. Donald McClanrock, a forensic scientist, testified that Smith had more barium gas on his left hand than on his right hand, and that this indicated that Smith shot a revolver with his left hand.[183]

Smith's trial counsel called no forensic experts for the defense; instead he relied on cross-examination. He was able to obtain some concessions at trial. Unfortunately, those concessions later proved fatal. Dr. Field admitted on cross-examination that the blood on the muzzle of Smith's .357 magnum was not "necessarily" the result of "blow back." Clearly this statement means that it could have been. Julien Mason admitted that the bullet that caused the back wound likely ricocheted off Conner's belt, and that the same bullet may have caused the head wound. Clearly, this means that maybe it did not. Mason further conceded that contrary to the testimony of Dr. Field, he had found no gunpowder residue in Conner's head wound. McClanrock conceded that the gases found on Smith's hands could have come from the rifle.[184]

In the federal *habeas* hearing, Smith presented new expert testimony aimed at proving that he did not shoot Conner in the head from inches away with the .357 pistol. Gary Laughlin, a forensic microscopist and metallurgist, testified that the metal fragments in Conner's head could not have come from

[181] *Id.*
[182] *Smith v. Angelone*, 111 F.3d at 1132.
[183] *Id.* at 1131.
[184] *Id.*

a .357 magnum or Smith's 9 mm. weapon, but could have come from Smith's rifle. He also testified that there was no powder residue in the head wound. Vincent DiMaio, a forensic pathologist, testified that Conner's head wound was caused by the rifle, and from at least 2 to 3 feet away.[185]

Perhaps the most important testimony came from Stuart James, a bloodstain pattern expert. He testified that the blood spatters on the tip of the .357 magnum were not blow back. James explained that blow back blood has directionality; i.e., the blood from the wound immediately blows straight back toward the weapon on a path that is perpendicular to the front surface of the barrel. Spatters that land on the front surface of the barrel will be round. Spatters that land on the side of the barrel will have streaks or tails and be elongated. Further, he testified that blow back spatter can travel 2 to 3 feet and occasionally farther.[186] His testimony absolutely contradicted Dr. Field's testimony at trial that the circular spatters on the .357 were blow back and that blow back spatter could not travel more than 6 inches from the target. Stuart James also testified to key evidence thus far overlooked. The clothing of Roy Bruce Smith was confiscated by the police the night of the killing. Smith's light brown cutoff shorts did not show evidence of high-velocity spatter. His brown shirt did not show evidence of high-velocity spatter. James opined that it is high-velocity blood spatter on the clothing of the shooter that is used to corroborate high-velocity blood spatter on a weapon. When there is blow back from a wound, the blood often spatters on the shooter's clothing as well as on the weapon.[187] Further, James opined that the blood on the .357 magnum, represented as circular in shape at trial and never preserved photographically, may have been produced as a result of the officers subduing Smith and throwing the gun on the grass. The grass was already wet with blood. Grass, wet with blood, can act like a spring and fling small droplets of blood when disturbed.[188]

Despite the testimony of these experts, the hearing judge found that this testimony was cumulative of the testimony previously elicited by defense counsel on cross-examination at trial. Thus, the federal district court held that Smith failed under the "performance" prong of *Strickland*, because trial counsel reasonably relied upon cross-examination of the state's own witnesses to establish its case.[189] And, on appeal, the United States Court of Appeals for the Fourth Circuit agreed.[190]

---

[185] *Id.* at 1132.
[186] *Id.*; Report of Stuart James Re: Roy Bruce Smith, September 6, 1995; and Findings of Fact and Conclusions of Law.
[187] Report of Stuart James; and Findings of Fact and Conclusions of Law.
[188] *Id.*
[189] Findings of Fact and Conclusions of Law.
[190] *Smith v. Angelone,* 11 F.3d at 1132.

Ineffective Assistance of Counsel — State Case

State of Florida v. Reichmann, a death penalty case like *Smith,* is still pending in the Florida state courts.[191] In 1988, Dieter Reichmann was convicted of murder and sentenced to death.[192] As a basis for the death penalty, the trial judge found that the "murder was committed for pecuniary gain and was cold, calculated, and premeditated without any pretense of legal or moral justification." The defendant presented no mitigating evidence at the sentencing phase.[193]

The conviction and death sentence were affirmed on direct appeal by the Florida Supreme Court in 1991. Reichmann then filed a petition for a writ of *certiorari* to the United States Supreme Court. *Certiorari* was denied the following year.[194] Thereafter, in 1994, he filed a motion to vacate the original conviction and sentence in state trial court.[195] Reichmann's motion consisted of 14 separate claims, 11 of which asserted ineffective assistance of counsel, with 24 subparts alleging separate instances of deficient performance. The remaining claims alleged newly discovered evidence; a *Brady* violation; and a claim of judicial misconduct in that the trial judge did not write the findings supporting the death sentence; rather, they were the prosecution's creation, per *ex parte* order of the trial judge. Because the trial judge would be called as a witness on the issue of misconduct, the Florida Supreme Court appointed a successor judge to preside at the hearing and rule on the motion to vacate.[196] The facts presented by the Supreme Court of Florida to support the conviction and sentence follow.

Dieter Reichmann and Kersten Kischnick, "life companions" of 13 years, were German citizens and residents. They were vacationing in Florida in October of 1987. Kischnick was shot to death in Miami Beach on October 25, as she sat in the passenger seat of a rental car driven by Reichmann. The prosecution alleged that Reichmann was her pimp and he killed her to collect insurance proceeds as she was too sick to work and had wanted to quit the life. The insurance issued automatically when Reichmann used his Diner's Club card to rent the vehicle. Further, it provided double indemnity coverage in the event of accidental death. Reichmann also had insurance policies on Kischnick in Germany. Those policies provided that murder was considered an accidental death. In all, the insurance proceeds totaled almost $1 million.

---

[191] *State of Florida v. Dieter Reichmann,* Crim. No. 87-42355, Eleventh Circuit Court, Florida, Order on Motion to Vacate Judgment of Conviction and Sentence [hereinafter cited as Order on Motion to Vacate].

[192] *Reichmann v. State,* 581 So.2d 133 (Fla. 1991).

[193] Order on Motion to Vacate at 2.

[194] *Id.*

[195] *Id.*

[196] *Id.* at 2–3.

At trial Reichmann testified that he and Kischnick had been touring in the rental car in an effort to videotape the Miami sights. They got lost and stopped to ask a stranger for directions. Realizing that they were close to their destination, Reichmann unbuckled his seat belt, reached behind to grab the video camera, and placed it on Kischnick's lap. He handed her her purse so that she could tip the stranger for his assistance. Reichmann saw the stranger reach behind, he got scared, stretched out his right arm, with the palm facing outward, and hit the gas pedal. At that moment he heard an explosion and Kischnick slumped over. She was shot on the right side of her head. Reichmann drove around looking for help, driving 10 to 15 miles before he hailed a police officer for assistance.[197]

To be sure, the state's case was circumstantial. The State's gunpowder residue expert testified at trial that gunpowder residue was found on Reichmann's hands. Based on the number and nature of the particles, the State's expert concluded that there was a reasonable scientific probability that Reichmann had fired a gun. Moreover, the gunpowder residue was not consistent with Reichmann's account that he was merely sitting in the car when Kischnick was shot. An expert for the defense testified that the gunpowder residue merely indicated that Reichmann was in the vicinity of the gun when it was fired.[198] The State's bloodstain evidence was much more damning. It was highlighted in the State's closing argument, and relied on by the Florida Supreme Court in affirming the conviction and death sentence.[199] At trial the State presented expert testimony of a crime laboratory serologist on the blood found on Reichmann's clothes and in the rental car. He opined that because there was high-velocity blood spatter on the driver-side door, that blood could not have gotten there if Reichmann were in the driver's seat when Kischnick was shot. Further, the pattern of blood found on a blanket that had been folded in the driver's seat evidenced high-velocity spatter and aspirated blood.[200] Reichmann testified at trial that the blood had gotten on the blanket earlier that summer in Germany. His dog had had surgery and bled on the blanket on the trip home from the hospital. He brought the blanket along to Miami to use on the beach, after which he intended to discard it. The defense presented no blood spatter expert of its own.[201]

At the post-conviction stage Reichmann's attorney, James Lohman, submitted two volumes, in excess of 400 pages, intricately setting forth the grounds for the motion to vacate. With respect to the bloodstain evidence, he asserted that "Defense counsel's failure to rebut in any way the devastating and

---

[197] *Reichmann*, 581 So.2d at 135–136.
[198] *Id.* at 136.
[199] *Id.*
[200] *Reichmann*, at 136.
[201] *Id.* at 136, n. 6.

patently erroneous bloodstain opinion testimony was unreasonable and contributed significantly to the adverse outcome of the trial."[202] In further support, he submitted a third volume containing expert reports and other
documentary proof. Relevant to this chapter, and found to be the most
troublesome new evidence for the hearing judge, was the report of Stuart
James, blood spatter expert for the defense.

Excerpts of the highly exculpatory report follow.[203]

> The victim in this case, Kersten Kischnick, received a fatal gunshot wound
> of entrance to the right side of her head while sitting in the front passenger
> side seat of a rented, 1987, red Ford Thunderbird. The projectile entered
> 2½ inches above and 1½ inches behind the right external ear meatus. There
> was evidence of powder residue and stippling around the entrance wound,
> which according to the pathologist, indicated a range of discharge distance
> of from several inches to 18 to 24 inches. (Trial testimony of Dr. Villa,
> p. 2919). There was no wound of exit. The thrust of the interpretation of
> the bloodstain evidence offered by the State at trial was to prove that the
> defendant, Dieter Reichmann, was not in the driver's seat at the time of the
> shooting of his girlfriend by an unidentified person as he stated to author-
> ities and testified at trial. If he were not in the driver's seat, his account of
> the shooting was false and he was the murderer, allegedly for financial gain.
> The importance of proper interpretation of bloodstain evidence in such a
> case cannot be overemphasized, especially when a defendant's version of
> events might be verified or contradicted by that evidence. The State here
> relied heavily upon the interpretation of bloodstain evidence and experi-
> mentation of a serologist to show that Dieter Reichmann was not in the
> driver's seat of the Thunderbird at time of the shooting.
>
> Based upon my extensive review, examination and analysis of the blood-
> stain evidence in this case, I can state with a high degree of scientific
> certainty that the major conclusions reached and presented by the serologist
> in this case were grossly inaccurate. In general, the bloodstains were signif-
> icantly misinterpreted. In addition, crucial bloodstains were completely
> ignored or overlooked. The serologist's primary conclusions are completely
> contrary to the overwhelming weight and significance of the bloodstain
> evidence, and the techniques he utilized in forming those conclusions are
> at odds with most basic professional norms and scientific principles upon
> which correct bloodstain interpretation is founded.

James' conclusions follow:

---

[202] *Reichmann*, Motion to Vacate, Vol. I, at 156.
[203] Stuart James, Report of Evaluation of Bloodstain Evidence, Re: Dieter Reichmann,
September 20, 1994.

In analyzing and discussing the photographs, physical evidence, reports and testimony in *State v. Reichmann*, I found a high degree of agreement and unanimity among my colleagues with regard to interpretations and conclusions that could be drawn from the bloodstain patterns in the automobile in which Kersten Kischnick was shot, on items within the vehicle, and on the clothing worn by her and the defendant, Dieter Reichmann. Based upon my review of the evidence, I make the following findings:

1. When the victim in this case, Kertsen Kischnick, received the gunshot wound to the right side of her head, her head went back to the head rest on its right side at which time blood and brain material accumulated on the head rest. Her head then either moved or was moved to its position on its left side as seen in the scene photographs. This is consistent with the Medical Examiner, Dr. Paul Villa's, deposition testimony on page 29, " that brain matter is more to the right of the body or the head."

2. At some point in time after bloodshed, the victim's seat was moved to the observed reclined position.

3. Transfer bloodstains on the face of the victim and the alteration of bloodstains on the chest of the victim indicate contact with her after bloodshed either by Mr. Reichmann, police personnel or paramedics, or some combination thereof.

4. Bloodstains on the hands of Dieter Reichmann are consistent with contact with a source of wet blood and are likely responsible for transfer bloodstains on the steering wheel of the vehicle. Blood from his hand may have been flicked onto the driver's door as well as possibly wiped on the blanket located on the driver's seat.

5. Bloodstains on the trousers of Dieter Reichmann are consistent with some blood transfer as well as some dripping of blood from above while he was in a sitting position. There are also some small spatters of blood on the right knee area that could have been produced by exhalation of blood droplets from the victim. These would appear to be the leftward extent of any possible exhaled blood within the vehicle.

6. Exhaled blood (not "aspirated blood") was deposited on the victim's left shoulder, left arm, thigh, pocket book and money that is exposed on her left thigh. In reviewing photographs and examining Ms. Kischnick's white slacks, there is no question that at the time of bloodshed, victim had three (3) one-dollar bills on her left thigh, based upon the void or clean area within the exhaled bloodstain pattern on left leg of the slacks. I find this to be one of the more significant aspects of the homicide scene, yet it was virtually ignored throughout the investigation and in those portions of trial testimony I have reviewed. In addition, Ms. Kischnick's left hand is directly below the currency in the few photographs depicting this part of the scene. This is consistent with the defendant's testimony that the assailant had turned away from the car momentarily, and that the victim was

taking out some money to "tip" him at the time the fatal shot was fired. It would also appear that she may have been holding a cigarette in her left hand or mouth at the time she was shot, based upon the observation in the Medical Examiner's "Scene Investigation Report" of October 26, 1987. "A burned out cigarette is evident on the left side of the passenger's seat on the lateral side of her thigh." Other than Dr. Villa's reference, this fact was also ignored by any investigative efforts to reconstruct what was taking place at the time of the homicide.

7. It is impossible to determine the height of the passenger door window based on the location of the bloodstains because the stains most likely did not come from the entrance wound at the time of the gunshot. The window was completely closed in all the scene descriptions and photographs, and stains as likely as not were deposited on the window sometime after it was closed. Hence, the stains are obviously of no value whatsoever in determining the height of the window when Kischnick was shot.

8. The blood on the driver's door was not high velocity blood spatter, i.e., it did not come directly from the gunshot wound of entrance on the right side of the victim's head. Even the serologist acknowledged several times that he "could not explain" how blood got from the entry wound on the right side of the head to the driver's door. (Trial testimony, pp. 3816, 3832, 3932). It is also extremely unlikely that this was exhaled blood from the victim's left nostril due to the unlikely position of the nose, in addition to the force that would be required to direct the exhaled blood to the driver's door. The six stains are too few in number and were not documented photographically. It appears that the stains were removed for presumptive blood testing and then the circled areas where they had been were photographed. Small circular stains as described by the serologist can be produced by other mechanisms such as flicking of blood from the hands or some object or other activity involving the driver, the paramedics or police personnel. It is also possible that these stains represent activity due to flies occurring at a later time but prior to the serologist's bloodstain examination done as late as one week after incident.

9. Based upon my analysis of all available crime scene evidence, descriptions, photographs and experiments, it is my opinion to a reasonable degree of scientific certainty, that there is no basis on which to conclude, as the serologist did, that the driver's seat of the automobile was not occupied at the time the victim was shot in the right rear of her head through the passenger side window. First, six spots on the driver's door are not high velocity impact blood spatter resulting from the gunshot wound. Second, it is unlikely that exhaled blood from the victim's nose traveled farther to her left than the right edge of the driver's seat or right trouser of the driver. The small blood spatters on the right trouser leg of Mr. Reichmann's trousers could be the

result of exhaled blood. Third, the method utilized to identify high velocity blood spatter or exhaled bloodstains on the blanket as high velocity spatter or exhaled blood by the serologist, after a negative stereo microscopic examination, was not scientifically valid and was a gross misinterpretation. My analysis of bloodstain evidence would indicate that there is no more likelihood that the driver's seat was unoccupied than occupied at the time Ms. Kischnick was shot. It is impossible to conclude with any degree of scientific certainty that the seat was unoccupied....

    I would have been available to provide expert assistance and opinion in 1987-1988. In discussing the evidence herein with several highly qualified professional colleagues, I can assert with confidence that any number of experts in my field would have been available at that time to present similar conclusions, in particular with regard to the poorly substantiated and inaccurate conclusions that were presented at trial.

In responding to the 14 claims set forth in Reichmann's motion to vacate, the trial court "took the liberty of restating the order of claims for purposes of addressing the most substantive ones first." The bloodstain interpretation and analysis by Stuart James was first to be addressed.[204] The post-conviction judge noted that bloodstain evidence was crucial in that it was the focal point of the state's closing argument at trial, and formed the basis for affirmance of the conviction on direct appeal.[205] The post-conviction judge also noted that, consistent with community standards as testified to by Steven Potolski, Esquire, an expert in capital defense, a reasonable attorney would have taken steps to present an "available" expert to rebut the serologist's conclusions. Notwithstanding this, the post-conviction judge stated:

[T]he Defendant failed to sufficiently meet his burden by demonstrating that, based on reasonable probability, Mr. James, or a similar expert, would have been found by an ordinary competent attorney using diligent efforts, and that such expert would have been prepared to rebut the State's serologist at trial. The fact that Mr. James was found years later, and has worked on the case since 1994, is irrelevant. Rather, the "reasonable probability" standard must be measured from trial counsel's perspective at the time, without resort to distorting hindsight. No testimony was offered that, given time limitations immediately before trial, Mr. James could have rendered the same opinions as offered at the post-conviction hearing. At best, Mr. James merely "presumed" that he would have been available if contacted "depending on scheduling." (T. May 14, 1996, Stuart James, page 74)...[206]

---

[204] Order on Motion to Vacate, at 10 n.3.
[205] *Id.* at 10–11.
[206] *Id.* at 15.

The court also concludes that trial counsel's comprehensive and extensive cross-examination of the serologist ... was effective in showing the weaknesses of the witnesses' testimony, and that such weaknesses were argued to the jury at closing.[207]

The court's reasoning was and is illogical. James never testified that he would not be available for consultation and testimony. His response was merely an honest and accurate attempt at extemporaneously recollecting what he had scheduled on certain days of trial, years prior. Moreover, in his report, excerpted *supra*, James explicitly stated that he, as well as other experts, would have been available to testify. Further, James has been called to testify during trial on numerous occasions.[208] In a notorious multidefendant murder case in Massachusetts, with only 1 day's notice, he flew from Florida to Boston, reviewed the testimony of the state's bloodstain expert at trial, the available evidence, and testified. Consequently, that defendant was acquitted of first-degree murder.[209]

The judge found that trial counsel's performance was not deficient because a reasonably competent attorney would not have been able to *find* a bloodstain expert.[210] Implicit in this finding is the judge's misperception of bloodstain pattern interpretation. It is not novel; it is not obscure. To be sure, he should have read *Knight*,[211] *Sturtivant*,[212] and *Lindsay*,[213] all decided well over a century ago. A superficial search would have revealed hundreds of cases, presenting hundreds of different bloodstain experts. Perhaps he would have also wanted them to extemporaneously testify, under penalties of perjury, whether or not they were available to testify on certain days, years prior.

Fortunately for Dieter Reichmann, the post-conviction judge found the trial judge's sentencing order invalid. Contrary to Florida law, and per *ex parte* order of the trial judge, the prosecutor, not the trial judge, drafted the death penalty sentencing order. Neither the *ex parte* communication nor the sentencing order were disclosed to defense counsel during the penalty

---

[207] *Id.* at 15–16.

[208] Telephone conversations with Stuart James.

[209] This author was present during trial. James was called to testify as a bloodstain expert for defendant, Ricardo Parks, and this request came during trial. The prosecution "sandbagged" the defense by only providing notice that a serologist would be testifying to blood typing. While on the stand that serologist engaged in a full-scale bloodstain interpretation, quoting from a publication authored by James. The defense moved for a mistrial based on unfair surprise. The trial judge denied the request and granted a short continuance. For a full discussion of the issue, *see Commonwealth v. Ventry Gordon*, 666 N.E.2d 122 (Mass. 1996) (affirming convictions of the other co-defendants and discussing remedial measures afforded when there is unfair surprise).

[210] Order on Motion to Vacate, at 16.

[211] 43 Me. 11 (Me. 1857); nn. 2–14, *supra*, and accompanying test.

[212] 117 Mass. 122 (1875); nn. 15–21, *supra*, and accompanying test.

[213] 63 N.Y. 143 (1875); nn. 22–24, *supra*, and accompanying text.

phase.[214] Further, at the post-conviction hearing Reichmann's attorney, James Lohman, presented 15 witnesses from Germany who would have been willing and able to testify at Reichmann's sentencing hearing had they been contacted and requested to do so. The court heard from landladies, friends, neighbors, and former lovers. All traveled from Germany at their own expense to speak on Reichmann's behalf. The court also received written statements from many others, including Reichmann's mother and brother, who would have been able to testify on his behalf at trial.[215]

Based on judicial misconduct, coupled with trial counsel's failure to present any testimony on mitigation, the post-conviction judge granted Reichmann's motion to vacate the death sentence. A new penalty phase proceeding was ordered before a new judge and jury.[216] The denial of the Motion to Vacate the Conviction is on appeal.

Conclusion

This journey has spanned over a century, from jurisdiction to jurisdiction; from trial court to appellate court; and often extending as high as the United States Supreme Court. It has delved into the quagmires of *Frye* vs. *Daubert*; and the illusive standards of review. Bloodstain pattern evidence has been the basis of issues of admissibility and expert qualifications on direct appeal. Bloodstain pattern evidence has formed the basis of ineffective assistance of counsel claims; *Brady* violations; newly discovered evidence; and expert perjury at the post-conviction/collateral attack stage.

To be sure, an attorney with the burdensome task of attacking a murder conviction, post-trial, should sift through the trial transcript and discovery. In a case in which no bloodstain evidence was presented, should it have been? What do the crime scene photographs show? Can the defendant shed any light on the subject? Did anybody examine the defendant's clothes? A bloodstain expert would be most helpful in these inquiries. In the case in which bloodstain evidence was admitted, was it accurate and effectively presented, or did counsel merely rely on the opportunity for cross-examination? If cross-examination was defense counsel's strategic vehicle, was there something more that could have been elucidated by retaining an expert for the defense.

Whether one is proceeding on direct appeal or *via* collateral attack in trial court, having the court agree that there was error is only the first hurdle. It is necessary to prove to the reviewing court that the defendant was harmed. As such, one should pay special attention to the trial record on appeal in an

---

[214] Order on Motion to Vacate, at 48–51.
[215] *Id.* at 53–55.
[216] *Id.* at 56.

effort to convince the appellate court that, while there may or may not be "overwhelming evidence of guilt," the bloodstain evidence was crucial. Likewise, when dealing with the conviction on collateral attack, an essential part of the presentation of proof should be how the new expert evidence is different from that educed at trial. And, have the expert explicitly state how his or her conclusions differ from all the bloodstain evidence elicited at trial, fully anticipating perceived "concessions" achieved on cross-examination which could later render your expert testimony cumulative.

And, aside from this diatribe, always be mindful that sympathetic fact patterns consistently help. Having a client accused of the murder of a police officer in the line of duty does not help. Having a client who is an alleged pimp who killed for pecuniary gain likewise does not help. This is not to posit that such cases are hopeless; rather they present the special challenge.

Outline of Basic Laboratory Experiments for Bloodstain Pattern Interpretation

8

STUART H. JAMES

Contents

Adequate training in bloodstain pattern interpretation includes hands-on performance of controlled laboratory experiments which duplicate the types of bloodstain patterns encountered at the scenes of violent crimes. The following descriptions of bloodstain experiments are typical of those performed by students attending basic bloodstain interpretation schools.

Experiment 1
The Volume of a Drop of Blood

The objective of this experiment is to determine the average volume of a single drop of blood falling from the tip of a 5-ml volumetric glass pipette for reference purposes. It is recognized that the average volume of a drop of blood will vary depending upon the type of object from which it falls.

Equipment

    Human blood
    Ring stand
    Burette clamp
    Hoffman clamp
    Glass volumetric pipette (5 ml)
    Rubber tubing
    Syringe
    Glass beaker (50 ml)
    Tissue

Procedure

Using the syringe, draw well-mixed human blood from the beaker up into the volumetric pipette beyond the calibration mark on the pipette.

- Tighten the Hoffman clamp and remove the syringe.
- Using tissue paper, wipe excess blood from the outside of the tip of the pipette.
- Carefully open the Hoffman clamp until the blood falls slowly enough to permit accurate counting of the individual drops.
- Begin counting blood drops when the level of blood in the pipette stem crosses the calibration mark and count all the blood drops from the start until the pipette is drained.

The volumetric pipette is calibrated TD (To Deliver) so the small amount of blood that remains in the tip should not be forced out and counted as additional drops.

The experiment should be run at least three times to record sufficient data to determine the average volume of a drop of human blood.

Work Sheet 1: The Volume of a Drop of Blood

	Run 1	Run 2	Run 3	Run 4	Run 5
Blood volume					
No. of drops					
Drop volume					

Average blood drop volume calculated _____

Reported average blood drop volume <u>0.0506 ml</u>
Deviation from reported value _____

The blood drop volume is calculated by dividing the number of drops of blood counted into the total volume of blood measured.

Experiment 2
Diameter of a Bloodstain Produced by Single Drops of Blood of Constant Volume as a Function of Distance Fallen and Surface Texture

The objective of this experiment is to determine the relationship between the distance single drops of blood of constant volume fall and the diameter of the resultant bloodstains on various horizontal surfaces. It will be demonstrated that maximum bloodstain diameters are achieved when the height of the blood source allows the blood drop to reach its terminal velocity.

Equipment

Human blood
Cardboard target surfaces
Fabric target surfaces
Glass target surfaces
Glass pipette or dropper
Plumb line
Tape measure
Tissue

Procedure

Three materials, cardboard, blotter paper, and glass, as listed on the work sheet are utilized as target surfaces for this experiment.

- Draw well-mixed human blood into the pipette and wipe off the excess blood on the outside of the tip of the pipette.
- Squeeze the initial drop onto tissue to remove any air bubbles.
- Using a plumb line for centering and a tape measure for accurate distances, allow a drop of blood to fall onto the target surfaces at the heights indicated on the work sheet.
- Mark each target for proper identification.

- When the bloodstains have dried, measure the diameters with a ruler and record the results on the work sheet.
- Plot the diameters of the bloodstains on the cardboard targets vs. the total distance fallen on the provided graph paper.

Work Sheet 2: Diameter of Bloodstain in Millimeters

Distance Fallen, in.	Cardboard	Fabric	Glass
3			
6			
9			
12			
18			
24			
36			
48			
72			
96			

Experiment 3
Effect of Surface Texture on Spatter of Blood Drops and the Size and Edge Characteristics of the Resultant Bloodstains

The objective of this experiment is to study and compare the effects of various target surfaces upon which drops of blood impact. The degree of satellite spatter produced as well as the variation in size and edge characteristics produced by impact with these surfaces will be studied.

Equipment

Human blood
Glass pipette or dropper
Plumb line
Tape measure
Tissue
Target surfaces:
- Wood

- Cardboard
- Linoleum
- Fabrics
- Newspaper
- Glass
- Concrete
- Carpet
- Skin
- Metal
- Wet surface

Procedure

The listed surfaces as well as others of choice may be utilized for this experiment.

- Draw well-mixed human blood into the pipette and wipe off the excess blood on the outside of the tip of the pipette.
- Squeeze the initial drop onto tissue to remove any air bubbles.
- Using a plumb line for centering and a tape measure for accurate distance, allow a drop of blood to fall onto the target surfaces at a single height of 48 in.
- Observe and record the features of the resultant bloodstains.

Material	Type of surface[a]	Observations
Wood		
Cardboard		
Linoleum		
Fabric		
Newspaper		
Glass		
Concrete		
Carpet		
Human skin		
Metal		
Wet surface		

[a] Type surface = Hard/Soft, Smooth/Rough, Porous/Nonporous

Experiment 4
Bloodstain Shape vs. Angle Of Impact

The objective of this experiment is to study the oval or elliptical nature of bloodstains produced by drops of blood falling onto nonhorizontal surfaces compared with blood drops falling onto a horizontal surface producing more or less circular bloodstains relative to the surface texture of the target surfaces. It will be demonstrated by this experiment that the more acute the angle of impact of the falling blood drop, the greater the degree of elongation of the resultant bloodstain becomes as the width of the bloodstain decreases and its length increases. The calculation of the angle of impact will be determined in the following ways.

1. Graphical plotting of the length-to-width (L/W) ratio vs. the angle of impact.
2. Graphical plotting of the width-to-length (W/L) ratio vs. the angle of impact.
3. The use of the following formula with a scientific calculator with the arc sin function:

$$\text{Angle of impact} = \text{arc sin } W/L$$

Equipment

Human blood
Cardboard and wallpaper target surfaces
Angle board (90 to 100°)
Glass pipette or dropper
Plumb line and tape measure
Tissue

Procedure

Two materials, cardboard and wallpaper, are utilized as target surfaces for this experiment.

- Draw well-mixed human blood into the pipette and wipe off excess blood on the outside of the tip of the pipette.
- Squeeze the initial drop onto tissue to remove any air bubbles.
- Using a plumb line for centering and a tape measure for accurate distance of 48 in., allow drops of blood to fall onto the target surfaces at the angles indicated on the work sheet. The initial drops are to fall onto a horizontal surface (90°) and thereafter at increments of 10°.

Note that the wallpaper targets are to be utilized at 90, 60, 30, and 10°. This will show the relative independence of target surface to degree of elongation of the bloodstain.

- Mark each target for proper identification.
- Allow the target surface to dry at the same angle at which it received the bloodstains.
- When the bloodstains have dried, accurately measure the width and length of each bloodstain with a ruler and record the results on the work sheet.
- Determine and record the length-to-width ratio L/W of the bloodstains for each angle increment on the cardboard target surfaces and plot these values vs. the angles of impact on the provided graph paper.
- Determine and record the width-to-length ratio W/L of the bloodstains for each angle increment on the cardboard target surfaces and plot these values vs. the angles of impact on the provided graph paper.
- Determine the angles of impact of the bloodstains for each angle increment utilizing a scientific calculator and the formula:

$$\text{Angle of impact} = \arcsin W/L$$

- Determine and record the length-to-width ratio L/W of the bloodstains for each angle increment on the wallpaper surfaces.
- Determine and record the width-to-length (W/L) ratio of the bloodstains for each angle increment on the wallpaper target surfaces.
- Compare the ratios obtained from the bloodstains on the wallpaper surfaces with those obtained on the cardboard surfaces.
- Compare the calculated angles of impact obtained with the bloodstains on the wallpaper target surfaces with those obtained on the cardboard target surfaces.
- Compare the three methods of angle of impact determinations.

Cardboard Targets

Impact Angle, °	Length (mm)	Width (mm)	L/W Ratio	W/L Ratio	Sine of Angle
90					1.000
80					0.985
70					0.940
60					0.866
50					0.766
40					0.643
30					0.500
20					0.342
10					0.174

Wallpaper Targets

Impact Angle, °	Length (mm)	Width (mm)	L/W Ratio	W/L Ratio	Sine of Angle
90					1.000
60					0.866
30					0.500
10					0.174

Experiment 5
Angular Impact Produced by Horizontal Motion

The objective of this experiment is to determine the effect of horizontal motion applied to falling blood drops to the resultant angular impact bloodstain patterns and to determine the direction of travel of the source of the blood. The edge characteristics of the bloodstains, degree of low-level spattering of blood, and wave cast-off bloodstains originating from the parent drop will be studied.

Equipment

> Human blood
> Glass pipette or dropper
> Paper
> Stop watch
> Tissue

Procedure

- Lay out the paper on a table for a distance of 10 ft.
- Draw well-mixed human blood into the pipette and wipe off the excess blood on the outside of the tip of the pipette.
- Squeeze the initial drop onto tissue to remove any air bubbles.
- Holding the pipette 4 in. above the target surface, walk at a normal constant pace the distance of 10 ft allowing blood drops to fall on the target surface.
- Measure with a stop watch the number of seconds it takes for the person to travel the distance of 10 ft. The movement of the person should begin several feet in front of the table and terminate beyond the table to achieve measurement of a uniform speed.
- Repeat the experiment with the person walking at a fast pace and at a running pace with the blood falling from the pipette 4 in. above the target surface.

- Repeat the experiment with the paper on the floor and the pipette of blood held 36 in. above the target surface utilizing a timed, normal, constant walk, fast walk, and run.
- Record the results on the work sheet provided.

Distance Fallen, in.	Seconds 10 ft.	Velocity ft/s	Amount Spatter	W/L Ratio	Angle of Impact
Normal Walk					
4	_____	_____	_____	_____	_____
24	_____	_____	_____	_____	_____
Fast Walk					
4	_____	_____	_____	_____	_____
24	_____	_____	_____	_____	_____
Run					
4	_____	_____	_____	_____	_____
24	_____	_____	_____	_____	_____

Notes: Velocity (ft/s) is calculated by dividing distance in feet/time in seconds or 10 ft/time in seconds. Amount of spatter can be characterized as none, minimal, moderate, or great.

Experiment 6
Drip Patterns of Blood and Splashed Blood vs. Distance Fallen

The objective of this experiment is to study the characteristics of bloodstain patterns produced when amounts of blood larger than a drop are subjected to minor impact or fall onto a target surface. These splashed bloodstain patterns will exhibit many radiating, satellite spatters of blood. In this experiment the characteristics of bloodstain patterns produced by drops of blood allowed to drip into itself on the target surface will be studied and compared with the splashed bloodstain patterns. These bloodstain patterns will also be compared with those produced by projected blood in Experiment 7.

Equipment

Human blood
Cardboard target surfaces
Plumb line and tape measure
Glass beaker
Glass pipette or dropper
Tissue

Procedure

- Measure 1 ml of well-mixed human blood into a small glass beaker.
- Using the plumb line for centering and a tape measure for accurate distance, pour the blood in the beaker onto the cardboard target from a height of 12 in.
- Mark the target for proper identification.
- Repeat the procedure using 1 ml of blood and pouring it from a height of 24 in. and 72 in.
- Draw well-mixed human blood into the pipette and wipe off the excess blood on the outside of the tip of the pipette.
- Allow the blood to fall from the pipette a drop at a time from a height of 24 in. creating a pool of blood on the target surface into which the subsequent drops of blood fall.
- Mark the target for proper identification.
- Compare and describe the bloodstain patterns.

Experiment 7
Projected Blood vs. Distance Fallen and Blood Projected on Vertical Surfaces

The objective of this experiment is to study the characteristics of bloodstain patterns produced by quantities of blood larger than a drop that are projected from the blood source rather than just falling onto the target surface. These bloodstain patterns will exhibit more dramatic radiating spatters of blood in addition to irregular, spinelike edges around the central bloodstain. Additionally, blood which has been projected under force or pressure such as occurs in arterial spurting often creates characteristic patterns on horizontal and vertical surfaces with clusters of bloodstains and drip patterns and flow patterns from excess blood depending upon the inclination of the target surface.

Equipment

Human blood
Cardboard target surfaces
Syringe
Plumb line and tape measure

Procedure

- Draw 1 ml of well-mixed human blood into a syringe.
- Using the plumb line for centering and a tape measure for accurate distance, expel the blood from the syringe onto the cardboard target from a height of 12 in.

- Mark the target for proper identification.
- Repeat the procedure using 1 ml of blood and expelling it from the syringe from a height of 24 in. and 72 in.
- Set up a vertical cardboard target surface and expel 1 ml of blood from the syringe from a distance of 24 in. from the target and 24 in. above the floor.
- Repeat the procedure with the vertical target and expel 1 ml of blood from the syringe 6 in. from the target and 24 in. above the floor.
- Describe and compare the bloodstain patterns in this experiment and with those patterns produced in Experiment 6.

Experiment 8
Cast-Off Bloodstains

The objective of this experiment is to study and characterize the types of bloodstain patterns produced by a bloody object in motion where blood is projected or cast off from an object other than the impact site. The swinging motion of a bloody hand, weapon, or other object will produce bloodstain patterns on nearby surfaces depending upon the arc of the swing. Determination of the approximate position of the assailant and victim at the time blows were struck may be determined and the number of blows struck may be estimated.

Equipment

Human blood
Overhead, front, and side paper target surfaces and masking tape
Wooden block and sponges
Weapons (baseball bat, pipe, poker, hammer, rock)

Procedure

- Set up the paper target surfaces.
- Moderately cover a hand with well-mixed human blood and swing the hand in a sideways and overhead motion and study the cast-off bloodstains produced.
- Place and secure a blood-soaked sponge on a wood block on a table floor, or other surface.
- Strike the sponge several times with a type of weapon in an overhead fashion and study the cast-off bloodstains produced.
- Count the number of blows struck and correlate this number with the cast-off trails on the overhead target surface.

- Correlate the position of the assailant and the victim from the locations and angles of impact of the cast-off bloodstains on the overhead target surface.
- Several weapons may be utilized as well as a left- and right-handed overhead swing.
- Strike the blood-soaked sponge on the floor with a rock or short weapon in a kneeling position and observe for cast-off bloodstains on the shoulders and rear of the pant legs of the person swinging the weapon.
- Record your observations.

Experiment 9
Medium-Velocity Impact Blood Spatter

The objective of this experiment is to study the bloodstain patterns produced when a strong force impacts upon an exposed source of blood. The size of individual bloodstains produced is usually within the range of 1 to 3 ml in diameter although smaller and larger bloodstains are not uncommon. A variety of impact spatter patterns will be produced and studied in relation to the type of object, target surface, and quantity and condition of exposed blood required to produce the patterns.

Equipment

Human blood
Cardboard and fabric target surfaces
Weapons (baseball bat, pipe, poker, hammer, rock, fist, shoe)
Shoes, sponge, wooden block

Procedure

- Set up the cardboard target surfaces 24 in. to the sides and front of the impact site vertically and horizontally.
- Secure a sponge on a wood block on a table, floor, or other surface and saturate with well-mixed human blood.
- Strike the sponge several times with a type of weapon, changing the target surface for different weapons.
- Apply some clotted blood to the sponge and strike several times with a type of weapon.
- Observe and record locations and quantity of blood spatter on the target surfaces as well as the person swinging the weapon.

- Measure bloodstain diameters for comparison to high-velocity impact blood spatter.
- Place 50 ml of blood on a horizontal cardboard target and step into the pool of blood with some force and observe the bloodstain pattern produced.
- Repeat this experiment allowing a hand to fall into the pool of blood and observe the bloodstain pattern produced.
- Repeat this experiment allowing a hand to slap into the pool of blood and observe the bloodstain pattern produced.
- Record your observations.

Experiment 10
High-Velocity Impact Blood Spatter

The objective of this experiment is to study the bloodstain patterns produced by high-velocity impact produced by gunshot. Many of the blood droplets produced by this type of impact are extremely small and create a mistlike dispersion with diameters of 0.1 ml and smaller although larger bloodstains are frequently seen in the patterns. These bloodstain patterns will be compared with medium-velocity impact blood spatter.

Equipment

Human blood
Sponges
Weapon (.22 caliber)
Target frame and bullet box
Wig, plastic, cloth, or rubber cover for sponge
Cardboard target surfaces
Tape measure

Procedure

- Set up vertical cardboard target surfaces 6 in. in front of and behind the impact site.
- Saturate the sponge with well-mixed human blood and attach to the impact site.
- Fire the weapon through the rear target so the slug passes through the sponge and on through the forward target into the bullet box.
- Repeat this experiment with the target surface distances at 12 in.
- Repeat this experiment with a single horizontal target surface below the impact site.

- Using the vertical cardboard target surfaces 6 in. in front of and behind the impact site, cover the blood-saturated sponge with hair, cloth, or plastic and fire the weapon.
- Record your observations and compare relative quantities of forward and back spatter in each situation. Measure the diameters of the high-velocity impact blood spatter and compare with medium-velocity impact blood spatter in Experiment 9.

Experiment 11
Recognition of Blood Transfer Patterns, Swipes or Smears, Smudges, and Wipes of Blood

The objective of this experiment is to study and recognize transfer patterns in human blood including hair swipes and other types of smearing of blood as well as alteration of existing bloodstains on a surface.

Equipment

Human blood
Weapons (baseball bat, pipe, poker, hammer, rock, fist, shoe)
Fabrics
Wig
Cardboard and clothing surfaces
Paper

Procedure

Soak various objects with well-mixed human blood and create contact transfer patterns on cloth or cardboard surfaces. Unlimited variations of this experiment are possible using hands, feet, numerous objects, and different type of activities.

- Create a hair swipe by soaking a wig with blood and dragging it across the cardboard surface. Determine directionality of the swipe by studying the feathered edge of the pattern.
- Create a wipe pattern by moving an object through an existing blood-stain and altering its appearance.
- To determine sequence of events, create a handprint in blood on a cardboard surface and then spatter some blood onto the transfer pattern and observe the location of the two types of bloodstain patterns on the surface.

- Step into a pool of blood with different types of footwear or bare feet and walk on paper or outside on pavement until visible blood is no longer transferred to the surface. Measure the distance traveled relative to the type of footwear or bare feet.
- Record your observations.

Experiment 12
Blood Volume vs. Bloodstained Area

The objective of this experiment is to create bloodstains on known surfaces, measure the surface area in square inches, and correlate this area with the volume of blood used. This information may assist with the estimation of blood accumulation at a scene when comparisons are made with similar surfaces.

Equipment

Human blood
Surfaces (carpet, wood, linoleum, concrete)
Graduated glass beaker or cylinder
Grid measuring device

Procedure

- Place 50 ml of well-mixed human blood into a graduated glass beaker or cylinder.
- Pour blood onto the chosen surface.
- Estimate the square inches of stain area with the grid measuring device.
- Pour an additional 50 ml of blood onto the original bloodstain and estimate the square inches of stain area with the grid measuring device.
- Pour additional blood in 100-ml increments up to 500 ml and estimate the square inches of stain area with the grid measuring device.
- Record the data on the work sheet provided.
- Plot the results as bloodstain area vs. blood volume.

Area of   50 ml of bloodstain _____
Area of 100 ml of bloodstain _____
Area of 200 ml of bloodstain _____
Area of 300 ml of bloodstain _____
Area of 400 ml of bloodstain _____
Area of 500 ml of bloodstain _____

Experiment 13
Bloodstain Size vs. Horizontal Projection

The objective of this experiment is to project blood drops of various sizes at a constant velocity and to record the distance traveled in relationship to the diameters of the resultant bloodstains.

Equipment

> Human blood
> Syringe
> Motor-driven device
> Cardboard target surfaces

Procedure

- Set up the motor-driven device approximately 3 ft above the floor.
- Lay the target surface on the floor in front of the device to a distance of 4 ft.
- Mark the target surface in 20-in. increments for a distance of 100 in.
- Start the motor-driven device.
- Draw 5 ml of well-mixed human blood into the syringe and expel the blood onto the blades of the device.
- Measure the diameters of 5 bloodstains at the 20-in. increments.
- Record the data on the work sheet provided.
- Determine the average diameters of the bloodstains at the five distances.

Diameter of Bloodstains in Millimeters

Number of Measurements	20 in.	40 in.	60 in.	80 in.	100 in.
1					
2					
3					
4					
5					
Average diameter (mm)					

Experiment 14
Clotting and Drying Time of Blood

The objective of this experiment is to study the formation and appearance of blood clotting and the drying of bloodstains as these processes progress over a period of time from the initial shedding of blood under average ambient conditions. Different quantities of blood and surfaces will be utilized.

Equipment

Freshly drawn human blood
Surfaces (carpet, floor tile, wood, newspaper, cloth, glass, skin)
Pipette
Glass rods
Filter paper
Timer

Procedure

- Set the surfaces in their locations and record the temperature and humidity.
- Place 1 drop, 1 ml and 5 ml of freshly drawn human blood on each surface and note the time.
- Record the time each bloodstain requires to dry.

Degree of dryness may be established by touching the bloodstain with a glass rod or filter paper and observing for transfer of blood.

Clotting of blood may be established by passing a glass rod through the bloodstain and observing for firmness or jelling of the bloodstain. Clot retraction and production of serum may be observed with the bloodstains after a period of time if the blood has not absorbed into the material. Note any appearance of clot retraction.

Drying Time for a Single Drop of Blood

	Material	Drying Time	Clot Formation
1			
2			
3			
4			
5			

Drying Time for 1 ml of Blood

	Material	Drying Time	Clot Formation
1			
2			
3			
4			
5			

Drying Time for 5 ml of Blood

	Material	Drying Time	Clot Formation
1			
2			
3			
4			
5			

Experiment 15
Presumptive Testing of Blood

The objective of this experiment is to test stains on various materials for the presence of blood utilizing catalytic color and luminescence presumptive tests for blood.

These chemical tests employ an oxidation reaction and the catalytic peroxidase activity of the heme portion of the hemoglobin molecule. Positive results are characterized by the production of color or luminescence. It is important to utilize both positive and negative controls when performing these tests. Although a negative test result may exclude a suspect stain as blood, all positive tests require confirmation to prove the presence of blood.

Equipment

Human blood
Various surfaces (cloth, wood, metal, carpet, tile, etc.)
Normal saline
Swabs and filter paper
Leucomalachite green reagent
Phenolphthalein reagent
Luminol reagent (demonstration)

Procedure

To obtain samples from the various surfaces, including the positive and negative controls, moisten a cotton swab or folded filter paper with normal saline and rub the surface to be tested.

Using the prepared reagents, perform the following tests:

1. **Leucomalachite Green**   Apply 1 to 2 drops of reagent on the test area of the swab or filter paper and observe for the production of a rapidly appearing blue-green color indicating a positive result. Record the results on the work sheet provided.
2. **Phenolphthalein**   Apply 1 to 2 drops of methanol on the test area of the swab or filter paper followed by 1 to 2 drops of phenolphthalein reagent followed by 1 to 2 drops of hydrogen peroxide. Observe for the production of a rapidly appearing bright pink color indicating a positive result. Record the results on the work sheet provided.

Leucomalachite Green

	Material Tested	Result		
		Positive	Negative	Questionable
1				
2				
3				
4				
5				
6 + Control				
7 − Control				

Phenolphthalein

	Material Tested	Result		
		Positive	Negative	Questionable
1				
2				
3				
4				
5				
6 + Control				
7 − Control				

Bloodstain Atlas and Terminology

STUART H. JAMES

The glossary presented in this section has been largely adapted from terminology compiled by the Terminology Committee of the International Association of Bloodstain Pattern Analysts. The suggested list of the Committee was proposed in 1996. Input was also received from many individuals throughout the forensic community both in the U. S. and Canada.

This glossary is offered as a guideline and is not designed to be all encompassing. It should be recognized that the terminology utilized in this text is not all-inclusive, and variations may exist in different texts and other sources. However, these terms have been carefully studied and represent definitions that will be useful in communication within the discipline of bloodstain pattern interpretation. It is felt that the terminology presented here does represent a significant agreement and consensus of opinion of many individuals. There is a need for consistent and uniform terminology in order to avoid confusion and misleading interpretation in the evaluation of written conclusions and oral testimony in court.

The color reproductions of bloodstains that comprise the atlas represent a variety of bloodstains and patterns that have been produced with human blood on a variety of surfaces. The bloodstains have been photographed at approximately 90° to minimize the possibility of distortion, and most contain a measuring device in millimeters to show their relative sizes. Another important feature of this atlas is the demonstration of the similarity of the size and distribution of the examples of bloodstain patterns that are in the range of medium- to high-velocity bloodstains that can be created by a variety of events (see Plate 1).

Glossary

Angle of impact The acute or internal angle formed between the direction of a blood drop and the plane of the surface it strikes.

Arterial spurting (or gushing) pattern Bloodstain patterns resulting from blood exiting the body under pressure from a breached artery.

Back spatter Blood directed back toward the source of energy or force that caused the spatter. Back spatter is often associated with gunshot wounds of entrance.

Bloodstain The resulting transfer when liquid blood has come into contact with a surface or when a moist or wet surface comes into contact with dried blood.

Bubble rings Rings in blood that result when blood containing air bubbles dries and retains the circular configuration of the bubbles as a dried outline.

Cast-off pattern A bloodstain pattern created when blood is released or thrown from a blood-bearing object in motion.

Clot A gelatinous mass formed as a result of a complex mechanism involving red blood cells, fibrinogen, platelets, and other clotting factors. Over time, the blood clot retracts, resulting in a clear separation of the mass from the more fluid, yellowish blood serum which remains at the periphery of the stain. (*See* serum stain.)

Directionality The directionality of a bloodstain or pattern which indicates the direction the blood was traveling when it impacted the target surface. Directionality of the flight of a blood drop can usually be established from the geometric shape of its bloodstain.

Directionality angle The angle between the long axis of a bloodstain and a predetermined line on the plane of the target surface which represents 0°.

Direction of flight The trajectory, or flight directionality, of a blood drop which can be established by its angle of impact and directionality angle.

Drawback effect The presence of blood in the barrel of a firearm that has been drawn backward into the muzzle.

Drip pattern A bloodstain pattern that results from blood dripping into blood.

Expired or exhaled blood Blood that is blown out of the nose, mouth, or a wound as a result of air pressure and/or airflow, which is the propelling force.

Flight path The path of the blood drop as it moves through space from the impact site to the target.

Flow pattern A change in the shape and direction of a wet bloodstain due to the influence of gravity or movement of an object.

Forward spatter Blood which travels in the same direction as the source of energy or force causing the spatter. Forward spatter is often associated with gunshot wounds of exit.

High-velocity impact spatter A bloodstain pattern caused by a high-velocity force impact/force of approximately 100 ft/s or greater such as that produced by a gunshot or high-speed machinery. It must be emphasized that blood does not spatter at the same velocity as the velocity of the wounding agent. This pattern is characterized by a mistlike dispersion which, due to the high surface area of small droplets, can only travel a short horizontal distance in its flight. The preponderance of individual spots of blood produced by these mistlike blood droplets are usually 0.1 mm, or smaller, in diameter, although some larger spots are also always produced.

Impact pattern Bloodstain pattern created when blood receives a blow or force resulting in the random dispersion of smaller drops of blood.

Impact site The point on a bloody object or body which receives a blow. Often, impact site is used interchangeably with point of origin. Impact site may also refer to an area on the surface of a target which is struck by blood in motion.

Low-velocity impact spatter Bloodstains produced on a surface when the blood source has been subjected to a low-velocity force approximately 5 ft/s or less to a blood source.

Medium-velocity impact spatter Bloodstains produced on a surface when the blood source has been subjected to a medium-velocity force between approximately 5 and 25 ft/s to a blood source. A beating typically causes this type of spatter. The preponderance of individual spots of blood produced in this manner are usually 1 to 3 mm in diameter, but larger and smaller spots also occur.

Misting Blood which has been reduced to a fine spray as the result of the energy or force applied to it.

Parent drop A drop of blood from which a wave castoff or satellite spatter originates.

Point or area of convergence A point or area to which a bloodstain pattern can be projected on a two-dimensional surface. This point is determined by tracing the long axis of well-defined bloodstains within the pattern back to a common point or area.

Point or area of origin The three-dimensional point or area from which the blood that produced a bloodstain originated. This is determined by projecting angles of impact of well-defined bloodstains back to an axis constructed through the point or area of convergence.

Projected blood pattern A pattern created when blood is projected or released as the result of force.

Ricochet or secondary splash The deflection of large volumes of blood after impact with a target surface that results in staining of a second surface. Ricochet does not occur when small drops of blood strike a surface.

Satellite spatter Small droplets of blood that are projected around or beside a drop of blood upon impact with a surface. A wave castoff is also considered a form of satellite spatter.

Scallop pattern A bloodstain produced by a single drop which is characterized by a wavelike, scalloped edge.

Serum stain A clear, yellowish stain with a shiny surface often appearing around a bloodstain after the blood has retracted due to clotting. This separation is affected by temperature, humidity, substrate, and/or air movement.

Skeletonized bloodstain A bloodstain that consists only of its outer periphery, the central area having been removed by wiping after liquid blood has partially dried. A skeletonized bloodstain is also produced by the flaking away of the central portion of a completely dried stain.

Smear A relatively large volume of blood, usually 0.5 ml or more, that has been distorted to such a degree that further classification is not possible. A smear is similar to a smudge, but a smear is a stain produced by a larger volume of blood.

Smudge A bloodstain that has been distorted to such a degree that further classification is not possible.

Spatter The dispersion of small blood droplets due to the forceful projection of blood.

Spine The pointed edge characteristics that radiate away from the center of a bloodstain. Their formation depends upon impact velocity and surface texture.

Splash A stain pattern created by a low-velocity impact upon a quantity of blood approximately 1.0 ml or greater striking a surface.

Swipe The transfer of blood onto a surface not already contaminated with blood. One edge is usually feathered, which may indicate the direction of travel.

Target A surface upon which blood has been deposited.

Terminal velocity The maximum speed to which a free-falling drop of blood can accelerate in air, which is approximately 25.1 ft/s.

Transfer pattern A contact bloodstain created when a wet, bloody surface contacts a second surface as the result of compression or lateral movement. A recognizable mirror image or at least a recognizable portion of the original surface may be transferred to the second surface.

Void or shadow Absence of bloodstain in an otherwise continuous bloodstain pattern. Often the geometry of the void will suggest an outline of the object which has intercepted the blood, such as a shoe, furniture, person, etc.

Wave castoff A small blood droplet that originates from a parent drop of blood due to the wavelike action of the liquid in conjunction with striking a surface at an angle less than 90 °.

Wipe A bloodstain pattern created when an object moves through an existing bloodstain removing blood from the original stain and altering its appearance.

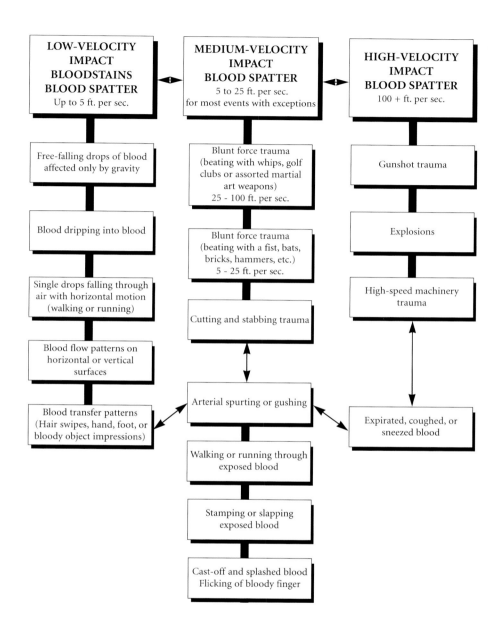

Plate 1 Diagrammatic summary of interrelationships of forces acting upon a source of blood.

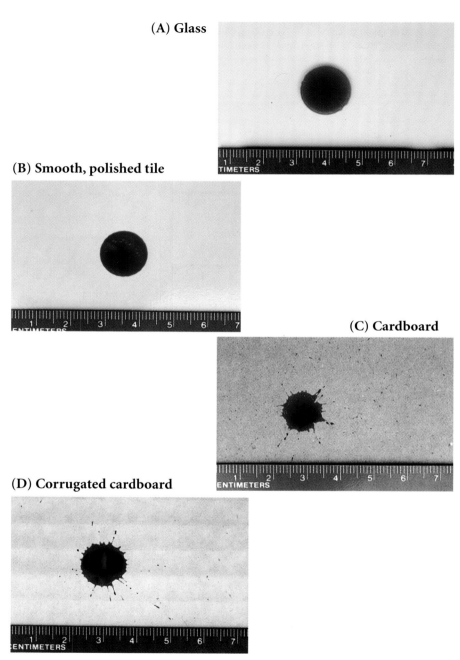

(A) Glass

(B) Smooth, polished tile

(C) Cardboard

(D) Corrugated cardboard

Plate 2 (A – H) Effects of target surface textures on bloodstain characteristics and degree of spatter produced from single drops of blood that fell 30 inches. Note the production of spines and small spatters around the periphery of the central bloodstain as the result of contact with rough surfaces.

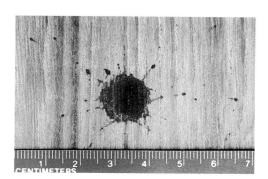

(E) Wood paneling

(F) Newspaper

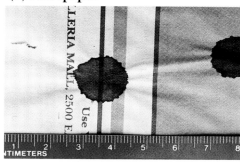

(G) Concrete

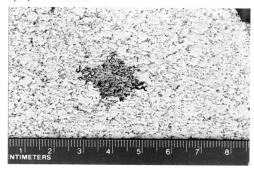

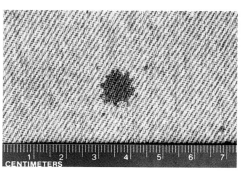

(H) Denim jean cloth

Plate 3 Appearance of a single drop of undiluted blood that fell from a distance of 36 inches onto smooth cardboard.

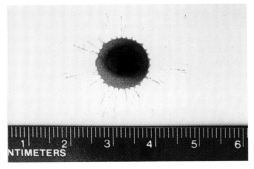

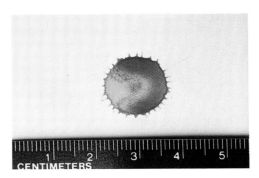

Plate 4 Appearance of a single drop of blood diluted with water (1:1) that fell from a distance of 36 inches onto smooth cardboard. Note the prominent peripheral rim with lighter center area of stain.

Plate 5 Appearance of bloodstains resulting from single drops of blood that fell onto outside of denim jean material. Note dark color and presence of small crusts of blood on the surface of the stains.

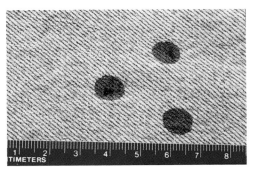

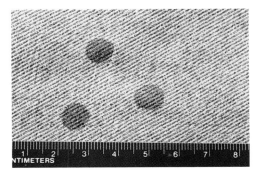

Plate 6 Appearance of the same bloodstains on the inside of the denim jean material that have soaked through the material to the opposite side. Note the lighter appearance of the stains.

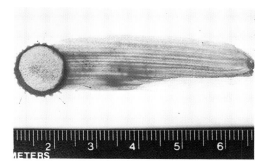

Plate 7 A skeletonized blood-stain produced by a wiping alteration of a partially dried bloodstain indicating activity shortly after the blood was deposited. Note the remaining peripheral ring of the original bloodstain due to drying around the edges.

Plate 8 A skeletonized blood-stain produced by the flaking of blood crusts from the center of a dried bloodstain. Note the remaining peripheral ring of the original bloodstain.

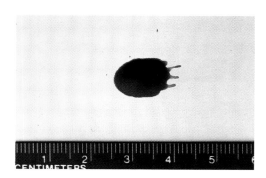

Plate 9 The appearance of a bloodstain produced by a single drop of blood that fell 30 inches with horizontal motion onto smooth cardboard as the result of dripping from a person in a fast walk. The direction of trav-el is from left to right.

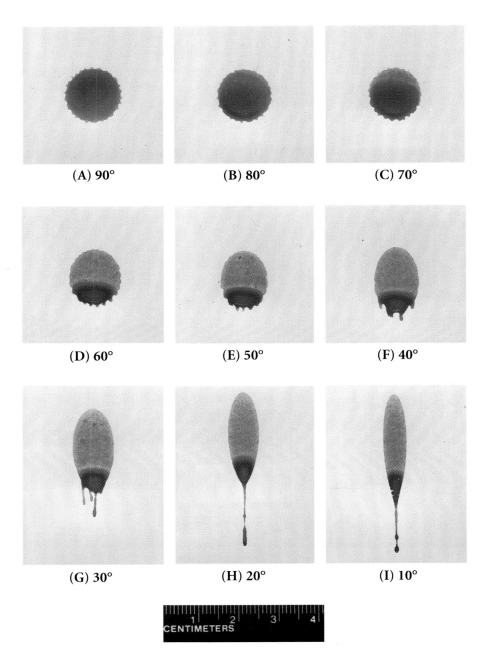

Plate 10 Shape and increasing elongation of bloodstains relative to decreasing angles of impact of single drops of blood falling 30 inches onto smooth cardboard (90° to 10° at 10° increments).

Plate 11 Formation of a wave castoff by a blood drop. The tail of the parent bloodstain points in its direction of travel whereas the tail of the wave castoff points back to the parent bloodstain.

Plate 12 Closer view of the wave castoff bloodstain.

Plate 13 Bloodstain pattern produced by 1 milliliter of blood that fell 36 inches onto smooth cardboard.

Plate 14 Closer view of satellite spatter produced by 1 milliliter of blood that fell 36 inches onto smooth cardboard.

Plate 15 Bloodstain pattern produced by 1 milliliter of blood projected downward 36 inches onto smooth cardboard.

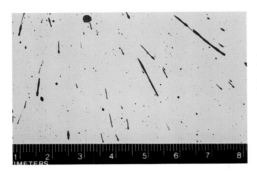

Plate 16 Closer view of satellite spatter produced by 1 milliliter of blood projected downward 36 inches onto smooth cardboard.

Plate 17 Drip pattern of blood produced by single drops of blood that fell 36 inches onto smooth cardboard.

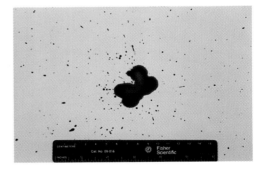

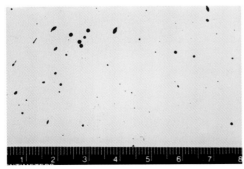

Plate 18 Closer view of satellite spatter produced by single drops of blood that fell 36 inches onto smooth cardboard.

Plate 19 Drip pattern of blood on concrete surface near edge of wall. Note the large quantity of satellite spatter on the vertical as well as horizontal surfaces.

Plate 20 Close view of satellite blood spatters on a vertical surface produced by blood dripping into blood.

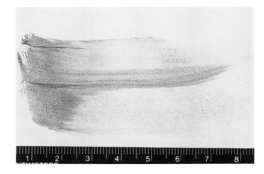

Plate 21 A swipe or transfer of blood onto a surface that was created by the edge of a hand. Note the feathering of the right edge indicating the direction of travel from left to right.

Plate 22 Transfer pattern produced by hair wet with blood. A detached hair is present within the stain. The direction of travel is from right to left.

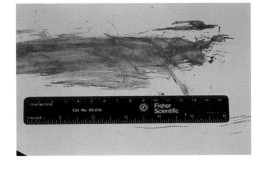

Plate 23 Closer view of transfer pattern produced by hair wet with blood. Note the beading effect produced by small blood droplets adhering to the individual shafts of hair.

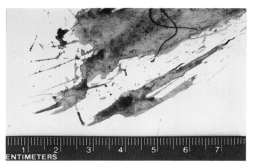

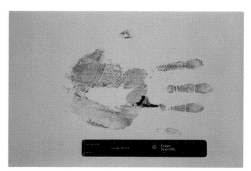

Plate 24 Transfer pattern of right handprint produced by hand wet with blood.

Plate 25 Transfer pattern of a partial fingerprint in blood. Note the clear ridge detail on the right side of the stain produced by the top area of the finger.

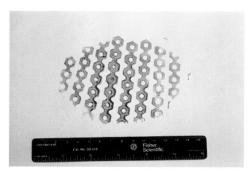

Plate 26 Transfer pattern of partial shoe print in blood exhibiting patterned sole.

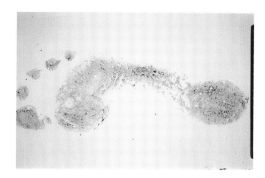

Plate 27 Transfer pattern in blood of right foot exhibiting ridge detail of the sole and toes.

Plate 28 Transfer pattern in blood of same right foot wearing sock showing distinct fabric weave pattern of the sock.

Plate 29 Transfer pattern in blood of claw type hammer on towel.

Plate 30 Multiple patterns of blood transfer on wall created by victim who survived gunshot wound to head for a period of time showing hair transfer, finger impressions, and movement of victim against wall.

Plate 31 Flow patterns of blood on door produced by contact with bloody source.

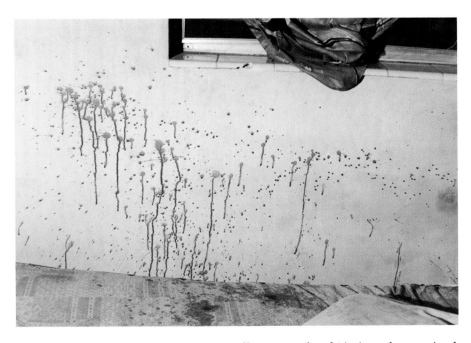

Plate 32 Arterial spurt pattern on wall as a result of victim who received stab wound to chest with severance of an artery.

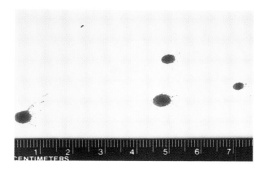

Plate 33 Cast-off bloodstain pattern produced on ceiling by overhead swing of broom handle wet with blood.

Plate 34 Continuation of cast-off pattern further from peak of backswing.

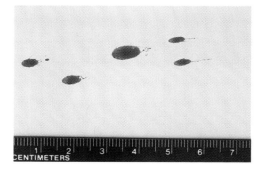

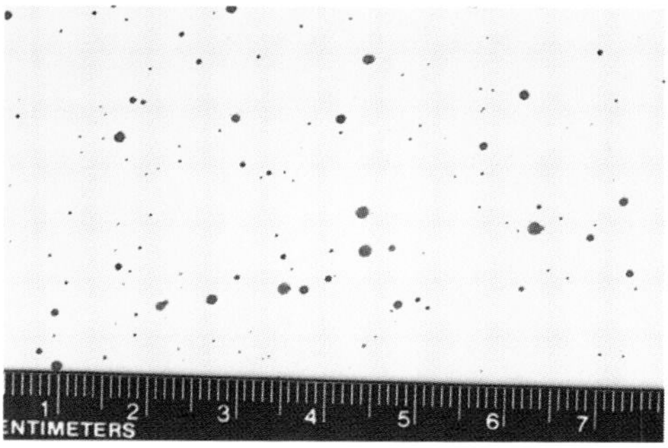

Plate 35 Medium-velocity impact blood spatter on vertical surface.

Plate 36 Medium-velocity impact blood spatter on horizontal surface.

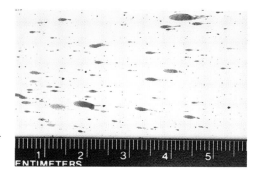

Plate 37 Appearance of medium-velocity impact blood spatter on denim jean material.

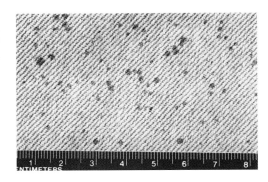

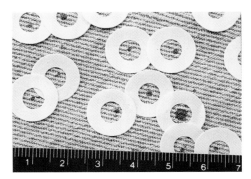

Plate 38 The use of circular ring reinforcements to illustrate the location of spatters on denim jean material.

Plate 39 Medium-velocity impact blood spatter with a void area produced by shoe.

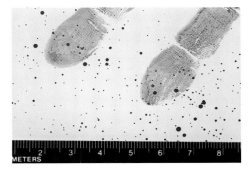

Plate 40 Medium-velocity impact blood spatter on top of partial bloody handprint showing production of handprint prior to spatter.

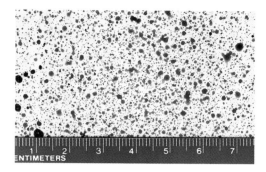

Plate 41 High-velocity impact blood spatter produced by gunshot.

Plate 42 High-velocity impact blood spatter produced by gunshot. Note the misting effect of minute bloodstains surrounding the projectile hole.

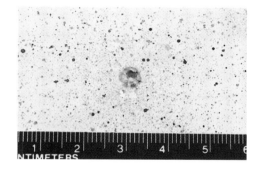

Plate 43 Appearance of high-velocity spinal fluid impact spatter on ceiling produced by contact shotgun wound of head that eviscerated the brain of the victim.

Plate 44 Appearance of small spatters of blood produced by exhalation of blood from mouth.

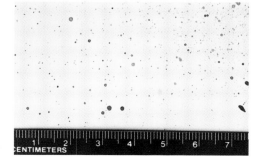

Plate 45 Appearance of small apparent spatters of blood actually produced by fly activity on denim jean material.

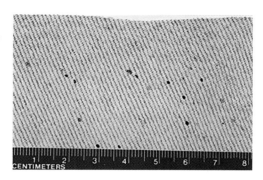

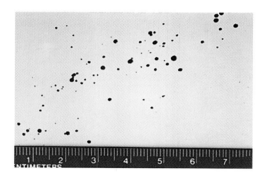

Plate 46 Small spatters of blood produced by flicking fingers wet with blood.

Plate 47 Appearance of pooled blood exhibiting partial drying, clot retraction, and production of serum.

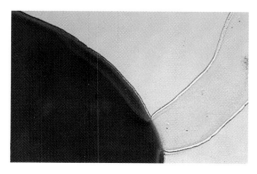

Plate 48 Appearance of pooled blood exhibiting partial clot retraction and production of serum.

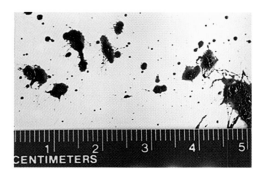

Plate 49 Appearance of clotted blood spatters produced by impact onto partially clotted blood. Note strands of fibrin and dense centers of spatters.

Plate 50 Closer view of clotted spatter with typical "fried egg" appearance at dense center of bloodstain.

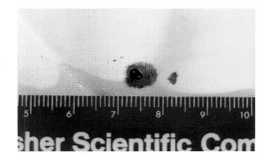

Plate 51 Positive leucomalachite presumptive test for blood on left with negative control on right.

Plate 52 Positive Hemastix® presumptive test for blood with negative control on right.

Plate 53 Positive phenolphthalein presumptive test for blood with negative control on right.

Plate 54 Positive luminol presumptive test for blood.

Bibliography

1. Balthazard, V., Piedelievre, R., DeSoille, H., and DeRobert, L., Etude des Gouttes de Sang Projecte, paper presented at the 22nd Congress of Forensic Medicine, Paris, France, 1939.

2. Bevel, T., Geometric bloodstain interpretation, *FBI Law Enforcement Bulletin,* Office of Congressional and Public Affairs, Vol. 52, No. 5, pp. 7–10, May, 1983.

3. Bevel, T. and Gardner, R. M., *Bloodstain Pattern Analysis — With an Introduction to Crime Scene Reconstruction,* CRC Press, Boca Raton, FL, 1997.

4. DeForest, P. R., Gaensslen, R. E., and Lee, H. C., *Forensic Science — An Introduction to Criminalistics,* pp. 295–308, McGraw-Hill, New York, 1983.

5. Eckert, W. G and James S. H., *Interpretation of Bloodstain Evidence at Crime Scenes,* CRC Press, Boca Raton, FL, 1989.

6. Hurley, M. and Pex, J., Sequencing of bloody shoe impressions by blood spatter and blood droplet drying times, *I.A.B.P.A. News,* Dec., 1990.

7. James, S. H., and Edel, C. F., In *Bloodstain Pattern Interpretation, Introduction to Forensic Sciences,* W. E. Eckert, Ed., CRC Press, Boca Raton, FL, 1997.

8. Kirk, P. L., *Blood — A Neglected Criminalistics Research Area, Law Enforcement Science and Technology,* Vol. 1, pp. 267–272, Academic Press, London, 1967.

9. Kirk, P.L., *Crime Investigation,* 2nd ed., pp. 167–181, John Wiley and Sons, New York, 1974.

9a. Kish, P. E. and MacDonell, H. L., Absence of evidence is not evidence of absence, *Journal of Forensic Identification,* Vol. 46, No. 2, pp. 160–164, March/April, 1996.

10. Laber, T. L., Diameter of a bloodstain as a function of origin, distance fallen and volume of drop, *I.A.B.P.A. News,* Vol. 2, No. 1, pp. 12–16, 1985.

11. Laber, T. L. and Epstein, B. P., *Bloodstain Pattern Analysis,* Callen, Minneapolis, MN, 1983.

12. Lee, H. C., Gaensslen, R. E., and Pagliaro, E. M., Bloodstain volume estimation, *I.A.B.P.A. News,* Vol. 3, No. 2, pp. 47–54, 1986.

13. LeRoy, H. A., Bloodstain pattern interpretation, *Identification Newsletter of the Canadian Identification Society,* January, 1983.

14. MacDonell, H. L., Interpretation of bloodstains — physical considerations, in *Legal Medicine Annual,* C. Wecht, Ed., pp. 91–136, Appleton, Century, Crofts, New York, 1971.

15. MacDonell, H. L., Preserving bloodstain evidence at crime scenes, *Law and Order,* Vol. 25, pp. 66–69, April, 1977.

16. MacDonell, H. L., Reconstruction of a homicide, *Law and Order,* Vol. 25, pp. 26–31 July, 1977.

17. MacDonell, H. L., Criminalistics, bloodstain examination, in *Forensic Sciences,* Vol. 3, C. Wecht, Ed., pp. 37.1–37.26, Matthew Bender, New York, 1981.

18. MacDonell, H. L., *Bloodstain Pattern Interpretation,* Laboratory of Forensic Science, Corning, NY, 1982.

19. MacDonell, H. L., *Bloodstain Patterns,* Laboratory of Forensic Science, Corning, NY, 1993.

20. MacDonell, H. L., *Bloodstain Patterns — Revised,* Laboratory of Forensic Science, Corning, NY, 1997.

21. MacDonell, H. L. and Bialousz, L., *Flight Characteristics and Stain Patterns of Human Blood,* United States Department of Justice, Law Enforcement Assistance Administration, Washington, D.C., 1971.

22. MacDonell, H. L. and Bialousz, L., *Laboratory Manual on the Geometric Interpretation of Human Bloodstain Evidence,* Laboratory of Forensic Science, Corning, NY, 1973.

23. MacDonell, H. L. and Brooks, B., Detection and significance of blood in firearms, in *Legal Medicine Annual,* C. Wecht, Ed., pp. 185–199, Appleton, Century, Crofts, New York, 1977.

24. MacDonell, H. L. and Panchou, C., Bloodstain pattern interpretation, *Identification News,* Vol. 29, pp. 3–5, Feb., 1979.

25. MacDonell, H. L. and Panchou, C., Bloodstain patterns on human skin, *Journal of the Canadian Society of Forensic Science,* Vol. 12, No. 3, pp. 134–141, Sept., 1979.

26. Pex, J. O. and Vaughn, C. H., Observations of high velocity blood spatter on adjacent objects, *Journal of Forensic Sciences,* Vol. 32, No. 6, pp. 1587–1594, Nov., 1987.

27. Piotrowski, E., *Uber Entstehung, Form, Richtung und Ausbreitung der Blutspuren nach Heibwunden des Kopfes,* K.K. Universitat, Wein, 1895.

28. Pizzola, P. A., Roth, S., and DeForest, P. R., Blood droplet dynamics — I, *Journal of Forensic Sciences,* Vol. 31, No. 1, pp. 36–49, Jan., 1986.

29. Pizzola, P. A., Roth, S., and DeForest, P. R., Blood droplet dynamics — II, *Journal of Forensic Sciences,* Vol. 31, No. 1, pp. 50–64, Jan., 1986.

30. Stephens, B. G., and Allen, T. B., Back spatter of blood from gunshot wounds — observations and experimental simulation, *Journal of Forensic Sciences,* Vol. 28, No. 2, pp. 437–439, April, 1983.

31. Sutton, T. P., *Bloodstain Pattern Analysis in Violent Crimes,* Department of Pathology, Division of Forensic Pathology, University of Tennessee, Memphis, 1993.

32. White, R. B., Bloodstain patterns of fabrics — the effect of drop volume, dropping height and impact angle, *Journal of the Canadian Society of Forensic Science,* Vol. 19, No. 1, pp. 3–36, 1986.

APPENDIX 1
Affidavit of Paul Leland Kirk: State of Ohio v. Samuel H. Sheppard

STATE OF OHIO	)		
	)	SS:	IN THE COURT OF COMMON PLEAS
CUYAHOGA COUNTY	)		Criminal Branch

No. 64571

STATE OF OHIO,	)	
	)	
PLAINTIFF	)	
	)	
vs.	)	AFFIDAVIT of PAUL LELAND KIRK
	)	
SAMUEL H. SHEPPARD	)	
	)	
DEFENDANT	)	

PAUL LELAND KIRK, of lawful age, being duly sworn, states that he resides at 1064 Creston Road, Berkeley, California; that he was graduated with the highest honors from Ohio State University in 1924 with a degree of Bachelor of Arts in Chemistry; that in 1925 he was awarded a degree of Master of Science in Chemistry by the University of Pittsburgh; that in 1927 he received a degree of Doctor in Philosophy in Biochemistry from the University of California; that he was an assistant in Chemistry at the University of Pittsburgh during 1924 and 1925; taught biochemistry at the University of California in 1926 and 1927; was Research Assistant in Biochemistry at the University of California in 1927 and 1928; Research Associate at the University of California in 1928 and 1929; Instructor in Microchemistry in the Biochemistry Division from 1929 to 1933; Assistant Professor of Biochemistry at the University of California from 1933 to 1939; Associate Professor of Biochemistry from 1939 to 1945; on leave to the Radiation Laboratory directed by Ernest O. Lawrence from 1942 to 1943. This was the first organization devoted to atomic energy research; from there he was transferred to the Metallurgical Laboratory of the University of Chicago, in 1943 to 1944, which was a branch of the Manhattan Project, concerned with the development of plutonium; Technical Specialist, Hanford Engineering Works, Richland, Washington, 1944 and 1945, in charge of Microchemical, Research and Development in connection with the manufacture of the atomic bomb fuel, plutonium, (explosive) used at Nagasaki, Japan; Professor of Biochemistry and Advisor in Criminalistics from 1945 to 1948; Professor of Biochemistry and Criminalistics at the University of California from 1948 to 1954; Professor of Criminalistics, School of Criminology, at the University of California from 1954 to the present time; member of the Medical School Faculty of the University of California from 1927 to 1950; Associate Professor in Physiology, Hopkins Marine Station (Stanford University), 1935; investigative work in Criminalistics in 1935 for the Berkeley Police Department in California, and investigation for the District Attorney of Alameda County, California, who was Hon. Earl Warren, now Chief Justice of the United States Supreme Court; continual investigative work in criminalistics for various public bodies and individuals until 1942, when the work was discontinued due to services required in the Atomic Energy Research Project; from 1945 continuous investigative work for district attorneys in Alameda and San Francisco Counties and other counties throughout the northern part of the State of California, this investigative work being principally on behalf of agencies of the State.

Affiant further states that prior to World War II he was placed in charge of the training program in Criminalistics of the University of California and wrote the curriculum; that after the War be renewed his activities in criminalistics; that he was consultant to numerous agencies, including the State Crime Commission of California, the Army, the Atomic Energy Commission, numerous industrial concerns with investigative problems, and private individuals.

Affiant further states that he has been accepted as an expert witness in Criminalistics for various Federal and State Courts, including the Federal and State Courts of California, Federal Court of Nevada, Federal Court

of Oregon, State Court of Arizona, Federal Court of
Idaho, and the State Court of Louisiana.

Affiant states that Criminalistics is the application
of the technique and principles of basic sciences,
particularly chemistry and physics, to the examination
and interpretation of physical evidence; that he is in
charge of the Criminalistics portion of the School of
Criminology of the University of California, which school
is concerned with the training of police laboratory
technicians, crime laboratory technicians, and the scientific investigation of crime; that the persons entering
and staying in said School come from all parts of the
United States and from all over the world; that many of
the State Crime Laboratories are staffed with graduates
of said School, which gives degrees of Bachelor of Arts,
Bachelor of Science, and Master of Criminology.

Affiant has been the author of at least 150 original
papers in the scientific literature and many of said
papers are on Criminalistics; that he is the author of
Quantitative Ultra-microanalysis, 1950, publisher, John
Wiley & Company; *Density and Refractive Index — Their
Application to Criminal Identification,* 1951, publisher,
Charles C. Thomas Company; *Criminal Investigation,* 1953,
publisher, Interscience Publishing Company. This work
has international circulation among state and governmental agencies in the United States and foreign countries, and is a guide to the use of physical evidence
by persons engaged in law enforcement.

Affiant is Associate Editor for Police Science of the
Journal of Criminal Law, Criminology and Police Science,
which is the official publication of the International
Association of Arson Investigators, the Illinois Academy
of Criminology, the Society for the Advancement of
Criminology; Associate Editor of *Mikrochimica Acta,* which
is an international journal of microchemistry, published
in German, English, French, and Italian.

Affiant is Vice President of the Microchemical Commission of the International Union of Pure & Applied Chemistry; a member of the National Research Council Committee
on Analytical Chemistry; a member of the American Chemical
Society Committee on Weights and Balances; a member of
the Belgian Royal Academy, the American Chemical Society,
the American Association for the Advancement of Science,
the American Society of Biological Chemists, and the
Society for the Advancement of Criminology.

Affiant states that he came to this County (Cuyahoga County, Ohio) at the request of William J. Corrigan, one of the attorneys for the defendant; that he arrived on January 22nd, 1955, and departed on January 26, 1955; that his purpose in coming to this County was to examine the physical evidence that was connected with the murder of Marilyn R. Sheppard; that he examined the premises at 28924 West Lake Road, city of Bay Village, Ohio; that he was informed that the house in which Marilyn Sheppard was murdered on the morning of July 4, 1954, had not been disturbed by anyone connected with the defense; that he was to make a careful appraisal of the technical evidence involved in said murder.

Affiant further states that said attorney agreed to pay this affiant his expenses and such other necessary fees as would compensate him for the time he would devote to his examination, investigation, and research, but with the specific understanding that his work in this region was to be entirely objective and his determinations would be without bias or prejudice to the case of the State of Ohio or the defendant, and that his work was to be on no other basis. He further states that no instructions or suggestions were made to him as to what to find or what not to find, by the attorney representing the defendant, or by any other party interested in the cause of the defendant; that his investigation, examination, and research would be strictly impersonal, and that the facts would be reported exactly as he found them to be.

Affiant states that with this understanding, he made an examination and investigation of the physical and technical evidence in the case and of the premises in which the murder was committed, and thereafter performed a number of experiments in his laboratory at the University of California, testing the significance of the facts which he found established in his examination and investigation during the period from January 22nd to January 26th, 1955, and made an interpretation of said evidence.

Affiant states that in order to properly interpret the evidence disclosed by his investigation and examination, and to arrive at ultimate facts, he examined the evidence presented in the case and determined the relation of such evidence to the facts disclosed by his examination, investigation, and research.

Affiant states that he examined certain physical materials of possible evidential value, as follows:

1. Premises of the defendant, Samuel H. Sheppard, 28924 West Lake Road, Bay Village, Ohio, on January 23 and 24, 1955.
2. Materials introduced as exhibits in the case of the State of Ohio vs. Samuel H. Sheppard, and held in custody of the Criminal Prosecutor of Cuyahoga County, Ohio, on January 25, 1955, in the presence of Mr. Parrino.

Items collected and removed from the premises of the defendant on January 24, 1955, follow:

a. Top cover (ticking) of the bed on which Marilyn Sheppard was murdered. This was cut with a razor blade around the outside stitched junction.
b. The bottom sheet from the adjoining bed, carrying blood spatter.
c. The yellow pillow-case from the adjoining bed, showing blood spatter.
d. A pair of nylon stockings from the wardrobe in the defendant's dressing room.
e. Debris swept from the carpeting of the murder scene, between the bed of Marilyn Sheppard and the adjoining east wall of the room. This was removed with a vacuum sweeper and special filter attachment.
f. A number of samples of carpet fibers pulled from selected regions of the carpeting in the same general area.

Additional items received at or about the same time were a set of photographs, copied from court exhibits, 16 books of transcript covering technical and some other testimony, a copy of the inquest report, a copy of the autopsy report, certain copies of written statements made by witnesses but not part of sworn testimony, and some miscellaneous papers.

On February 18, 1955, there were received by registered mail two samples of dried blood, collected from two previously identified spots on the wardrobe door of the murder room.

On March 9, 1955, there was received by special delivery mail one package containing an envelope with cotton and two bottles of nail polish, one Revlon's "Cherries in the Snow" and one "Bachelor's Carnations".

Examinations and Results

Detailed analysis of the blood pattern in the bedroom in which Marilyn Sheppard was murdered constituted the bulk of the analysis of physical evidence. It is in this room and only here that the story of the actual murder is written.

Evidence introduced in the trial was examined at the County Prosecutor's office. Only visual examination was possible since no alteration whatever of the materials there was allowed; no samples were allowed to be removed. Numerous items in custody in that office should be examined thoroughly which apparently was not done previously. These include particularly:

a. The lower bed sheet from Marilyn Sheppard's bed.
b. Pillow slip from Marilyn Sheppard's bed.
c. Teeth fragments.
d. Nail polish. This latter item was not found. The container (Ex. 44) so labeled was searched with magnification, and was apparently completely devoid of anything that could be identified as nail polish. The same was true of the slide allegedly containing nail polish from under Marilyn Sheppard's finger nails. (See discussion of nail polish elsewhere.)
e. Defendant's trousers.

Numerous experiments were also performed to allow reliable interpretation of certain observations. The complete absence of careful interpretation shown in the trial transcript leaves nothing tangible, only inference. Experiments designed to test their reliability of interpretation but not dealing directly with materials involved in the case itself are appended to the affidavit, not written into it. The actual investigative details and results are broken into suitable categories which follow, along with a discussion of the status of the case as it was presented by the prosecution and on which the present guilty verdict rests. It is considered important to review these matters because they are either indicative of guilt and accepted by the jury, or they are fabric of errors of omission, commission, or both.

Technical Evidence of the Prosecution

Careful appraisal of the technical evidence presented by the prosecution shows it to be completely worthless as proof of the guilt (or innocence) of the defendant. Only the autopsy and pathology findings are really pertinent to the case. With two minor exceptions, it shows no circumstantial value whatever. There are

(a) Water under defendant's watch crystal.
(b) Loss of T shirt.

The first point, (a), is self-contradictory. If the watch was in the lake after the murder, fresh blood on it would have been removed to a degree which would make any effort to group it completely futile. (See Appendix A.) Since it was considered to be sufficient for grouping, the watch could not have been in the lake after the murder, and the water must have been under the crystal previously.

Point (b) has no ready explanation which can be shown so definitely. It is consistent with the story told by the defendant, as well as with the version presented by the Prosecution. It is not impossible that the murderer removed the T shirt to be used in cleaning blood from his own person. An unbiased observer would surely be struck by the fact that the defendant, if he removed his T shirt because it was bloody, would surely put on another one to cover loss of the first.

Other semi-technical points of the Prosecution that deserve comment are

a. The claimed drying of blood on Mrs. Sheppard's wrist before her watch was removed; and
b. Drying of blood on defendant's watch before it was inserted in the green bag.

These items are equivalent since both involve the time necessary for freshly shed blood to dry. Naturally, both temperature and humidity influence the rate of drying, and these are not known with certainty for the early morning of July 4, 1954. It is known that blood dries rapidly when in thin layers or small drops. Curvature of a small drop markedly increases its vapor pressure, and a thin layer exposes a great deal of surface for a very small volume.

Experiments to check this point are reported in Appendix B. The time necessary for blood to dry under reasonable conditions is certainly short enough that it could well have happened between the time of the murder and the time that the stage was set to simulate a burglary. In fact, unless some large drops or thick layers were involved, the time becomes reasonable if the watches were removed about immediately after the commission of the crime.

Blood Trails

The presence of blood trails throughout the premises has no bearing whatsoever on the guilt or innocence of the defendant. Whoever the murderer may have been, these would have occurred in a similar extent and degree. The fact that only five or six spots of blood were proved to be human in origin, and that these would or may have alternative explanations make it extremely doubtful if any of the blood trails, with a possible exception of spots on the main stairway, were in any way connected with the murder.

Experiments on these points are appended (see Appendix C) and show clearly that the blood trails claimed probably have no connection with the murder and could not have been used properly to prove the guilt or innocence of any accused person.

Ways in which blood might have been transported throughout the house by the murderer are by the

A. Clothing. Blood spatters do not drop from clothing unless the cloth is water repellent, in which case the loss of liquid blood is almost instantaneous. (See Appendix D.) Blood in the alleged trails did not come from this source.

B. Weapon. An occasional drop of blood may fall from some weapons some time after the weapon is immersed in it. Most of the excess blood drains almost immediately but when the wet surface is large, the slow drainage of the viscous blood allowed distances as much as fifty feet to be covered in normal walking before the last blood was lost. Most objects tested as weapons lost the last drop within fifteen (15) feet of normal walking. Blood may adhere to a static or swinging weapon for as much as forty-five (45) seconds after dipping in fresh blood. In every instance, the blood is lost as a few large drops, unless the weapon is shaken vigorously to dislodge the smaller accumulations. (See Appendix E.) No such large drops were found anywhere in the alleged blood trails. It should be noted that blood is so viscous and sticky that unless a weapon is actually dipped in it, or carries comparable amounts of blood, the latter is removed only by shaking and will not drip spontaneously. A vigorous movement will displace small drops, but carrying it normally displaces either nothing at all or large drops, depending on the amount of the accumulation. If any of the blood were shaken from the weapon after leaving the room, it still is not reasonable that this process would continue to the basement, the garage, etc., and in any instance, it tells exactly nothing about the hand that held the weapon.

C. Skin of hands (or face, etc.). Blood drops from an immersed hand in the same manner essentially as from a weapon. All considerations of B, above, apply.

D. Shoes. Tracking of blood on the shoes is a highly probable method of leaving a blood trail. Such trails may persist visibly as far as fifty feet (50) (see Appendix F) after stepping in an actual puddle of blood and walking at normal rate. The appearance of the trail is very different from the small spots claimed, and in no case could such spots be placed on the risers of stairs, as shown to have occurred. Heel smears containing blood might be placed in careful descent of stairs with bloody shoes. No definite record of such bloody smears is found in the testimony. In summary, the shoes are the most probable carriers of blood, but no evidence was adduced that remotely indicated this origin of any of the trails. Also, the presence of such trails would indicate the passage of the murderer but give no indication whatever of his identity. One further point of great importance — if any significant amount of blood was transported on shoes by the murderer, the shoes, even after soaking in water, would be expected to show evidence of the original presence of blood. (See Appendix G). No such indications were claimed in testimony, and inspection of the shoes did not reveal the slightest indication that blood was or had been present on them. It should be noted that the amount of blood would in any case be too small for extensive tests, but there should be enough around stitching and in small recesses to allow chemical blood tests to yield positive results.

Green Bag and Contents

Clearly, the presence of blood on the green bag is not indicative in any way of the guilt or innocence of any accused person, because it may be presumed to have been put there by the murderer regardless of who he may have been. This is equally true of all of the contents of the bag, since it must be accepted that the murderer stripped from both the victim and the defendant the items in the bag.

If the defendant was the person doing the stripping, two facts require explanations: (a) The presence of a four-inch tear in defendant's trousers below the right side pocket; and (b) the damage to the watch band of defendant's watch. Both of these items are things that are highly improbable if defendant stripped the key chain and the watch from himself. It would have been next to impossible for him to tear the pants as they are torn in removing the key chain since the only movement of his hand that is possible without contortion is upward and outward, not downward as required. Regardless of how excited or disturbed one is, he also tends to protect his watch, from sheer habit, if for no other reason. Ordinary removal would be normal and damage during it would have to have an accidental origin. This assumes that the damage to the watch band was not a pre-existing condition caused by an earlier accident. It is difficult to accept the idea that a person would remove his own watch so violently as to damage the band to the extent that exists.

Regardless of interpretations that may be placed on any of this evidence, it clearly has no value of proof of the guilt of the defendant, and actually is better interpreted in the contrary terms.

Blood on Defendant's Clothing

The comparative absence of blood on the clothing of the defendant is highly significant. It is entirely certain that the actual murderer received blood on his person, and no portion on his clothing that was exposed could have been exempt from bloodstaining. The amount on his person would not probably be very great. (See Appendix H.) His face and hair were probably spattered also in some degree, and his hand would have to be quite bloody, almost certainly from the blood of the victim and from his own blood (see elsewhere in this affidavit).

Complete washing in the lake would unquestionably be sufficient to remove the blood from the skin, and possibly from the hair, but only if the hair was well washed. Whether all blood would be removed from the clothing is doubtful, though it is possible that it might be removed from the trousers to a point of being undetectable. It would not be expected to be completely removed from the shoes, as indicated above, and crevices around belt buckles or similar recesses might well persist.

The presence of blood on the knee of defendant's trousers is particularly significant, because it appears to be hemolyzed blood, and restricted to the single relatively small area. Had other blood on his trousers been washed out completely by the lake water, this also would have been. If his wet trousers were placed against blood on the sheet in the bedroom as is strongly indicated by the examination of the sheet, such blood would have hemolyzed and spread throughout a restricted region, thinly and rather uniformly as is found.

Summary

Analysis of the technical evidence offered by the prosecution shows it to be superficial, incomplete, and erroneous in interpretation. Little if any of it had a direct bearing on guilt or innocence of Dr. Samuel H. Sheppard. At the most, it established that the victim was beaten to death by a weapon of unknown type; that there was some blood found in various places in the house; that the murderer attempted to give an impression of a burglary; that it was amateurish and clumsily performed as to fool nobody; and that certain details appeared to be inconsistent with the story told repeatedly by the defendant. Even these apparent inconsistencies were so minor as to be of little value if correct, and no certainty of the correctness of interpretation was established. Briefly, no actual proof of a technical nature was even offered indicating guilt of the defendant, and the facts that were established and offered are even

more readily interpreted in several respects in terms
of another murderer than the defendant.

The Murder Scene

The bedroom in which the murdered body of Marilyn Sheppard
was found is shown in approximate scale diagram in
accompanying Photograph No. 1.[1] The diagram represents
the condition at the time it was examined by the
undersigned. The two twin beds and bureau, shown in the
drawings, are in the same position as indicated in
prosecution photographs. The drawing omits the rocking
chair in the northeast corner of the room, which carried
no visible blood or other significant evidence, and the
small telephone stand between the two beds which did
not figure in testimony, or in this investigation.

Blood distribution. By far the most significant evidence
to be found was the blood distribution in the murder
room. Proper interpretation of this distribution must
give the reconstruction of the crime because every blow
struck placed its signature in the room in blood. It is
also the most significant, and possibly the only significant evidence, that can be offered based on blood
studies. It was virtually disregarded by the earlier
investigators as determined by examination of the trial
transcript.
    Blood spots were present on every wall of the room,
and were distributed over all of the defendant's bed.
The extent of blood on the floor, and on the items of
furniture could not be determined at the time of this
investigation, but some indication is available from
testimony and exhibits of the prosecution.

Distribution on the walls. The east wall of the room,
and particularly the wardrobe door and the open hall
door at the south end of that wall showed blood spatters
in very large numbers as indicated in trial exhibits
and in accompanying photographs. The distribution was
most significant, being roughly triangular on the two
doors, and discontinuing completely at the north end of
the wall for a distance of nearly four feet. Nearly all
spots on the wardrobe door were below the level of the

---

[1] Photographs not included.

door handle. On the open hall door, the spots ranged almost to the top of the door on the edge nearest the hall. The approximate limitation of blood spots on the doors is shown in Photograph No. 2. The last of the blood spots north of the wardrobe doors are approximately eight inches from the door jamb facing. A photograph of the most concentrated portions of these spots is given in No. 3. No spots were present on the north portion of the east wall for a distance of about four feet.

The south wall had on it a limited but considerable number of spots which were heaviest in the vicinity of the head of the bed on which the victim was found.

The west wall had almost no spots except that the window blind on that side of the room had few small ones. This was not because many drops did not start in that direction as indicated by the very large number on the adjoining bed, but merely because of the considerable distance which allowed only a very few velocity droplets to reach that far.

The north wall was very significant in respect to blood spots. On the west offset there were approximately ten spots which were relatively large and retained high velocity up to the time of impact. They had been thrown ten feet or more. A similar number was almost present and scattered over the east side offset on the north wall (see Photograph No. 4). The spots in both locations showed the beading around their periphery that is characteristic of a drop impacting with a considerable velocity. On the extreme east end of the wall, past the offsets for about two feet, there was an area containing no spots, and a continuation of the corresponding space on the east wall.

This single region in the entire periphery of the room in which no blood had traveled through the air must by necessity be the region in which the attacker stood, since it is the only place in which the blood drops have been intercepted. It is shown in the photograph of the sketch of the room, appended No. 1, and in Photographs No. 5 and 6. Close to the edge of the bed slightly overlapping it, the width of the cone would be about two feet which approximates the width of a man's body. It placed the attacker very close to the foot of the bed on the east side. Other details of the analysis will place him more precisely.

Defendant's bed. At the time of viewing this bed, the covers had been arranged to correspond with the arrangement shown in the exhibits of the prosecution, vis., the bloody side of the pillow upward, the pillow occupying the blood-free region of the lower sheet, and the top covers turned back so that all the exposed area showed blood spotting. On the bed, chiefly on the exposed portion of the lower sheet, and the turned-back portion of the upper sheet, on the top of the pillow, were a large number of small blood spots. On the side nearest to Marilyn's bed there was a region of larger spots, one over ¼ inch in diameter. Over the remainder of the bed the spots were much smaller, and showed by their shape that the droplets were moving at relatively high velocity and numerous drops moved in an arc approaching the horizontal. Many of them had dropped more nearly vertically, representing higher arcs of flight.

The Radiator. On top of the radiator were several blood spots. All of these had approached nearly horizontally and at high velocity. One in particular had been at so low an angle and with so high a velocity that it had "skipped" like a stone on water, leaving a series of about eight spots extending in a line one foot three and a quarter inches in length (1'3¼").

Point of origin. Because of the characteristic shape of blood spots striking in different directions and at different velocities, it is possible to trace the direction of a drop through air, and to estimate the velocity with considerable certainty. Utilizing the spots on the defendant's bed, it was noted that all those that gave elongated patterns had originated at a single center of origin which corresponded exactly with the region of Marilyn's mattress on which the blood intensity was greatest, and which was occupied by her head at the time she was found. It can therefore be stated with certainty that her head was in essentially the same position during all of the blows from which blood was spattered on the defendant's bed. This distribution is illustrated in Photographs No. 7 to 11.

One further point is evident from the blood on the defendant's bed, viz., Marilyn Sheppard's head was on the sheet during most, if not all of the beating that led to the blood spots. This is shown by the presence of nearly the same intensity of blood on the lower edge of the pillow on the defendant's bed, below the seam, as above the seam. The pillow must have been in north position, with this position forming an actual undercut on the end surface, or there would be folded regions free of blood on the top, which do not occur. For blood to spatter to this position of the pillow requires that the head be close to the same level as the mattress. The conclusion is further confirmed by the "skipping" effected drop on the top of the radiator. Since the blood travels in a trajectory which is essentially parabolic, its rate of drop due to gravity would be considerable at the distance of the radiator (about eight feet). To give the "skipping" effect would require an angle of incidence on the radiator of less than 15° which could only occur if the origin of the trajectory were lower than the radiator top. No blood drops were present on the ceiling, nor were there any high on the walls with the exception of a few on the hall door that were close to the top of the door.

Blood spots on the north wall, the spots that were thrown to both the east and west offsets in that wall, were examined for their trajectory and origin. They also originated at the same point as the spots on the defendant's bed, or very close to that spot.

Blood spots on the south wall (some spots illustrated in Photograph No. 12) were of more than one origin. Many of them were direct spatter from impact, and these aligned also with the position of Marilyn Sheppard's head when found. Others were thrown at a flat angle to the wall and did not originate from impact spatter, but impinged tangentially to the arc of the weapon.

Blood spots on the east wall were exceptional in their indications. Nearly all of them contrasted sharply with other spots in the room in that they were placed by low-velocity drops. Most of them impacted the wall nearly at right angles to it as is clearly demonstrated from their essentially round shape (Photograph No. 13), and the fact that the edge of the open door shows an exact pathway of one drop whose impact point is also clearly shown on the other door. Other drops in a minority, impacted at a variety of angles, and without any clear pattern, such as is shown by nearly the entire remainder of the room. (Photographs No. 14 and 15.)

These drops with low velocity and mixed pattern of impact predominantly horizontal could not have originated in the same manner as the remainder of the blood in the room, and gives the clue to the entire pattern of the event.

Extensive experiments show that many, and probably nearly all, of the blood drops on the east wall were thrown there by the backswing of the weapon used, since this is the only method by which low-velocity drops could have reached that wall, and it is the only way in which they would have been predominantly at right angles in impact direction. It can be stated very positively that they did not originate as impact spatter, which is the source of most of the drops that impacted other parts of the room. The low and triangular distribution of the drops on the two doors corresponds with the swing of the weapon which started low in a left-hand swing rising through an arc, and striking the victim a sidewise angular blow rather than one broken downward vertically. The absence of blood on the ceiling at a time when blood was thrown to other directions from the weapon demonstrates that no vertical "chopping" blows were used. A swing similar to that used with a baseball bat with a left-handed batter is the only one consistent with the blood spot distribution.

Cause of distribution.   It is established where the attacker stood during the murder. It is also established that Marilyn Sheppard's head, which was the source of most of the blood in the room, was down on the bed throughout most of the beating, and that its position was essentially constant during that time. It follows that any reconstruction of the crime must account for all of the blood spot distribution on the basis of the physical events that threw blood. It must also account for the location and character of the wounds insofar as they are independent of the exact nature of the weapon, which is not known.

Extensive experiments on the nature of blood thrown by different events were made. (See Appendix I). It was shown that fine, high-velocity drops were formed ahead of some bloody weapons when they were used to strike an object. These were from throw-off from the rapidly moving weapons. They were also formed from a certain set of conditions as impact spatter, in front of the weapon when struck vertically, or in the direction of movement of the weapon when struck angularly. At no time were any significant numbers obtained on the opposite side of an angular blow. The predominance of such fine, high-velocity drops that struck the defendant's bed, the radiator, and even the window shade at the opposite end of the room means that the blows were struck toward that end of the room, regardless of the particular origin of the fine spatter. Such blows would be struck in two ways only:

1. By a right-handed person striking vertical blows, and situated slightly to the left of Marilyn Sheppard's head, i.e., toward the hall doorway. This is not possible, because the attacker did not intercept blood spots at this location; and vertical blows would have placed some blood on the ceiling.
2. By a left-handed person, situated at the known position of this attacker, striking either angular or vertical blows (the latter excluded). This is completely consistent with observed facts.

It is further shown that large drops (predominantly less than ¼ inch in diameter) could be formed by

1. Impact spatter of any type of weapon. The direction of flight is determined by the shape of the weapon and its relation to the surface struck. A flat object, like a hammer, striking a flat surface throws such drops in every direction. A bar throws them only to the right, and left, etc. The great preponderance of the blood thrown by impact consisted of low-velocity, large drops which were thrown from a few inches up to about two feet from the point of impact. So much more blood constituted this local low-velocity spatter than traveled in any other way as to be striking. Some weapons produced almost nothing else. This corresponds to most of the blood in the immediate vicinity of the head, excluding the blood which simply flowed from the wounds to the bed, leaving a pool.
2. Throw-off from weapon. Large drops were regularly formed when a bloody weapon was swung through an arc, the predominant throw-off occurring at the ends of the stroke. The less energetic backstroke threw backward the largest drops at the lowest velocity. The vigorous movement of striking an object rarely threw large drops, and any drop thrown

was at high velocity. The spots on the doors in
the bedroom are predominantly the size described
above, most of which correspond only with backthrow
of a weapon, or with local low-velocity spatter.
The latter is ruled out completely by the distance
between the location of the victim's head and the
door (about seven feet). The distance from the
weapon to the door on the backthrow is only about
one and a half feet which allows low-velocity throw-
off to travel readily to the door.

High-velocity relatively large drops could be formed
in one of two ways:

1. Impact spatter from a very low angle or from a very
    flat impact by the weapon. These were always ahead
    of the direction of movement if the surfaces did
    not meet flat (e.g., hammerhead on flat block).
2. Throw-off in a violent movement of a very bloody
    instrument. This is difficult to produce because
    most of the blood is removed in a backthrow, and
    the necessary velocity of movement is difficult to
    get on any but a forward throw. In attempting to
    get these spots, usually the large drops leave at
    low velocity on the backthrow, and small, high-
    velocity ones are only formed on the forward. Blood
    spots, relatively large (about ⅛ inch diameter) on
    the north wall offsets correspond to high-velocity
    impact spatter from a left-handed blow. Both their
    direction and distribution are different than could
    be obtained by a right-handed throw-off spatter by
    a right-handed blow.

Very large spots (greater than ½ inch diameter) were
not obtained by weapon throw-off, even from a weapon
dipped in blood and swung while still dripping, though
a scoop-shaped weapon might collect and hold enough blood
if properly applied. Such spots were never accumulated
from impact spatter at greater than about one foot from
the point of impact.

The only method by which such very large spots could
be placed was to take blood into the cupped hand and
toss it at low velocity. In no case was it possible to
obtain a very large spot from higher-velocity blood

because the larger volume broke up into smaller drops. The requirements for obtaining very large spots are

1. Accumulation of relatively large volume — greater than will adhere to a surface, however irregular; and
2. Movement which impacts only at low velocity and is delivered very near to the surface impacted by the blood. No large volume of blood can be thrown far, because higher velocities break up the drops, and a low-velocity blood volume does not travel far. One or two feet is about as far as it can be kept intact and delivered.

One very large blood spot was present on the wardrobe door. (Photographs No. 14 and 16.) It measured about one inch in diameter at its largest dimension. It was essentially round, showed no beading, and had impinged almost exactly perpendicular to the door, i.e., horizontally and at right angles to the door. This spot could not have come from impact spatter. It is highly improbable that it could have been thrown off a weapon, since so much blood would not have adhered during the backswing for so long a distance, and then separated suddenly at just the right moment to deposit as it did. This spot requires an explanation different from the majority of the spots on the doors. It almost certainly came from a bleeding hand, and most probably occurred at a time different from the time that hand was wielding a weapon. The bleeding hand could only have belonged to the attacker. The origin of the injury is dealt with elsewhere, as is supplementary confirmation of the different origin of this spot. It should be noted that this spot is probably not unique in origin, and other spots on the east wall are possibly elsewhere and may have had the same origin, but this spot was unique in size and appearance and was consequently selected for more extensive study.

Blood Groups and Individuality

No serious question can be raised that the origin of most of the blood in the murder room came from the victim. This assumption was evidently made by the prosecution investigators who did little or nothing toward analysis of blood in that room, assuming that all of it was from the victim. It was established by them that the victim was of universal group O, and carried the M factor. It should be noted that nearly half the population is a group O, about 40 to 45%, and that a large majority, about 80%, carry the M factor. At no time was the group of Dr. Sam Sheppard determined or mentioned as determined during the trial. His group was determined as to A or B factors in this investigation. It was found that Dr. Sam is group A, probably M. The subgroup is inferred only from the weakness of the reaction when inhibition or agglutination by dried blood extract was used in the grouping. Only dry blood could be studied under the available circumstances.

Blood removed from the mattress, unquestionably the blood of the victim, was grouped and found to be devoid of A and B factors. Further, the blood was readily soluble in distilled water, and agglutination after treatment with anti-serum and cells was immediate as compared with controls of anti-serum and cells alone. The same results were found with a second rather large spot (½ inch in diameter) (Photographs No. 14 and 14A) from the same door panel as the very large spot discussed above. There was no sign of delayed agglutination, and solubility of the blood was excellent.

Grouping of the large spot was performed simultaneously with the same sera and cells and in identical manner. Several differences were immediately apparent. The blood from the very large spot was definitely less soluble than that from the small spot, or from controls from the mattress. In running the agglutination tests, in every instance and with tests for both A and B factors, agglutination was much slower and less certain than the controls. The fact that delayed agglutination occurred indicated clearly that this blood was also O group, but its behavior was so different as to be striking. These differences are considered to constitute confirmatory evidence that the blood of the large spot had a different individual origin from most of the blood in the bedroom.

It may be of interest that blood on both watches was stated to contain M factor but was never assigned a universal group in the prosecution testimony. This would be entirely understandable if the blood on those items was from the same source as the large spot on the wardrobe door. Since A and B factors are ordinarily more

readily determined in dry blood than is the M factor
the testimony is inexplicable otherwise.

Tooth Fragments

The fact established by the prosecution that one medial
incisor tooth of the victim was broken completely across
and that two other chips of considerable size were also
found is one of the most significant facts established.
Curiously, no attempt was apparently ever made to explain
it in testimony during the trial, though it absolutely
demanded explanation.

The tooth fragments were examined in the prosecutor's
office. The large fragment represented the entire lower
portion of the medial incisor, broken approximately to
the gum line on the front, and the break tapered downward
at the rear, so that a sharp projection from the root
would remain on the lingual side. The broad dimensions
of the fragment were ⅝ and ¼ inch. The smaller fragment
from the bed was ³/₁₆ × ⅛ inch and the fragment under
the bed was ⁵/₃₂ × ⅛ inch.

It is well known to everyone that teeth do not fracture
to this extent except under very unusual stress, or
people would be spitting out teeth all the time. A strong
blow to the teeth would be capable of breaking them,
but would inevitably injure the lips seriously. No
indication of such a blow was ever found according to
the testimony, the autopsy report, or the photographs
of the victim's face. The prosecution witnesses left the
matter totally unexplained, and by doing so admitted
their inability or lack of desire to explain it.

Two points are highly significant in the explanation:

1. The teeth were found outside her mouth, not inside,
   or in her throat as would be expected if broken by
   an external blow; and
2. The medial incisor fractured at an angle that is
   consistent only with a pull outward, not a blow
   inward. Because it was not stated in the testimony,
   it is not clear what portion of additional teeth
   contributed to two smaller fragments. If they were
   chipped from the labial surfaces, as they appeared
   to be, this could hardly happen from a blow. It
   seems very clear that the teeth were clamped on

something that was forcibly withdrawn with removal
of the fragments completely from the mouth. The
only reasonable article would be the attacker's
hand, possibly placed over the mouth to prevent an
outcry — which is consistent with defendant's story
and the fact that nobody heard such an outcry,
including Chip in the next room. It is certain that
she did not bite the weapon used to beat her. It
is highly improbable that she wasted time biting
clothing. It is entirely reasonable and highly
probable that she bit her attacker's hand. It is
equally certain that a bite of this ferocity would
have left distinct injury to such a bitten member,
and that blood would have been shed. This is not
pure speculation but reasoned approach to the
established facts, and it must represent at least
a close approximation of the truth. Blood shed from
the hand after being bitten could have placed the
large blood spot on the wardrobe door, and in fact
flowing blood from a wound is about the only
reasonable manner in which this spot could have
been placed. Certainly the murderer did not take
the time or trouble to scoop up blood in his hand
and gently toss it to the door. If blood was flowing
freely, as he pulled his hand away and swung it
back, the rapid accumulation of blood during the
swing could have and very probably did deposit as
the large spot discussed. If this is true, it
explains the definite differences shown by this
blood and other blood at the scene; and it explains
how so large a spot could have been placed with
the required low-velocity and large volume. It is
the opinion of this examiner that the murderer had
a definitely injured hand or finger on July 4, 1954.

Blood-Stained Bedding

Examination of the mattress top (Photograph No. 17) as
well as superficial examination of the under sheet and
pad of the bed on which the victim was murdered shows
certain interesting and possibly pertinent facts not
developed in the above discussion of the blood spot
pattern.

Examination of the bedding shows the presence in
considerable quantity of a fluid other than blood, most

heavily concentrated in the lower portion of the bedding, and forming a large pad of the large central bloody area. This fluid was urine, probably voided at or shortly before death. It was probably hypotonic, i.e., less concentrated than the blood for it appears to have produced hemolysis of the blood corpuscles as it mixed with the blood. The lighter portions of the large central bloody area represent a dilute solution of blood in this urine, which soaked into the bedding, spread laterally, and finally dried. It is of interest to the investigation in an indirect manner only, as will be developed below.

On the east side of the bed, visible on the lower sheet, corresponding to the edge of the mattress, and just south of the center point of the sheet is visible a region which appears bloody, but with very dilute blood. This spot is nine inches wide at its widest point, the south edge being three feet, three inches from the south edge of the sheet, and the north edge three feet, nine inches from the north edge of the sheet. Examination of this spot visually and with magnification (in the prosecutor's office) showed the blood to be highly dilute, and almost certainly hemolyzed. This could happen by mixing the blood with any dilute water solution or water itself, as well as with urine. Its position, shape, and size are most consistent with it having been made by a wet knee placed against the sheet. Inspection of the spot showed that blood was present in spattered drops before the other fluid was present, since the blood had been carried laterally with the flow of fluid, and original blood spots are still present, only partially displaced by the diluting fluid. It is clear that the diluting fluid was definitely placed on a region carrying whole blood spots.

The obvious and probably correct interpretation of this finding is that the defendant placed his knee at this position after coming from the lake. The water from his wet pants would have produced exactly the effect observed. It is to be noted that this region did not show in the mattress directly below, or on the pad below the sheet. Thus, it is shown that the amount of diluting fluid was quite limited, such as would be carried by a single layer of cloth.

The single alternative explanation would be that the murderer dipped his knee in the pool of urine (containing blood), lifted it out carefully enough that no smear of the material was left on the sheet, and placed the spot as a separate act. This could have happened, but would be expected to leave indications at the point of dragging the knee from the pool of urine. No such indications are present. It is also likely that the amount of liquid carried in this case would be great enough to soak further into the bed than is observed. The position of the spot is also inconsistent with the known position of the murderer. This explanation can be checked by testing the area on the sheet for the presence of urine. If the urine is absent, it shows that the first explanation is correct, and that the blood on the defendant's left knee was acquired after coming from the lake — not before.

A further observation of the blood pattern on the sheet is significant. This consists of an area approximately twelve to eighteen inches to the right of the wet spot discussed in the above paragraph, and eighteen inches from the edge of the sheet to the center of the area. This area contained numerous original, undiluted blood spots which had been strongly smeared in the north-south direction, or lengthwise with the bed. The area involved was at the exact spot that the attacker must have occupied to intercept the blood spots on the walls as they were intercepted. It lies just where a knee would have to be placed to balance him during the wielding of the weapon. It also seems indisputable that these smears, which do not occur elsewhere on the bed, accurately depict the position of the murderer's knee and confirm the previous analysis of his position. It indicates that he had one foot on the floor, the opposite knee being on the bed, so that his body was actually over the northeastern portion of the bed. This detail of position allows also some inference regarding the length of the weapon, and in closeness of approach to the east wall of the room on the backswing, all of which are important considerations in the overall analysis of the crime.

The Weapon

Some indications of the nature of the weapon are available from consideration of the details of the crime, as well as from the nature of the wounds. When a person is struck in the region of the face they automatically and instinctively lower and turn the head away from the blow as for protection for the face and especially the eyes. Further, they automatically and instinctively raise the hands in a protective gesture to shield the face, and they may grab other objects in the vicinity that may add to the shielding. The evidence is completely clear that the victim's hands were employed in this manner, resulting in severe injury to them. It is because of this fact that a straight type of weapon like a bar is most probable, since the injuries to the victim's forehead are parallel to the axis of the head which would require that she face the attacker directly and without defensive reflex action — a virtual impossibility.

This fact, and the nature of the wounds, indicates that the actual edge that cut through the scalp was at approximately right angles to the axis of the weapon. If the victim's head were turned to her right, essentially as she was found, and assuming this type of injury edge, nearly every one of the injuries visible in the photographs of the autopsy photographer can be accounted for on the basis of left-hand blows. They cannot, on the basis of right-hand blows, though some of them are consistent with right-handed blows only if her head were turned sharply to her left. The latter idea is inconsistent both with her final position, and with some of the injuries, notably those on the right of her head.

The weapon was short, as shown by the reconstruction diagram (Photograph No. 18). Having fixed the position of the attacker and knowing the position of the victim's head, the length of area is exactly what would be true of a man's arm wielding a weapon less than one foot in length, i.e., about thirty-six inches. Naturally, the torso and arm lengths influence weapon length calculation, because the distance that can be established is the sum of the arm and weapon length. Even with a short arm, the length of one foot covers the available and necessary distance.

This investigator did not view the wounds themselves, and the photographs of them are possibly misleading. It is still clear that the injuring edge of the weapon was more or less angular or possibly rounded with a small radius. This is necessary to produce the injuries as described in testimony, which are not sharply cut, but were parted through to the bone and beyond. A small bar-type instrument could have produced this effect but only if bent at a sharp angle from its axis. The necessary narrowness of such an instrument argues against it having enough weight to shatter the skull and separate the individual bones at the sutures.

A larger cylindrical instrument like a piece of pipe flared on the end is more reasonable, and consistent with the type of injury and the reconstruction of its mode of application.

If the weapon was carried into the room to be used as it eventually was used, a wide variety of possibilities exist. If it was acquired at the time it was needed, it would have to have been present in the bedroom prior to the murder which is improbable. A third possibility exists, viz., that it was an object carried for another purpose, but serving as a murder weapon when needed. Such an item is a heavy flashlight, several designs of which fill nearly all of the necessary specifications. The most serious argument against this possibility is the (presumed) absence from the room of glass which would be likely to have broken. A plastic lens might answer this objection. There still remains a puncture-type wound on the right side of the victim's head which is difficult to explain unless the rim had collapsed so as to form a sharp angle which could puncture.

With the available limited information, it is not possible to infer an exact weapon but certain of its characteristics are quite definite and can be safely assumed.

Miscellaneous Items

1. Victim's slacks. The blood pattern on the victim's slacks is definitely significant in the overall interpretation of the crime. Her legs were probably drawn up, also a defensive act, as indicated by the fact that when she later relaxed, they straightened out so as to protrude under the crossbar of her bed. Whether the legs were drawn up or not, the most exposed portion of the slacks, if on the victim, were the tops of the thighs and it is inevitable that this region would have accumulated the greatest amount of blood. Examination of the slacks and of photographs of them shows that this was not the case, the bottoms of the legs having the strongest blood spotting. This shows quite definitely that the slacks had been removed partially from the victim before the murder, and

substantiates the idea that the crime started as a sex attack, rather than as a murder.

2. Top sheet of victim's bed. The statement of the defendant that he spread the sheet over the victim's lower quarters is reasonable, both because of the appearance of the sheet at the time of photographing, and the apparent scarcity of blood spots from the top of the sheet as photographed. Naturally, portions of the sheet would have contacted the pool of diluted blood on the bed, and the pattern of blood is highly confused. It would be extremely difficult to reconstruct the position of the sheet during the murder, though the opportunity to examine it carefully in terms of the reconstruction and the available photographs would assist in this effort.

3. Pillow. The pillow from the victim's bed indicates far more than what was stated or implied in the testimony regarding it. Solid regions of bloodstain are present on both sides of the pillowcase. One of these can be explained by contact with the pool of blood on the bed which seems to have spread far enough to be soaked up from the sheet. Blood spatter from the blows themselves show that the side opposite to the alleged instrument mark was upward during the beating. That it was earlier in contact with liquid blood in quantity is shown definitely by the large bloody area on that side which could not have been placed during the beating had the pillow remained as it was found. It is certain that the pillow was either used to prevent outcry earlier, or that the victim attempted to shield herself by holding the pillow on her face or head. In either case, the pillow had to be moved at a subsequent time, and was probably doubled down on itself and folded in such a manner as to produce a mirror image blood impression later interpreted as an "instrument" impression. It is hoped to conduct experiments to check this point.

4. Nail polish fragments. Exhibits stated to contain nail polish (Ex. 44, and a set of slides) and examined in the Prosecutor's office in Cleveland appeared to be devoid of any such material at the time of examination, even when examined with reasonable magnification. Whether the material was in some way overlooked, or whether it has been lost since the time of the trial is not known. Numerous

small fragments similar to nail polish were, however, recovered from the rug in the bedroom at the time of this affiant's investigation. They were compared with samples of nail polish which were sent to the affiant by Dr. Richard N. Sheppard, which were represented to be the nail polish used by Marilyn Sheppard. The relative opacity of the materials found on the floor as compared with nail polish raised a strong presumption that the material actually is not nail polish, but is a red lacquer such as is used to coat small objects, and which is available commercially in many stores, and could conceivably be chips from the weapon.

5. Leather fragment. A leather fragment, approximately triangular in shape and measuring about $\frac{1}{4} \times \frac{1}{4} \times \frac{3}{8}$ inches on the sides was examined in the Prosecutor's office. It appears to be leather rather than a synthetic substitute. It also appeared to have been torn off recently, as indicated by the fresh appearance of the torn surface. Its significance cannot now be interpreted since its origin was not successfully traced by the prosecution investigators or by this investigator.

Reconstruction

From the known and demonstrable facts of the case, a reconstruction of the murder is possible. A limited amount of inference is unavoidable, but in the main, the facts are clear, and the conclusions inescapable.

1. The original motive of the crime was sexual. Examination of the slacks in which the victim was sleeping shows that they were lowered to their approximate final position at the time the blood spatters were made, as discussed above. Leaving the victim in the near nude condition in which she was first found is highly characteristic of the sex crime. The probable absence of serious outcry may well have been because her mouth was covered with the attacker's hand.

2. The victim was not moved after being beaten. This follows from the fact that her head was at the same point as the center of the blood spot pattern.

Since her legs protruded under the lower crossbar of the bed, it follows that she had drawn up her legs in a defensive action, and moved downward during the early stages of the struggle. At the time of death or unconsciousness, her muscles relaxed and the legs straightened to a position similar to that in which she was found.

3. At some point in the activities of the attacker, the victim obtained a firm grip on him with her teeth. His defensive reaction of jerking away was violent enough to break two or three of her teeth. The evidence indicates that blood welling from the resulting wound to a bitten member was thrown as a very large drop to the wardrobe door.

4. Presumably inflamed by the resistance and pain, the attacker utilized some available weapon to strike the victim down. She instinctively turned her head (probably to her right) and shielded it with her hands which were in turn severely injured in the beating that ensued. She may also have grabbed a pillow as a shield, pressing it in front of her head and depositing much blood on it. Whether an early blow produced unconsciousness or whether her head was held down with the other hand of the attacker is uncertain, but one of these two events must have occurred.

5. She was beaten by a weapon held in the left hand, swung low in rapid and vicious blows to her head after it was puddled with blood from earlier injury, and possibly after her actual death. Whether any beating occurred after death or not, her head was certainly beaten for some time in almost exactly the same position — the one in which it was found.

6. The weapon was almost certainly not over a foot in length, and had on it an edge, quite blunt but protruding. This edge was almost certainly crosswise to the axis of the weapon and could have been the flared front edge of a heavy flashlight. It was not similar in any serious respect to the alleged impression of a surgical instrument on the pillow case, not to any of a large variety of possible weapons that have been suggested by the Prosecution.

7. During the beating, the attacker stood close to the bottom of the bed and balanced himself with one

knee on the bed. The weapon swung to about ½ foot from the wardrobe door in this position.

8. After the commission of the crime, the attacker faked a very clumsy attempt to indicate that a burglary had been committed. This included removing watches, keys, etc. and stuffing them in a bag (the green bag) which was later thrown away during the retreat; upsetting the papers from the living room desk; disarranging the den; breaking the trophies; etc.

Defendant's Account

No crime reconstruction is complete or reliable unless it is at least consistent with all the known facts. Several obvious inconsistencies are certainly present between the reconstruction and the theory that the defendant was the attacker. It remains to show that the reconstruction is consistent with the version of the events given by the defendant.

His account is vague, with few details. It is not a well-thought-out story such as might be expected of an intelligent person who was faking the account. The vagueness itself is a characteristic which must be consistent with the known facts, if the account is to be considered true. That a true account would necessarily or probably be vague is indicated by the following known or claimed facts:

(a) The defendant was asleep on the couch when last seen by his visitors, the Aherns. A person suddenly awakened from a sound sleep often is confused and at a loss to act or understand what is happening, especially if it is not commonplace or customary.

(b) Sworn testimony is available to indicate that he suffered a dislocation or other injury to the vertebra of the neck, sufficient to inhibit his normal reflexes. Sworn testimony is also available to indicate that he suffered a blow to the face sufficient to loosen teeth, and cause swelling and discoloration around the eye. These circumstances strongly imply the probability of unconsciousness, which is certainly consistent with vagueness.

(c) On one special point, it was possible to conduct an experiment to determine whether vagueness was consistent with the fact, viz., the "light form" in the bedroom. The night light in the dressing room was turned on with a 50-watt light. All other lights in the house were extinguished. This investigator went downstairs after placing a subject in the bedroom in the position of the attacker. The subject had on a white shirt and dark trousers. After closing the eyes for a short time this investigator ran upstairs as rapidly as possible to the bedroom door. In the very dim light a whitish region was seen corresponding to the white shirt. The head could not be distinguished, nor could the portions below the lower limit of the shirt. The boundaries of the shirt itself could not be distinguished, and what was seen was as precisely what was described by the defendant as could be imagined.

The experiment was repeated with the night light on 100-watts. Again the results were similar though now the boundaries of the shirt could be dimly distinguished. It was still not possible to see anything but the white shirt.

It remains to determine whether other specific points of the account of the defendant are consistent with the interpretation of his investigation. Numerous points emerge from the consideration:

1. It was entirely possible that the defendant was struck on the back of the neck by the same weapon used to kill Marilyn Sheppard. If the weapon was of the type indicated by the studies made, and was a cylindrical object with a flared end, all that must be assumed is that it was the cylindrical portion that contacted the back of his neck rather than the flare. It may be pointed out that in the experiment described in the above paragraph, the subject on one occasion merely moved around as the investigator arrived at the door, and delivered a light blow to the back of the neck without the movement being seen or anticipated by the investigator.

2. The method and clumsiness of removal of the watch and key chain from the defendant's pocket certainly appears to be the work of another person. As pointed out earlier, it would be difficult and completely unnatural for a person to rip his trousers pocket

downward in removing a key chain, but this would be extremely probable if someone else stripped it from a prone body. It is also unlikely that a person removes his own watch so as to damage the band, even if he were faking a burglary.

3. The abandonment of the green bag in the woods is not the work of a person who is deliberately setting a scene as it was postulated that the defendant did. If he took time to wash off all the blood, to sponge the stairs and take the other precautions attributed to him, he would not carelessly throw away the green bag where it would not reasonably be in a real burglary. Rather, its abandonment was the act of a person in an unnatural hurry, as would be true of an intruder being pursued as claimed by the defendant.

4. One portion of the account given by the defendant can be accurately confirmed, viz., the return to the bedroom with wet clothing, and leaning over the bed (water spot on the sheet).

5. Another point of importance that was apparently not fully developed before is the question of the amount of sand in the defendant's shoes. If he waded out into the lake to wash off blood, he would not sink into the wet sand very far, and would pick up in the shoes minimal quantities of sand. Also, he would not pick up any sand in the pockets. If he were lying on the beach, as he stated, he would accumulate large quantities of sand in his shoes, and some in his pockets, as was the case. Further, the toes of his shoes had pressed into the insoles and linings much more sand than the heels of his shoes. While this scarcely constitutes proof that he lay face down in the water and sand, it at least is more consistent with that idea than with any alternative, for the sand would work down into the shoes and inevitably more would remain there than in the heels.

6. It is not reasonable to believe that the defendant would deliberately break his own and his wife's trophies, as occurred. Under no conditions, would this assist in establishing the event as the work of a burglar, for it is equally unreasonable for a true burglar. It is completely consistent only for someone who hated the Sheppards or who was jealous of their athletic tendencies and abilities.

7. It is not reasonable that the defendant would mistreat his surgical and medical equipment as was done. Even to establish the event as the work of a burglar, a doctor who likes his work (as it appears he did) would have faked the theft from the bag entirely differently, rather than merely upsetting it in the hallway, disrupting the contents of his desk, etc.

8. By no stretch of the imagination can it be conceived that the injuries to the defendant were self-inflicted. As a person who was fully aware of the danger associated with a blow to the back of the neck, and faced with the almost insurmountable difficulty of delivering such a blow at all, and certainly of doing it under control, no doctor would ever risk trying it. It is also peculiarly difficult to deliver a blow of any force to one's own face. Neither of these injuries can be reconciled with self-infliction.

9. It is equally ridiculous to assume that these injuries were sustained in falling from the landing platform at the beach. That type of fall would inflict many abrasions, bruises and secondary injuries to the limbs, with the serious possibility of broken bones. It could not under any circumstances select the back of his neck and his face for the only injury. No satisfactory explanation except THAT GIVEN BY THE DEFENDANT has been advanced for his injuries.

10. The type of crime is completely out of character for a husband bent on murdering his wife. In such instances, the murder does not start out as a sex attack with the single exception of an unfulfilled and frustrated husband, which is completely contrary to the indications of this event.

11. Tests of the large spot of blood on the wardrobe door which were conducted by this Affiant establish in Affiant's opinion that it is human blood, that it is not the blood of the Defendant, Dr. Samuel H. Sheppard, and that it is not the blood of Marilyn Sheppard, the murdered woman.

There is attached hereto and made a part hereof as though fully rewritten herein Appendices "A to J," referred to in this Affidavit. There is also filed herewith photographs numbered "1 to 45," all of which photographs were

taken by this Affiant and all the negatives of said
photographs were also developed by this Affiant.

_____

                                        PAUL LELAND KIRK

SWORN TO before me and subscribed in my presence, this
26th day of April, 1955.

_____

                                        WILLIAM J. CORRIGAN

```
STATE OF OHIO      )
                   )  SS:      IN THE COURT OF COMMON PLEAS
CUYAHOGA COUNTY    )                Criminal Branch


                                   No. 64571


STATE OF OHIO,          )
                        )
          PLAINTIFF  )
                        )
    vs.                 )      APPENDICES  A  TO  J
                        )      IN SUPPORT OF THE AFFIDAVIT OF
SAMUEL  H.  SHEPPARD    )         DR.  PAUL  LELAND  KIRK
                        )
          DEFENDANT  )
```

APPENDIX A

Blood on Watch Band

Fresh blood on a smooth non-absorptive surface dissolves and washes away rapidly in water. In order to determine how long blood would remain on an expansible metal watch band under these conditions, such a band (Photograph No. 19) was daubed liberally with freshly shed blood in separate experiments. In the first instance the blood was allowed to remain twenty minutes after deposition and the band was then dipped in freshwater and moved slowly back and forth. In the second, the blood was allowed to dry for 1¼ hours and treated similarly. In both instances, the blood dissolved rapidly and was essentially gone in less than one minute. In the latter experiment, a bit of clot in recess in the band persisted for about three minutes but was washed colorless in less than two minutes. In no case could the blood have been grouped after one minute in the water, and less than half a minute removed approximately 90% of it. This experiment emphasizes the great importance of the type of surface on which blood is deposited because it is very difficult to remove blood completely from absorptive surfaces. It also is conditioned by the fact that the amount of blood necessary for grouping is far in excess than that necessary for detection, and greater than is required for precipition tests.

APPENDIX B

Time of Drying of Blood

The same watch band illustrated in Appendix A was daubed liberally with fresh blood from a punctured finger. The time was taken at the moment of wetting the band, and the temperature and humidity were recorded. The temperature was 68° F — humidity 56% relative. Blood on smooth surfaces was completely dry in 1½ minutes. Blood which collected in the recesses between the individual bars of the band required longer but was completely dry in less than ten minutes.

Blood from the same source was smeared over the back of the hand (Photograph No. 20) and the same observations were taken under the same conditions. Within 2¼ minutes, the blood was completely dry.

APPENDIX C

Blood Trails

It will be shown in succeeding Appendices that long trails of blood are not to be expected if the blood is carried on the weapon, the clothing, or the shoes which are the three most likely ways in which blood might be transported and deposited on other objects by dripping.

Blood, or any viscous liquid, will shake off an object in small droplets. It will not fall spontaneously in small drops but only after enough has collected to form a large drop. Had any significant blood trails been left by the murderer in the house, the blood would not have been predominantly on the risers of the stairway, but would be on the treads in far greater quantity, regardless of the manner of its removal from the person and regardless of the object or material from which the blood was removed. The explanation that the blood was washed from the treads and horizontal surfaces after the murder but that the risers were missed is the only explanation consistent with the case of the prosecution. That this is not a sufficient explanation can be shown.

The steps throughout all of the house were very varnished or bare wood with the exception of the treads of the steps from the kitchen to the landing. They had been worn enough to leave indentations and irregularities in their surfaces. Blood dropped on them and washed up, unless most thoroughly done, would inevitably have left deposits in these irregularities and also washed areas which would have yielded the luminol test at least. This would reveal washing the blood, which was never demonstrated, though quite possible to do. Some blood would be expected on the main staircase, certainly on the treads and possibly on the risers. Beyond this, the murderer would be unlikely to leave more than the most occasional and minute sample. It is noted that it was the main staircase that yielded nearly all of the spots that were proved to be human as well as being proven to be blood. If it can be assumed that the spot on the stairs to the basement were left by the murderer, the only reasonable explanation is that his injured member started bleeding, since the distance and the time required to get this far are too great to allow liquid blood to be carried from the murder room. Even more important it appears that no comparable blood spots were located between the main staircase, the step or the basement. This is fully consistent with the idea that the blood on the basement steps was freshly shed by the murderer, since the intervening space would certainly have accumulated more of the victim's blood than would a place so remote from the crime. The only reasonable explanations are either that the blood in that location was not connected with the crime, or that it was freshly shed by the murderer.

APPENDIX D

Shedding of Blood from Clothing

Cloths may be considered as predominantly absorptive or repellent of aqueous solutions, including blood. Cottons and regenerated cellulose fabrics tend to be absorptive, though not invariably so. Wools, silks, and a variety of synthetics such as nylon tend to be repellent as a rule. Regardless of the type of cloth worn by the murderer, loss of blood by dropping from the clothing after leaving the murder room is extremely improbable. Absorptive cloths would soak it up but not drop it unless they approached saturation which is almost impossible in existing circumstances. Repellent cloths would rapidly shed most of the blood, holding and absorbing only the residue that was not drained or shaken off immediately. The following experiments were performed to test this concept.

A series of cloths, five in all, and including a variety of cottons, wools, rayons, and silk (Photograph No. 21), were suspended and liquid human blood was thrown against them by means of a brush dripped in blood. It was applied plentifully so that much of it flowed immediately from the garment. The time was taken when the blood was applied and measured until the last drop fell spontaneously from any of the garments. The condition of the cloths and the three or four drops that fell after the first rapid drainage are illustrated in Photograph No. 22. The three or four drops fell within 2½ minutes after which no further drainage occurred and the remaining blood dried on the clothing. Shaking of a cloth after application of liberal amounts of blood caused the removal of nearly all of the excess immediately. Thus, whether clothing is shaken by the movement of its wearer, or allowed to stand completely quiet, no blood drains after a short interval of time, and that which is retained is either absorbed by the cloth (predominates) or dries in a crust on the surface.

APPENDIX E

Spots from Weapon

The weapon is the only object which is certainly in contact with fresh flowing blood from the wounds inflicted. It is not dipped, but the side that contacts a region carrying much blood can be considered as having a comparable amount of blood on that limited surface.

Two series of experiments were performed with a variety of objects which would illustrate effects similar to some common weapons. They were:

1. A large bread knife, with a roughly triangular blade eight (8) inches in length and a breadth at the widest point of one and a half (1½) inches.
2. A large monkey wrench, fifteen (15) inches in length, with a jaw one and three-quarters (1¾) inches deep and a maximum opening of four (4) inches.
3. A brass bar, eleven and three-quarters (11¾) inches in length, three-quarters (¾) inches wide, and one-eight (⅛) inch thick.
4. A bar of soft wood, twenty-three (23) inches long, one inch wide and seven-sixteenths (7/16) inch thick.
5. A small ball pean hammer, with a head length of two and a half (2½) inches and a face three-quarters (¾) inch in diameter.

The first experiment involved dipping the objects in liquid blood, removing them, and holding them over paper with recording of the time necessary for all blood to drain as drops from the object. This was supplemented by a similar timing while the objects were swinging at a moderate rate in the hand.

1. Bread knife, immersed two inches. Static, it lost four drops, the last drop of which required twenty-eight seconds. Swinging, it lost nine drops, also requiring twenty-eight seconds for the last one.
2. Wrench, immersed to cover the main jaw. Static, it lost seven drops requiring forty-two seconds; swinging, nine drops requiring forty seconds.
3. Brass bar, immersed two inches. Static, it lost two drops in thirty-five seconds; swinging, seven drops in thirty-three seconds.
4. Wood bar, immersed three inches. Static, it lost two drops in forty-seven seconds, swinging, six drops in eighteen seconds.
5. Hammer, entire head immersed. Static, it lost five drops at intervals of one, two, thirteen, twenty-one, and forty-three seconds. Swinging, it lost two drops at four and fifteen seconds. Repeated, swinging it lost four drops at one, two, seven, and twenty seconds.

It is clear that the time of drainage controls the time lapse before the last drop. Swinging speeded up the first drops but not the last. Violent shaking removed all blood much faster than the force applied.

In order to determine in the more tangible terms of distance, a similar set of experiments was made with three of the objects above, nos. 1, 2, and 3, in which the dripping weapon was carried over long strips of paper at ordinary quick walking speed, and the distance was measured to the last drop that fell.

1. The bread knife was immersed two inches in the blood. It lost three drops to the paper strip, the last of which was fifteen feet, five inches from the origin.
2. The wrench was immersed so as to cover the entire upper jaw. Because of the great irregularity of surface and the presence of horizontal surface as carried, it retained more blood and for longer than the others. The last spot was lost after walking fifty feet, though the next to last drop was lost after only about thirty feet.
3. The brass bar, immersed three inches in the blood lost the last drop at ten feet. A second trial with the same bar lost the last drop at fourteen feet.

Two significant points must be mentioned. No weapon for a murder would be nearly so loaded with blood as these objects were, and the blood would be undergoing clotting whereas the blood used here was not, and was therefore less viscous, allowing it to drain more completely from the object. It is also to be noted that the number of drops was always small.

One major point of difference was noted as compared with the alleged blood trails at the murder scene: All drops lost were large (approximately ½ inch diameter spots) because the adherence of the sticky blood to the object could not be overcome until enough blood had collected to give a heavy drop. This could only be altered by shaking of the object to throw off the small accumulations. Perhaps as important was the fact that in dropping approximately two feet from the object to the floor, the large drop on impact separated to form a large central spot with several smaller surrounding spots and in every instance formed a very irregular outline. Not a single drop was ever described in the trails in the Sheppard house that indicate it to be comparable in size or appearance with the drops formed in this experiment.

APPENDIX F

Transport of Blood by Shoes

By far the most probable method of leaving a trail of blood is transport on the bottoms of shoes. The amount of the blood so carried is necessarily small because the first few steps serve to press out and deposit all but the residual film of blood and liquid held in recesses of the surface of the shoe.

Test of the distance through which blood will be carried by this method was performed by stepping repeatedly in a region of heavy blood spots on a floor until the shoe soles were thoroughly blood smeared. The subject then walked normally along a strip of wrapping paper until no more visible blood could be seen on the paper. The last footprint showing any visible trace of blood occurred fifty feet from the origin. The first shoe print is shown in Photograph No. 24. Minute amounts of blood detectable chemically may, naturally, be carried further than the last visible print.

The important aspect of this experiment is that the bloody footprint is not a series of drops or spots as claimed in the Sheppard house, but rather a diffuse area of thin deposit, retaining a semblance of the shape of the shoes' contact with the surface. It must also be remembered that the murderer may have stepped in very little blood as compared with the rather large amount used in this experiment.

APPENDIX G

Blood Removal from Shoes

In order to determine the likelihood that all blood would be washed from Dr. Sam Sheppard's shoes by his alleged washing in the lake, a shoe with leather sole and stitching was daubed with about two dozen spots of freshly shed human blood. (Photograph No. 25.) Most of this was placed along the stitching but various spots were placed at random on the leather of the sole.

The shoe was allowed to stand for thirty-five minutes to allow complete soaking of the blood into the leather and complete drying which actually required a very short time. The shoe was then immersed in water and forced back and forth in the water to simulate the washing action of water movement for five minutes. At the end of that time some of the spots had disappeared, and all were reduced in size but sixteen spots could still be observed with the eye, as shown in Photograph No. 26. Because the treatment used did not apply mechanical action to remove the blood spots as would walking, the wet spots were rubbed vigorously with paper toweling until no actual spots could be seen as such. The shoe was then returned to freshwater for five more minutes, after which it was removed and allowed to dry.

Inspection with magnification revealed that blood was still visible in three places, twice where it had soaked into the stitching, and the largest visible quantity was in a small cut in the sole of the shoe.

This experiment shows that blood adheres to surfaces into which it can soak, with considerable tenacity, as has been previously shown with clothing, and in contrast to the behavior on smooth, non-absorptive surfaces such as metal watch bands. It is very probable that even the visible blood would have disappeared with walking, but certainly not to a point at which chemical blood test methods would not have revealed its original presence.

APPENDIX H

Amount of Blood Spatter on Clothing

Without knowing the details of a weapon and the exact conditions of its use, it is not simple to predict the amount of blood that might spatter on the person wielding the weapon. In the series of experiments reported in Appendix I, and discussed briefly in the Report, a wide variety of objects of various sizes, shapes, weights, and configuration were used to spatter far more blood than was spattered in the commission of the Marilyn

Sheppard murder. During the entire series of experiments, the same set of coveralls was worn without washing or disturbing blood on the garment.

The appearance of the garment is shown in Photographs No. 27, 28, and 29. The surprising thing is that the amount of blood that was spattered backward was uniformly less than that spattered sidewise or forward, even though the blows were delivered in a number of ways and under all the variations listed above. While the amount of blood is definitely significant, it shows that the murderer could well have escaped without having accumulated enough blood to drip or leave any blood trail whatever from that source. If his garments were as absorptive as the garment used in these experiments, it is very certain that they would not have lost blood by dripping at any time.

APPENDIX I

Nature of Blood Spots from Different Origins

In order to determine the nature and appearance of blood spots resulting from spatter under different conditions, from throw-off by objects simulating weapons and similar questions, a considerable series of experiments were conducted. A wooden block was taken as approximating the hardness of a skull. Over it was placed a layer of sponge rubber ⅛ inch thick which approximates the thickness of the subcutaneous layer of the forehead and scalp, and over this was placed a sheet of polyethylene plastic to simulate the skin which is impermeable to liquids. The arrangement so prepared (Photograph No. 30) was placed on a stool of wrapping paper to collect blood spatter. Around the region was built a rectangular wall carrying removable paper strips to collect all flying blood on the sides and in front of the swings of the object used as a weapon. Similar paper strips were placed over the top to collect blood flying upward as well. Only on the operator's side was the structure open, the operator collecting the blood that traveled backward, as discussed in Appendix H.

The objects used as weapons included the small ball pean hammer described in Appendix E, a metal two-cell flashlight with a flared rim, and three metal objects illustrated in Photograph No. 31. The shortest is an inch steel bar, fifteen inches long; the second is a brass rod about twenty inches in length and bent on the end to an approximate right angle; the longest and heaviest is a brass bar, 3/8 inch in diameter and two feet in length.

Blood was puddled on the top of the plastic cover of the sponge sheet, to the extent that it just did not flow off. This required about three to four ml. at the beginning, and frequent renewals with one or two ml. of blood. Heavy enough blows were dealt that at least with one object, the heaviest bar, the plastic sheet and rubber sponge were cut completely through to the underlying wood. One such cut is shown spread with forceps in Photograph No. 32. The paper strips were removed from the walls after each series of blows of a certain type and object, and photographed.

It was found that the character of the spattered blood from impact varied somewhat in direction and velocity as well as size of drop formed as the conditions were varied, as would be expected. However, certain regularities emerged and were found to be invariably true:

a. Large drops formed by impact spatter do not have enough velocity to travel more than one or two feet.

b. All high-velocity drops which traveled up to twelve feet, and in some instances traveled almost straight up were medium to very small, i.e., not more than ⅛ inch diameter for the largest. Clearly, it is possible that some set of conditions might be found that would throw spatter drops that are larger, and it is also true that the higher-velocity drops would spread more on impact with the receiving surface than would slower drops. It can be stated unequivocally that spatter drops that travel more than a couple of feet will never be very large.

c. The smallest, high-velocity spatter droplets occurred to some extent with most blows, and tended to occur ahead of the direction of stroke, and in front of the impact point, i.e., away from the person wielding the object. When the spatter included both high and low flying droplets, the higher flying included a much higher percentage of the small drops as shown by comparing high spots in Photograph No. 33 with lower flying ones from

the same blows in Photograph No. 34. These drops
were formed by use of the flat surface of the ball
pean hammer, and drops were thrown as far as twelve
feet from the origin and as high as seven feet in
the air at the point of impact. If the wall had
not intervened, they would have traveled as far as
about twenty feet. The smallness of drops ahead of
the object is illustrated in Photograph No. 35,
which were made by the heavy brass bar.

Photographs No. 36 and 37 show that the spatter
from use of a flashlight is comparable in characteristics with spatter spots from other objects.

The other significant regularity that must remain undis-
puted, is that large spots, ¼ inch or more, will only
be obtained at any distance over a very few feet by
throw-off from the weapon. To test this, various objects
were dipped in blood and the blood thrown from them in
various ways:

a. In front of an object thrown forward violently as
    in delivering a blow, the spots were predominantly
    small and high velocity, as was true of many spots
    on Dr. Sam's bed. They often could not be distin-
    guished from the small spatter spots, which also
    tended to move in the same direction. A typical
    range of sizes is shown in Photograph No. 38,
    showing forward throw-off from the light bent bar.
    These included as large spots as are to be expected
    with this motion if delivered with the violence of
    a true blow.

b. Throw-off on the backstroke was different in that
    the velocity of the object was invariably smaller.
    An object dipped in blood and thrown back as in
    preparing for a blow deposited large drops, mixed
    with a considerable proportion of small ones.
    Photograph No. 39 shows this effect with the hammer;
    40 shows it with a bar, and 41 shows it with a
    flashlight. It will be noted as being of interest
    that the flashlight produced backthrow spots most
    nearly like that on the east wall of the murder
    room, ranging almost, but not quite up to ½ inch
    diameter, and down to very small spots. It will
    also be noted that the roundness of the drop was

readily duplicated by the back motion postulated in this report and used in this experiment. The distance from the paper wall was close to that known to have occurred in the bedroom. While this does not prove that a flashlight was the weapon used, it does show that an object of that general shape and size produces the results found. It is also demonstrated quite definitely that the spots on the east wall could only have come from backswing of the weapon, which in turn requires a left-handed blow. One further conclusion depends on the fact that by every means that could be devised, no spot as large as the single one discussed at length in this report was ever approached by throwing blood from any type of object like a weapon, nor by any type of impact spatter.

It can be concluded from these experiments that the interpretation and analysis of the blood spot pattern in the murder bedroom is (a) fully consistent with the demonstrable facts; and (b) that any other interpretation is not consistent with the result of experiment.

APPENDIX J

Breaking of Teeth

Two questions suggest themselves with regard to the broken teeth of Mrs. Marilyn Sheppard.

1. Is the shape of break consistent with and only with a fracture of the tooth by a pull outward?
2. What is the magnitude of the force necessary to break a tooth completely off close to the gum?

To answer these questions, a considerable number of human teeth were collected from dentists who had extracted them. Only a portion of some fifteen or twenty teeth were incisors, and the condition with respect to decay and dental repair was quite variable. Seven incisors were chosen for experimentation as shown in Photographs No. 42 and 43.

To anchor the roots of the teeth solidly as in the jaw, holes were drilled in a heavy brass. A hole was filled with molten "Woods" metal, an antimony alloy that melts below the boiling point of water, the root was held in the liquid metal until the alloy was solid and all teeth so mounted could not be moved until the metal was remelted. The method of breaking the teeth varied but usually consisted of pulling steadily on them by means of a hooked notch cut in a brass bar as illustrated (Photograph No. 44).

The force necessary to cause fracture was in general greater than the maximum capacity of the largest spring scale available, i.e., greater than ten pounds, and at least one tooth required a very heavy pull. One badly decayed tooth broke with a relatively light pull. It can only be concluded that the force necessary to break the tooth is primarily a function of the tooth's condition. Some further tests were made to break an unmounted tooth with the bare hands. These were not successful with any of several teeth tested.

Most significant of the findings of this study was the manner of fracture. All but one tooth was broken with the force from the lingual toward the labial surface. In every instance the fracture was diagonal and similar to the tooth found in Marilyn Sheppard's bed (Photographs No. 44 and 45). The one tooth broken with a blow delivered to the labial surface (Photograph No. 46) yielded the fracture in the opposite manner. It was complicated by a splitting of the tooth but verified the indication given by the fractures in the opposite.

A limitation on the experiment was the fact that tests were made on incisors similar in size to the tooth from the bed. These were few in number in the series available for study.

APPENDIX 2
Illustrative Testimony — A Motion in Limine* for the Admissibility of Bloodstain Pattern Interpretation

The following is an example of direct and cross-examination of an expert witness appearing on behalf of the State to establish the admissibility of bloodstain pattern evidence and the qualifications of individuals offered to give testimony in this discipline.

Direct Examination by the Prosecutor

After the witness is sworn in and states his name for the record.

Q: Sir, please tell the Court what your occupation is?
A: Yes, I am a forensic consultant and I provide scientific investigation for both prosecutors and defense attorneys.

Q: And just, generally, what do you do when you provide such services without going on for an hour or so?
A: My main area of concentration is that of crime scene reconstruction, which includes the discipline of bloodstain pattern interpretation. I also provide some scientific services in the area of accelerant testing in suspected arson cases.

Q: You are primarily employed by what organization?
A: I am self employed as a forensic consultant.

Q: Are you a consultant for blood spatter analysis for any organizations or state governments?
A: In terms of governmental agencies, I consult with law enforcement agencies, district or state attorneys, public defenders, and private attorneys.

---

* Depending upon the particular state or jurisdiction this Motion in Limine may be referred to as a *Frye* or *Daubert* Hearing.

Q: Generally, what services do you perform for these agencies?

A: Well, in cases that I have worked directly for law enforcement there have been probably a dozen or more cases in the past two or three years involving scene reconstruction using bloodstain pattern interpretation. I have also been involved in what they call their cold case group, meaning agency members and myself have gotten together to review old cases, which they call cold cases, looking for other avenues of evidence.

Q: If you can look at SF-l, which I have placed in front of you, and tell the Court what it is?

A: State's exhibit F one is a copy of my curriculum vitae.

Q: Is that essentially up to date?

A: Yes. The only addition would be on the last page under the category of consultation and testimony. I have testified in the State of Georgia since this copy was made.

Q: Now can you advise the Court of the educational background that you have that relates to blood spatter analysis?

A: I should begin with my college degree in biology and chemistry. I received that in 1962 from Hobart College located in Geneva, New York. I also have completed nine hours of graduate study in forensic science. That was accomplished at Elmira College in Elmira, New York. There were three courses taken between 1977 and 1979. The first was bloodstain pattern interpretation. The second was homicide investigation and the third was forensic microscopy.

Q: Are there any additional workshops or courses relating to blood spatter analysis?

A: Yes, in terms of additional training in bloodstain pattern interpretation, I have received in excess of two hundred hours in bloodstain training and many of these hours were accomplished through what used to be referred to as advanced bloodstain institutes. These were yearly conferences which began in 1983, attended by persons who had completed a basic course in bloodstain pattern interpretation. I was a charter member of that group. That group eventually became the International Association of Bloodstain Pattern Analysts and we had annual meetings and training sessions, which are continuing every year. I have also attended some workshops in places such as John Jay College of Criminal Justice with an emphasis on bloodstain pattern interpretation.

Q: Now you mentioned professional organizations. Are you a member of any professional organizations that relate specifically to blood spatter analysis?

A: Yes, I am a member of a professional organization specifically related to bloodstain pattern interpretation. That would be the International Association of Bloodstain Pattern Analysts, which is the group derived from the advanced institutes that I mentioned.

Q: How long have you been a member of that organization?
A: Since 1983. I am a charter member.

Q: Can you basically tell the Court what that organization is and what it does and who the members are?
A: The organization is comprised of I believe to date more than three hundred members in the United States and Canada. I don't know any foreign countries that are represented at this time other than Canada. The basic requirements to become a member or receive a membership would be a completion of a recognized course in bloodstain pattern interpretation, which is a forty hour course. Some members of this group are actively involved in the study of bloodstain pattern interpretation through case work and research and many in case work and testimony. Members include a variety of types of individuals. There are several private consultants, as myself, who do not represent a specific organization. Many of the members are in the area of police work, either as detectives or in many instances, crime scene technicians, who are part of either sheriff or police agencies. There are also several attorneys who are members. I can remember there are at least two forensic pathologists who are members of this organization. So it is a whole variety of individuals.

Q: Now, what was the other organizations that you belong to that deal with the area of bloodstain pattern interpretation?
A: I am a fellow member of the American Academy of Forensic Sciences in the Toxicology Section. That's a general organization of forensic experts and there are many members of that organization who are involved in bloodstain pattern interpretation, both pathologists and non-pathologists. But it is a general forensic group.

Q: That's one discipline within this general group?
A: That's correct. The American Academy of Sciences has sections in pathology, jurisprudence, criminalistics, toxicology, questioned documents, and jurisprudence to mention the major ones.

Q: You advised the Court — can you advise the Court of your work experience in the area of forensics?

A: My initial forensic work-related experience was as a forensic toxicologist and that began in 1969 at Wilson Memorial Hospital in Johnson City, New York.

That laboratory where I was Chief Toxicologist began also providing other types of scientific analyses for police agencies, in addition to doing the coroners' work in postmortem toxicology. We expanded that into other areas and my major work area, as a forensic person, subsequent to that would have been my involvement with the forensic — the crime laboratory, which I was part of the setting up of procedures at Binghamton General Hospital located in Binghamton, New York. We had a crime laboratory which provided scientific services to approximately eight or nine counties in upstate New York. And that's where we provided in large part our scene investigation and analysis of bloodstains, hairs, fibers, and other types of forensic evidence. That was between 1977 and 1981.

Since 1981, I have been primarily a forensic consultant, although I have had a lot of activity with a private investigating firm as a forensic chemist testing samples for accelerants in fire debris.

Q: Essentially, how many years have you been involved in bloodstain pattern analysis?

A: Well, I began to take a serious interest in the subject in the early seventies 1974, 1975, and looked at some cases at that time. I have been to many scenes with the coroner looking at other aspects in addition to bloodstains. But it was 1977, when I actually took a formal course in the subject and felt comfortable in looking at the various types of stains. So I would say most actively since 1977.

Q: Now have you received a formal teaching appointment in the area of forensics and, specifically, within the area of bloodstain analysis?

A: Formal teaching appointments between 1972 and 1980 include an adjunct lecturer at the State University of New York at Binghamton, which is now referred to as Binghamton University. At this institution, I taught courses in forensic science and these courses included topics of death investigation, analysis and collection of physical evidence, but also in part bloodstain pattern interpretation. It was not a course solely dedicated to that subject but part of the overall curriculum. A similar course was also taught at Broome Community College. This course was entitled Death Investigation and also included some lectures on the area of bloodstain pattern interpretation. I also was on the staff of the Basic Recruit Academy for training of police officers in the Broome County area. Part of that instruction did include some crime scene teaching and bloodstain pattern interpretation.

Q: Have you, specifically, taught in the area of bloodstain pattern analysis?
A: Yes, I have.

Q: Can you describe that course?
A: My initial teaching in a bloodstain pattern course in the variety that I referred to as a forty hour type course of a five day duration was lecturing as a guest of Herbert Leon MacDonell, who is a consulting criminalist in Corning, New York. I lectured to students within his bloodstain training group at that time. I have done that on several occasions.

   I also have been a co-lecturer with Herbert Leon MacDonell at two bloodstain institutes that were held at police academies. One in Springfield, Illinois at the State Police Academy and another at the Tampa Police Academy in Florida.

   In 1990, I did organize myself and teach with the assistance of a William Fischer, who is a private investigator and person who is trained in bloodstain interpretation and Paul Kish an assistant to Herbert MacDonell. The three of us directed a Bloodstain Institute in Oakland County, Michigan, which is near Detroit. Other specific training in bloodstain pattern interpretation, would be one or two day lectures or workshops. I had done this at several locations, one being the Southern Police Institute in Louisville, Kentucky. Also, I had given several hour-type lectures and presentations for the Florida Homicide Investigators Association and also for a Police Training Institute in Jacksonville, Florida.

Q: Now have you made any presentations in the area of bloodstain pattern analysis?
A: Yes, I have.

Q: And, specifically on your resume, SF-l, would those presentations be generally covered in pages ten through fourteen?
A: Yes, that's correct.

THE PROSECUTOR: Your Honor, would you like a copy of the resume?
THE COURT: Yes.
   Thank you.

Q: Essentially, the ones that relate to bloodstain pattern analysis, that are specifically referred to in those pages, are pretty self-evident. Would that be a fair statement?
A: Yes. I have listed the title of the presentation, and also the location and the date.

THE PROSECUTOR: Your Honor, do you feel you have the need to have the witness specifically go through those?

THE COURT: No.

I'll take a look at it and if there is any question I am sure the defendant will elicit it on cross-examination.

BY THE PROSECUTOR:

Q: Sir, have you published any articles or books concerning bloodstain pattern interpretation?

A: I have not published anything. I co-authored with Doctor William G. Eckert, a forensic pathologist, a text entitled "Interpretation of Bloodstain Evidence at Crime Scenes." That was in 1989. I have also contributed to a book entitled the "Practical Methodology of Forensic Photography" in terms of providing input on the photography of bloodstain evidence. That was 1991. Aside from that I have both authored and co-authored several articles, which have been published in scientific journals. For example in the "American Journal of Forensic Medicine and Pathology" I co-authored with Doctor Eckert an article with respect to disinterments and their value in associated problems, forensic type material.

Q: On approximately how many occasions have you been hired by a state or a prosecuting agency or defense attorney to render a bloodstain pattern analysis?

A: I would estimate several hundred times over the last twenty years.

Q: And, generally, what law enforcement agency would that generally encompass?

A: When I was involved with the hospital and crime laboratory, I was involved in a lot of prosecution work at that time. But if you go from 1981, when I have been actually a full time private consultant, I worked for numerous police agencies, prosecutor's offices, as well as defense attorneys. I can give you some examples. I have done probably ten to twelve cases in the past eight or ten years for Dauphin County, Harrisburg, Pennsylvania.

Over the most recent years I have done work for the Palm Beach County Sheriff's Office and the Florida Department of Law Enforcement. I have done some work for the Martin County Sheriff's Office, Stuart, Florida.

I would estimate at the present time, looking back over twelve months, that I have probably — at this point am doing about sixty to sixty-five percent defense work and the remaining thirty, thirty-five percent prosecutorial in nature.

Q: Approximately, how many occasions have you been hired by the defense?

A: Well, as I said, in the past year I worked on approximately thirty-two cases. That is major investigations and approximately sixty-five percent of those have been for defense.

Q: Approximately about how many cases have you conducted such an examination overall, including state, defense, or private attorney?
A: As I said initially, several hundred over the last twenty years.

Q: And have you ever been qualified in a court as an expert in the area of bloodstain analysis?
A: Yes, I have, sir.

Q: And, approximately, how many occasions?
A: I would say at least one hundred times in the area of bloodstain pattern interpretation.

Q: And, generally, could you describe the various courts that you have been so qualified in?
A: I have testified — qualified and testified in approximately nineteen states within the Continental United States. I have also been qualified and testified in Canada, in the U.S. Virgin Islands, specifically St. Croix, and I also testified in South Korea, not at the request of the South Korean Government, but, rather, a military court-martial, having been hired by the United States Army and I did in fact qualify and testify at Camp Casey located near the DMZ.

Q: Have you been qualified in New Jersey?
A: Yes, I have.

Q: On how many occasions?
A: My best recollection is I have qualified and testified on two occasions in New Jersey.

Q: Can you recall the county or locations?
A: Yes. I testified on behalf of the Public Defender's Office in Morris County in Morristown and I also testified in a homicide case in Hudson County in Jersey City.

Q: And do you recall who retained you in Hudson County in that matter?
A: It was a private attorney in Hackensack. I don't recall his name right at the moment.

Q: Now have you ever been rejected by any court as an expert in bloodstain or blood spatter analysis?
A: No, sir, I have not.

Q: Have you ever participated in a case where blood spatter testimony had been rejected by the court as not being a sufficient area for expert testimony?

A: I have not, no.

THE PROSECUTOR: Your Honor, I don't know if it is necessary but at this point I move to have Mr. James qualified as a forensic scientist with an expertise in bloodstain pattern analysis.

DEFENSE ATTORNEY: No objection.

THE COURT: All right.

Then I will grant that request.

BY THE PROSECUTOR:

Q: Mr. James, can you tell the Court how many individuals or organizations are currently involved in conducting bloodstain pattern analysis?

A: Well, I can only give an estimate. For example, I believe I testified that there are approximately three hundred members of the International Association of Bloodstain Pattern Analysts and most of them are actively involved in this area.

There are a lot of individuals who are doing bloodstain interpretation, who are not members of the organization. I couldn't give you an exact number.

Based on my knowledge in the forensic area and the cases that I have worked on both for the prosecution and defense, I am aware that, for example, the Federal Bureau of Investigation, the FBI, does bloodstain pattern interpretation as an organization as well as numerous agencies both at the city, county, and state level. That is — for example in Broward and Dade County, Florida and also Palm Beach County, the sheriffs' departments have forensic units. There are specifically trained individuals who respond to crime scenes. And many of these individuals have received bloodstain pattern interpretation training who document, collect and preserve, and interpret bloodstains. I am sure every state has a significant number of individuals who are practicing in this area.

Q: Now I direct your attention to SF-2. Can you tell the Court what that document is?

A: Yes. This document is an affidavit that I prepared at your request dated on December 7th, 1993.

Q: Specifically, does that document list several Supreme Court decisions relating to bloodstain interpretation?

A: Yes, it does.

THE DEFENSE ATTORNEY: If I can interject? I believe the State's other witnesses have entered the courtroom. I feel it is appropriate that they be excused during this witness's testimony.

THE PROSECUTOR: No objection.

THE COURT: All right. Would the other witnesses, whoever they are, please leave and wait out in the hallway?

(The witnesses are excused.)

THE PROSECUTOR: I apologize. I keep forgetting that different states have different rules.

THE COURT: All right.

BY THE PROSECUTOR:

Q: Now the decisions that you list in your report, what was the result in those decisions with regard to the admissibility of bloodstain pattern analysis as a proper subject area for expert testimony?

A: Well, in the decision that I have listed here, the Supreme Court of the respective state upheld the admissibility of bloodstain evidence.

Q: Are you aware of any Supreme Court or other case throughout the country that has held that bloodstain pattern analysis is not a proper subject matter for expert testimony?

A: I am not aware of any.

Q: Are you aware of any individual who either writes or practices in the area of forensic science who takes the position that bloodstain pattern analysis is not a proper subject matter for expert testimony?

A: I am not aware of any nor seen such writings.

Q: Can you generally describe — before I get into that. Are you familiar with the literature concerning bloodstain pattern analysis?

A: Yes, I am.

Q: And can you tell the Court the first time that — at least to your knowledge that this matter was addressed in a publication?

A: Well there are numerous references made to the interpretation of bloodstain evidence in the forensic literature dating back to the 19th century, mainly in Germany and England. The earliest publication that I have seen personally and which I have with me was published in 1895 and this was the translation from the German — and it was written by Doctor Eduard Piotrowski, P-I-O-T-R-O-W-S-K-I. First name is Eduard, E-D-U-A-R-D. This deals with various experiments performed by the author to demonstrate how various types of bloodstain patterns may be produced.

Q: Can you tell the Court when this discipline first was utilized in the United States?

A: Yes. The most significant use of bloodstain evidence in what we would refer to as the 20th century and recent years was in 1955. And that was in the case of State of Ohio v. Sam Sheppard. In that instance Doctor Paul Kirk, who is now deceased, at the time was a consulting criminalist and also a professor at the University of California at Berkeley. He was one who had done a lot of bloodstain pattern experiments and did in fact prepare an affidavit and eventually testified in the retrial of Dr. Sam Shepherd. That was a milestone in terms of the significant use of bloodstain evidence. Evidence of this type has always been there in cases of violent crime and bloodshed. But bloodstain evidence typically was often overlooked and not utilized. Since 1955, the area of bloodstain pattern interpretation has been greatly enhanced by Herbert Leon MacDonell. After conducting research and experiments in 1971, Herbert Leon MacDonell published a treatise or publication concerning bloodstain evidence entitled "Flight Characteristics and Stain Patterns of Human Blood." The only other publication prior to that time, since the 1940s, was a chapter devoted to bloodstain interpretation in one of Dr. Paul Kirk's books which was entitled "Crime Investigation." And since 1971, organized courses have been developed mainly through the efforts of Herbert Leon MacDonell and this has resulted in the training of numerous individuals, including myself, in the area of bloodstain pattern interpretation. There are now numerous individuals, who I can mention if you desire, who instruct bloodstain pattern interpretation, as well as practice in the area, themselves, and there are numerous types of schools, both basic and advanced, which are available for individuals to receive training. There are many publications, some we have mentioned already, but other scientific articles that have appeared in various journals in the area of bloodstain pattern interpretation.

Q: You have mentioned Mr. MacDonell and some of the literature. Are you familiar with the most recent publication, as far as a book in the area of bloodstain pattern analysis?

A: Yes, I am.

Q: And is Mr. MacDonell the author of that book?

A: Yes he is.

Q: And does that book essentially take a position with regard to the admissibility of bloodstain pattern interpretation as a proper subject area of expert testimony?

A: Yes, it does.

Q: And what is that opinion?

A: That it is in fact considered within the context of this book a proper subject for courtroom testimony.

Q: Now can you generally describe for the Court what bloodstain or blood spatter — which is the better term to utilize. Bloodstain pattern or blood spatter pattern analysis?

A: To be most general it is easier to say bloodstain pattern interpretation. Spatter is one type of bloodstain.

Q: Generally, describe what does bloodstain interpretation consist of; generally, what you do and what can you learn and things of that nature?

A: Well, to begin with the area of bloodstain pattern interpretation is a discipline. The theory of bloodstain pattern interpretation is certainly based on principles of the natural sciences, including biology, since blood is a biological fluid and has, therefore, biological characteristics.

Also when you talk about bloodstain interpretation, you are talking about for the most part, but not exclusively, blood which has been shed. That is, blood which has exited the body. And once blood has done that, it is then subjected to external forces, and that is where the discipline then invites the area of mathematics and physics. Because you are now talking about what blood does in motion, when it is affected by various forces. So that's how these three natural sciences kind of form the basis of the discipline of bloodstain interpretation.

What can be determined from interpretation of bloodstain patterns is in my opinion within the scope of overall crime scene reconstruction. The whole basis for any investigation of a violent crime is the observation, collection, and interpretation of what is generally known as physical evidence and bloodstains are certainly physical evidence in an event involving bloodshed. On the one hand we have the serologist, who types the bloodstains, ABO grouping, genetic markers, and performs DNA profiling.

On the other hand, we have the nature of the actual bloodstains, as they appear at a scene of a violent crime, and this is where the interpretation becomes involved with the size, shape, orientation, and distribution of these stains on various surfaces and what information can be derived from the proper interpretation of the bloodstains.

Q: Can you advise the Court of what information can be derived and how you go about obtaining that information?

A: Various types of information may be derived. Every case does not allow every question to be answered. But the types of things that generally would be of a general scope would be the origin and source of the bloodstains as to whether they are coming from a victim for example in a standing or lying-down position. It helps affix the position of a victim at the time the bloodshed is occurring.

Proper interpretation may permit an evaluation as to the relative position of an assailant and a victim. At the point of or subsequent to death, movement of a victim after bloodshed or after death may be documented by observation of bloodstain evidence. The type of weapon may be correlated with the type of injuries that occurred. For example, you have in many cases shootings and beatings. Very specific types of bloodstains are produced relative to those types of events for the reconstruction of the scene. This takes on more importance when you arrive at a scene and the body has been moved to a different location. Interpretation of bloodstains may give you an indication as to what type and how serious injuries are to a victim, who has not yet been located.

I think each case has its own merits in terms of bloodstain evidence. One of the key areas that may encompass cases in general is that bloodstain evidence may corroborate other areas of forensic investigation.

In other words bloodstain evidence does not stand alone as a single solver of all mysteries. It has to be used in connection with forensic pathology, criminalistics, and the other areas of forensic expertise. It is part of the overall investigation and, with that in mind, often a version of events offered by witnesses or defendants may be either verified or contradicted. That is probably the most significant area that bloodstain interpretation can offer.

Q: Now can you generally describe how you would conduct such a bloodstain pattern analysis or investigation?

A: Well, there are two aspects of this. One being the actual on-scene investigation, which would involve proper observation, documentation, and collection of physical evidence. With respect to bloodstains, the various types of bloodstains should be photographed in an overall and close-up fashion. Bloodstains should be measured with respect to their widths and lengths in order to determine the angle of impact. A string method may be used to show, based upon the angle of impact, the origin of the bloodstain. When this type of reconstruction is done it should be utilized with a sufficient number of bloodstains. Not just one or two.

I think the best adage about scene work on bloodstains is simply that one or two blood spots do not a pattern make. That should be adhered to by everyone. After these types of things have been accomplished at a scene, you have the general collection of physical evidence, which would include if necessary lifting of bloodstains using various lengths of tapes. Diagrams and photographs come into play in interpretation.

The second part of how this is done is something I probably do more frequently than scene work presently. That is the interpretation of photographs. It is certainly better to get to a scene as soon as possible. However, often I have to rely upon interpretation of photographs, which are taken by a police agency, which is why in teaching we stress proper photography. If you have adequate photography, one is able to draw certain conclusions more effectively than otherwise.

In connection with looking at photographs, I request copies of the autopsy report, copies of crime laboratory reports and other significant evidence relating to the case. And I also like the opportunity to look at collected physical evidence. From my perspective that's how I utilize all available information for the interpretation of bloodstains.

If I were asked a question is it always better to look at the evidence as opposed to the photograph, I would say usually but not always. Physical evidence sometimes has a tendency to become altered in appearance. There are cases where the original photograph of a piece of evidence may be better and more like the actual crime scene than evidence that has been altered in terms of improper packaging and deterioration. Prior testing procedures may have removed some pre-existing bloodstains.

Q: Now without being repetitive, if you could, advise the Court how the bloodstain pattern analysis you just described — how that would be utilized in general to enhance the understanding of the average juror when you are testifying in these hundreds of occasions?

A: Well, I think that bloodstain pattern interpretation can assist the jury, as much as other types of forensic evidence can, to reach a conclusion in a case. I would go back to my original statement that bloodstain evidence, criminalistics, and pathology all have to be in corroboration. If I can show as a witness that my interpretation of the scene based on bloodstain evidence is in corroboration with the wound interpretation of a forensic pathologist and the blood typing of the serologist and the hair and fiber analysis of the criminalist, then it gives the jury a better overall graphic of the significance of the scientific evidence.

Q: Now sir, do you have an opinion as to whether bloodstain pattern analysis has been generally accepted in the forensic science community?

A: Yes.

Q: And what is that opinion?

A: I would say that based on my involvement within the field of forensic science and with my professional associates and other members of the forensic community that bloodstain evidence is accepted within our community.

Q: And I think your answer basically stated what you base that opinion on. Is there anything else you base it upon that you have not just told us?

A: I think that's the best general answer. This could also relate to the appearance of bloodstain evidence articles in scientific literature and the overall increased use of this area in investigations.

THE PROSECUTOR: Your Honor, I have nothing further.

THE COURT: All right. We'll take a short recess before we start cross-examination. You may step down, sir.

(A recess is taken.)

THE COURT: All right. Cross-examination.

Cross-Examination by the Defense Attorney

Q: Sir, you testified earlier that bloodstain pattern analysis to some significant extent is based upon the natural sciences; is that correct?

A: Yes, sir.

Q: What are the natural sciences?

A: Well, as I would perceive them, there is biology, chemistry, physics, and mathematics.

Q: And do you have any formal educational training in those natural sciences?

A: Yes, I do.

Q: And what is that training or education, I should say?

A: Well, I have a BA degree in biology and chemistry from Hobart College, which I testified to. Part of that curriculum also included a college level course in physics and also a college level algebra and mathematics.

Q: Why is formal educational training in biology important to a bloodstain pattern analyst?

A: I consider, since I am trained in biology and also as a medical technologist, it helps me understand some aspects of blood distribution, blood clotting, and things of that sort. Understanding blood as a biological fluid is valuable for me.

Q: Can that sort of educational experience assist you in interpretation of bloodstains?

A: In some cases.

Q: Why is formal educational training in chemistry important to bloodstain pattern analysis?

A: Well, depending upon the specific situation, probably chemistry is the least significant natural science with respect to bloodstain interpretation, although in many death investigations analysis of the blood from a chemical point of view can be helpful but not specifically for pattern interpretation, but rather for some other biological values such as toxicology and perhaps postmortem interval based upon body chemistry.

Q: If you had a crime scene that was outdoors and there were some bloodstains in the area where the victim was, would the injection of rain or water into those stains have any effect or any significance in your opinion on that particular crime scene?

A: Yes, the effect would be in the case of rain on bloodstains on an outdoor surface would certainly be the potential of eradication of those stains or dilution of the stains by water, which would alter their appearance.

Q: And would a background or formal educational training in chemistry help you identify those sorts of problems?

A: I don't think you need formal education in chemistry to identify a diluted bloodstain.

Q: Why is physics important, formal education of physics important to bloodstain analysis?

A: I think it gives you a bit of a foundation. It is not required so much for the practical application of interpretation as it is, perhaps, more for the overall understanding. In other words, when I teach a course in bloodstain interpretation to, say, for example, thirty students and none of them has ever taken a course in physics, it takes a little longer to get some of the theory across to them. So having taken a course in physics, that part of the theoretical, didactic lecturing becomes a lot easier for them to understand since blood in motion is based on physics.

Q: If there were two drops of blood falling on a floor, such as I am standing on, one from ten feet and one from twenty feet, would there be a different visualization for those two drops of blood?

A: There could be.

Q: And your background in physics would assist you in interpreting the distance from which those blood droplets fell?

A: For one thing the interpretation of that particular difference in distance would be a little risky since the size or volume of the original drop is not known. But physics — the knowledge of physics would tell you why that was — why that was true. But I don't think that you would need to be a physicist to make that determination.

Q: I didn't say you need to be a physicist. But a background, formal educational background in physics is important to interpret bloodstains; is that correct?

A: It is more important to just have an overall understanding, maybe an easier understanding of the mechanics of what is going on, but not so much for the interpretation.

Q: How about mathematics? Why if at all is mathematics important to a bloodstain pattern analyst?

A: In order to determine the angle impact for example, one needs to measure the width and length of the stain in question. And that's a trigonometric function based upon the mathematics of a right triangle and the ratio is easily accomplished, width over length, and taking the arc sin of that. That can sound like Chinese to someone who has not taken mathematics. With the advent of hand-held calculators, it is a process of pushing three or four buttons on the calculator to get the information automatically. The calculator has helped in terms of that.

Q: You mentioned on your direct examination an individual by the name of Herbert MacDonell; is that correct?

A: Yes.

Q: How would you characterize his standing in the bloodstain analysis community?

A: I would say that Herbert MacDonell is certainly responsible for the increased awareness of bloodstain pattern interpretation and is certainly a well-respected criminalist and I think highly of his work.

Q: And do you respect his opinions and his writings?

A: I don't always agree with him, but I do respect him, yes.

Q: In your suggested reading attached to your C.V. — excuse me — attached to your affidavit, you list eight publications, four of them were written by Mr. MacDonell; is that correct?

A: Yes, I believe so.

Q: You also mentioned earlier on direct examination a certain book or treatise published by Mr. MacDonell. That would be "Bloodstain Patterns," 1993 publication?

A: Yes, I just received that from him personally about two weeks ago.

Q: And he described — he described you in the beginning of the book, did he not?

A: He was very kind to me there.

Q: May I direct you to page 113 of this to the second full paragraph?

A: "To begin with, although the author."

Q: Actually just above that. Two sentences above that at the end of the first paragraph. Would you agree with this sentence: "Unfortunately, not all who offer such schools are as well qualified as they should be, however" — in there he is referring to people who teach these seminars and schools — whatnot in your discipline.

Would you agree with that statement?

A: Yes.

Q: I direct your attention to the next paragraph. Mr. MacDonell states: "I completely agree with Doctor Peter DeForest in his concern that there are those who feel they are qualified beyond their actual ability. In a recent journal DeForest wrote 'numbers of individuals without scientific backgrounds have been trained in these courses. With this type of training these individuals have stepped beyond this important investigative role to offer scientific evidence as expert witnesses in court. The danger inherent in this development cannot be overemphasized.' "

Do you agree with that statement?

A: No, I don't.

Q: Why don't you agree with that statement?

A: Because it kind of flies in the face of the training that Professor Mac-Donell is offering to individuals around the country.

Mr. MacDonell does not make it a prerequisite of a scientific background to take his course and he trains students in his course. They receive a certificate of completion at the end of the course if they pass a written examination. If this were criteria for which it would be necessary to learn bloodstain interpretation, then he should not allow people in his course that don't have a scientific background.

Q: Do you make a distinction between people who learn about bloodstain interpretation and can serve in an investigatory role as opposed to people like yourself who come up here under oath and serve as an expert witness?

Do you see a difference between those two categories of people?

A: I do in a sense of experience. I think if I can be permitted to —

Q: Please.

A: There are many people who receive training in bloodstain interpretation through Herb MacDonell or other individuals around the country, who I feel are qualified to interpret bloodstains.

Some individuals are from very small police agencies. They take the bloodstain course, they may have one, two, or perhaps, three homicide investigations a year. And these are the individuals, I believe, that have to be very cautious because of their lack of both prior experience, before they take the course, and the limited opportunities that they have to apply what they have learned.

Comparing this to individuals in Broward County Sheriff's Department Forensic Division, who constantly go to crime scenes on a daily basis, the experience factor enhances their capabilities.

You have two different levels of investigative type individuals. Those who don't have a lot of opportunity for experiences are the ones I think who are more apt to get in trouble for overstating what they are seeing, because they lack experience.

Q: Can field experience supplant the educational background that you, for example, have in these natural sciences?
A: Well, no, I don't think that field experience can replace formal training in biology or physics, no.

Q: Well, I direct your attention then to what I questioned you about a minute ago, that middle paragraph on page 113 of Mr. MacDonell's treatise.

Are you saying that there is no danger in people who take these courses coming into court and testifying as expert witnesses in bloodstain interpretation? Are you saying there is no danger inherent in that?
A: Oh, no. I have great concern about numerous people who have been permitted to testify, who some have been trained in a one-week course, some have not, and still have been permitted to testify. And I have been aware and I have been able to controvert, I would say, many outrageous opinions that have been offered by some of these individuals.

That's an area of concern in forensic science and it is not limited to bloodstain interpretation. But I think the ability of someone to properly interpret bloodstains is a combined effort of education and experience and the ability to know when you are overstepping your boundaries and saying I have a particular case where I think I need to engage the assistance of a forensic pathologist or a serologist or another bloodstain pattern analyst. Knowing when you are at the limit of your ability, I think, is as important as being trained.

Q: I direct your attention to page 117 of the same text. Top of the page, first full sentence.

A: Yes, sir.

Q: I quote: "This author believes that a bachelor's degree in either science or a recognized program in criminal justice wherein the sciences are included should be an absolute minimum requirement before anyone is accepted as an expert witness in this discipline."
Do you agree with that sentence?

A: No, I do not.

Q: Why not?

A: Because I believe that the interpretations that are made by a well-trained forensic investigator can be quite valid in the absence of a degree in chemistry, physics, or biology.

But I make the criteria of one who is trained, one who does a significant amount of case work, and also one who is willing to seek out assistance when needed. There are various levels of investigators. I am not saying that everyone who has taken a bloodstain course should be qualified in court. I don't think you can make it a prerequisite in biology, chemistry, or physics for this discipline. I think that's more appropriate for a person who is conducting DNA testing for example. I sincerely believe they should have a degree in biology, in genetics, training in genetics, to make those interpretations. That's a different science and different level of forensic area. For bloodstain pattern interpretation, it is the documentation, at the scene, drawing conclusions, and I believe very truly as a teacher on this subject, to be always willing to give the alternative explanations for the occurrence of bloodstains and be willing to be conservative about interpretation.

I think that's where some other individuals get into trouble. For example, if I may, I was recently involved in a case with a trained blood-stain expert on the opposing side, who found it necessary to say that he was 110 percent sure of his conclusions. And I felt that was totally wrong and that's the kind of statement that is very, very dangerous. This discipline, as well as the others in forensic science, are not 110 percent certain of conclusions and I think the good expert, the qualified expert will acknowledge that.

Q: Are you familiar with the report prepared by _____ in this case, *State v.* _____?

A: No, sir, I am not.

Q: Have you seen it?

A: No sir, I have not.

Q: Do you know anything about the facts of this case?

A: Only through very limited discussion with the prosecutor. I just have a sketchy amount of detail about the case. I have not seen any materials or photographs relating to it.

Q: Again, going back to Mr. MacDonell's text at page 117, he states in the first full paragraph:

> "It is recognized that some persons with only a high school education or possibly not even that have been accepted as experts and allowed to present testimony on this subject. It has also been proven that in many instances these individuals have made grievous errors through their ignorance of basic scientific principles."

Do you agree with those two sentences?

A: I do agree with the fact that, first of all, there are individuals who are members of the Bloodstain Pattern Association whose formal education is high school and then going on to do other things, whether police-related work or medical investigator work, or what have you. I don't know that I can make a correlation between those individuals and the second statement that Mr. MacDonell has made. I think people that are well-trained can make grievous errors, as well. The prerequisite for being wrong is not just a lack of education.

Q: Would it be fair to state that this section of Mr. MacDonell's book here, Chapter 21, "Areas of Forensic Concern," this section is trying to identify what problems exist with people coming into court and testifying as expert witnesses when they really don't have the qualifications, training, education, and experience to do so.

Would you agree with me?

A: Yes. I believe that Herb MacDonell is addressing this problem. I think the problem is much broader than the area that he has gotten into. And it is not a matter of so much of training and education, as it is being a neutral witness.

I think in every discipline, in forensics and otherwise, there are people who will give you any opinion, as long as you pay for it. That's just a general problem in the criminal justice system anyway. Hopefully a small problem.

Q: You are not saying the legal system, are you?

A: Criminal justice. It's all encompassing.

To get back to this. He's making some valid points here but I don't think the solution is to require every person to have a degree in natural sciences to be able to testify about bloodstain interpretations. I don't think it's practical or necessary.

Q: Are there some cases that factually are much more difficult for someone in your discipline to interpret than other cases?

A: Oh, yes, myself included. I have had a couple of cases that I have been baffled by. In terms of the interpretation of the bloodstains, cases can be very complex. You may have multiple victims. There are situations that occur. One of the things I do in a complex case is seek out the opinion of someone else in my field. Everybody should have the ability to seek advice if they need it.

Q: So you could not give an opinion about the _____ case, whether it's, say, relatively easy, mildly complex or a very complex case, because you don't know anything about it?

A: I haven't seen the case.

Q: What does it take to get into the International Association of Bloodstain Pattern Analysts. What requirements are there for that?

A: Well, since I am a member I should know. The basic requirements are to be actively engaged in the field of bloodstain interpretation. The main requirement is to complete a forty-hour course in bloodstain pattern interpretation, which has been taught by a qualified instructor. Although, I don't know what the criteria for that are. But in order to get into the organization, you have to be sponsored by somebody. Somebody has to recommend you.

Q: Some other member, you mean?

A: Yes, a member must recommend you and then the application is reviewed so, therefore, the organization then knows who the instructor was, so they can decide whether the course training is adequate, based on their knowledge of the instructor. I believe those are the major criteria.

Other questions are asked relative to has this person done research in the field, have they testified in the field, in court, but the major criterion is the completion of the basic bloodstain course.

Q: Forty-hour course, recommendation of another member of the association — I assume twenty or thirty dollar annual fee of some kind?

A: I think it is $30.

Q: $30. And that's it, correct?

A: Basically, yes.

Q: Well, my point is, being a member of this voluntary association, certainly in no way qualified you to testify as an expert witness in this area; is that correct?

A: Mere membership in the organization is certainly not. It is one of other types of qualifications.

Q: It is voluntary. I can be a bloodstain pattern expert and not a member of that association, correct?

A: Yes. There are people who have qualified as an expert who do not belong to the organization.

Q: This association is not some form of governmental licensing board or anything like this?

A: No, there is no national certification, if that's what you are getting at.

Q: That's what I am getting at.

A: No, sir.

Q: Are there any standards promulgated by the International Association of Bloodstain Pattern Analysts with regard to minimum standard before you can testify as an expert witness in a case?

A: I haven't looked at the bylaws recently. But I don't think the organization makes any ruling on whether — on what is necessary for someone to be qualified. Basically, members must have taken the basic course but the organization does not qualify people. That's done by the court based on individual credentials.

Q: There is nothing in the organization or association that sets up any minimum standards to your knowledge?

A: No.

Q: I noticed earlier on direct examination, that you testified about this forty-hour course that I believe you took in 1977. Did I hear you say that?

A: Yes, you did.

Q: Who was that course taught by?

A: That course was taught by Herbert Leon MacDonell.

Q: You mentioned earlier that there is a Dr. Paul Kirk who has some significant influence in this discipline, insofar as the Sam Sheppard case, is that right?

A: Yes.

Q: And do you recognize him as one of the pioneers and leading experts in this field prior to his death?

A: Yes, I believe that he made significant contribution to the field of bloodstain pattern interpretation.

Q: If I told you that he said that at least one year of college physics is a prerequisite to any criminalistic activity and "the student of criminalistics must be well equipped in the fields of general inorganic and organic chemistry with a minimum of three years of lecture and laboratory courses and that knowledge of biology was important and at times absolutely essential," would you agree with that?

A: Do you mean in relation to the field of criminalistics?

Q: Yes.

A: In my opinion, bloodstain pattern interpretation is not criminalistics in the sense that Dr. Kirk was referring to in that statement. I believe that he is referring to scientific examinations that are conducted in the forensic or crime laboratory such as serology, hair, fiber, glass, and soil analysis. I would also include forensic toxicology, drug analysis, and the analysis of fire debris for accelerant content. The latter types of examinations require the knowledge and use of sophisticated laboratory instrumentation such as liquid and gas chromatography and mass spectrometry. I fully agree that individuals engaged in those specialties need a college degree in the natural sciences.

Q: Do you know who Dr. Peter DeForest is?

A: Yes.

Q: And who is he?

A: Peter DeForest is at the present time, professor of forensic science at John Jay College of Criminal Justice in New York City.

Q: And you mentioned that you studied there at one point in time, did you not?

A: Yes, John Jay College sponsored a full-day workshop on bloodstain interpretation in 1985. The main lecturer was Bart Epstein from the Department of Public Safety in Minneapolis, Minnesota.

Q: Are you familiar with the writings of Dr. DeForest?

A: Yes, I have read several articles he has written.

Q: And you certainly read a book he co-authored, "Forensic Science — An Introduction to Criminalistics." Is that correct, 1983?

A: If that is the book that is co-authored with Dr. Henry Lee and Dr. Robert Gaensslen, the answer is yes.

Q: Dr. DeForest has written that a number of individuals without scientific backgrounds had been trained in workshops and have stepped beyond an investigative role to offer scientific evidence as expert witnesses in court. Do you agree with that general proposition that that has happened?

A: Yes.

Q: Dr. DeForest continues, "The danger inherent in this development cannot be overemphasized. No amount of experience can supplant scientific knowledge and the thought process based upon a careful adherence to the scientific method."

Would you agree with those two sentences?

A: Yes.

Q: What is the scientific method?

A: The scientific method is a basic and logical approach to a problem or a research matter relating to the organization of the solving of that problem. It is the determination of the preparation and methodology employed and the interpretation of the conclusions that are drawn. It is the adherence to a systematic approach to problem solving in the scientific community.

Q: Sir, is it important to have continuing education in the field of bloodstain pattern analysis?

A: Yes.

Q: And do you do so?

A: Yes I do.

Q: And in fact in your curriculum vitae you have a number of pages — I believe it is two — which are entitled continuing education and training in forensic science, is that correct?

A: Yes sir.

Q: And I see for nearly every year for at least the past ten years you have had some form — fairly significant twenty or forty hours of continuing instruction each year, is that right?

A: Yes.

Q: And it is your opinion that it is important to do that to keep up on things?

A: Yes, I believe that it is highly desirable but not always possible. For example, I have been unable in the last two years to attend the International Association of Bloodstain Pattern Analysts meeting because I have been in court. However, continuing education is important and available for individuals and I would encourage it.

Q: What is the International Association for Identification?

A: It is an organization whose main interests are fingerprint identification, firearm and toolmark identification, crime scene examination and photography. I am not a member but I am aware of the organization.

Q: And do they have a bloodstain pattern committee as far as you know?

A: Yes, I believe they do.

Q: We already know, since you have testified to it, what the requirements are for membership in the International Association of Bloodstain Pattern Analysts. You are a member of other scientific organizations? How about the American Academy of Forensic Sciences? What requirements are there to enter into that organization?

A: The requirements to gain entrance to the first category which is as a provisional member is to be actively engaged in a field of forensic science which includes the legal profession since the Academy has a jurisprudence section. You also must be recommended by a member in good standing of the section to which you intend to apply for membership. Advancement to full membership and eventually to fellow member requires continuing active work in the forensic sciences, attendance at yearly meetings, presentation of a paper at one or more of the meetings, as well as adhering to the ethical standards of the Academy.

Q: Are you familiar with the publication known as "Bloodstain Pattern Interpretation" by Herbert MacDonell in 1982 or thereabouts?

A: Yes I am.

Q: And Mr. MacDonell was expressing concerns in 1982 and I quote as follows from page 26. "Formal academic study in physics and mathematics is necessary for more complete understanding of bloodstain patterns. Without such knowledge, often an investigator cannot accurately correlate more complex interrelationships that are essential to the correct interpretation of evidence of this type. While it is not suggested that a minimum academic standard be set as a requirement before testimony should be accepted, certainly, the lack of formal courses in science might raise a question as to the potential witness's ability to represent himself as a scientist capable of competent technical testimony in this discipline." Do you agree with that statement back from 1982?

A: Yes I do in part. If someone is representing themselves as a scientist, I would adhere to that statement. I don't believe that a bloodstain-trained person has to represent himself as a scientist with a strong physics, mathematics, or biology background. If he or she is, all well and good, but I don't think that is necessary to make proper interpretations. It is important that the person has been well trained and has sufficient experience and if during the training period and the early experience the person has their interpretations reviewed by a more experienced individual. I think the concept that Herb has described is good but directed more at some individuals and situations where completely unqualified and untrained individuals have been able to testify and some grievous errors have been made in bloodstain interpretation.

Q: And that's a concern for you as well, in this profession?

A: Absolutely, any grievous error or gross misrepresentation of the evidence reflects back on the forensic science profession and hurts everybody.

Q: And you want to be very conservative in this discipline when you are only dealing with photographs or, let's say, items recovered from crime scenes that are, perhaps many years old, is that a fair statement?

A: Yes, I think being conservative in terms of the interpretation of photographs is correct. I don't know that the age of the photograph plugs into that necessarily.

Q: I meant the age of items of physical evidence. For example, if you have clothes that have blood on them and you are seeing them three or four years or one or two years after a particular incident, you want to be careful about drawing conclusions, is that correct?

A: Well, yes in the sense that it depends upon how the evidence was collected and maintained. It could be quite different from what it was originally. If you can ascertain that the evidence appears to be in its original state, perhaps compare it to photographs taken originally, then there should not be much of a problem. I have examined bloodstains on clothing over 15 years old and other than the color of the blood being darker, there was no real difference.

Q: But you did say that it is important to know how the items were packaged or maintained initially upon their retrieval from the crime scene, is that right?

A: Yes, if there is contamination then, obviously, there are going to be some problems with interpretation.

Q: What do you mean by contamination?

A: Bloodstained clothing can become contaminated by folding and or packaging when it is still wet. This creates artifacts on the material that have nothing to do with the events that created the original bloodstains. Additionally, wet bloodstained clothing may become infested with bacteria, fungi or be exposed to insect activity which may cause difficulty with interpretation.

Q: So your testimony then is that if you are at a crime scene or you are viewing pictures of a crime scene and you later find out that the clothing was soaked with blood at the time it was packaged, you would want to be very careful about rendering some conclusions or opinions from that, is that a fair statement?

A: Absolutely.

Q: Would it also be important to know or least have some idea whether or not an assailant or assailants may have handled bloodstained clothing before they were finally deposited at a crime scene? Would that be important to know?

A: That activity may be able to be determined from the bloodstain pattern interpretation of the clothing.

Q: Let me put it to you like this. Let's say you have an article of clothing that is removed from the victim and is partially soaked in blood. That item is then handled by an assailant and it is moved and repositioned. To interpret bloodstains isn't it important or wouldn't you think it is important to know that it was moved before you start drawing conclusions or that there may be a possible explanation for a certain stain somewhere else on that particular article of clothing?

A: I don't know if that information first of all would be necessarily known, but if I were told that someone handled the clothing while it was wet, I would take that information into consideration and determine if the bloodstains were consistent with that activity occurring or not.

Q: The point is you have to be very conservative in your discipline in drawing conclusions and you must look at everything and take everything into consideration before you come to any conclusion, is that a fair statement?

A: Yes, I think I made it clear earlier that bloodstain pattern interpretation helps to correlate the other facets of the case.

Q: Thank you. That's all.

Re-Direct Examination by the Prosecutor

Q: In your opinion is _____ qualified to render an expert opinion in court?

A: I know that _____ has been qualified numerous times in court. I have worked on cases with _____ both on the same side as well as an adversary. I would say of any person in the field of bloodstain interpretation that I can only evaluate their conclusions in a given case and I could agree or disagree with them. I think that _____ has certainly done a lot with bloodstain interpretation in case work as well as teaching and generally maintains a high degree of respect throughout the bloodstain community.

Q: That's all, your Honor. Thank you.

Re-Cross-Examination by the Defense Attorney

Q: So when you were asked whether or not _____ is qualified as an expert witness, your real answer would be it depends upon their conclusions, right, and the sophistication of the evidence presented?
A: I don't qualify people. I can look at work other individuals have done and I may either agree with them or not. This is the case with _____ or any other expert. I would leave it at that.

Q: And you haven't looked at their work in this case, so you don't know whether you would agree with it or not.
A: No sir, I don't.

Q: Thank you.
A: You are welcome.

THE COURT: You can step down.

APPENDIX 3
Court Decisions Relating to Bloodstain Pattern Interpretation

State

ALABAMA

Leonard v. State, 551 So.2d 1143 (Ala. App. 1989)
Robinson v. State, 574 So.2d 910 (Ala. App. 1990)

ALASKA

Crawford v. Rogers, 406 P.2d 189 (Alaska 1965)
Pederson v. State, 420 P.2d 327 (Alaska 1966)

CALIFORNIA

People v. Carter, 312 P.2d 665 (Cal. 1957)
People v. Hogan, 647 P.2d 93 (Cal. 1982)
People v. Clark, 857 P.2d 1099 (Cal. 1993)

DISTRICT OF COLUMBIA

Eason v. United States, 687 A.2d 922 (D.C.App. 1996)

FLORIDA

Castro v. State, 547 So.2d 111 (Fla. 1989)
Cheshire v. State, 568 So.2d 908 (Fla. 1990)
Morris v. State, 561 So.2d 646 (Fla. 1990)
Reichmann v. State, 581 So.2d 133 (Fla. 1991)

GEORGIA

Droke v. State, 314 S.E.2d 230 (Ga. 1984)
Coleman v. State, 348 S.E.2d 70 (Ga. 1986)
Coleman v. State, 357 S.E.2d 566 (Ga. 1987)
O'Toole v. State, 373 S.E.2d 12 (Ga. 1988)

IDAHO

State v. Rodgers, 812 P.2d 1227 (Idaho 1990)
State v. Rodgers, 812 P.2d 1208 (Idaho 1991)
State v. Raudebaugh, 864 P.2d 596 (Idaho 1993)

ILLINOIS

People v. Driver, 379 N.E.2d 840 (Ill. 1978)
People v. Erickson, 411 N.E.2d 44 (Ill. 1980)
People v. Knox, 459 N.E.2d 1077 (Ill. 1984)
People v. Owens, 508 N.E.2d 1088 (Ill. 1987)
People v. Smith, 633 N.E.2d 69 (Ill. 1993)

INDIANA

Fox v. State, 506 N.E.2d 1090 (Ind. 1987)
King v. State, 531 N.E.2d 1154 (Ind. 1988)
Hampton v. State, 588 N.E.2d 555 (Ind. 1992)

IOWA

State v. Hall, 297 N.W.2d 80 (Iowa 1980)

KANSAS

State v. Satterfield, 592 P.2d 135 (Kan. 1979)
State v. Ordway, 934 P.2d 94 (Kan. 1997)

LOUISIANA

State v. Graham, 422 So.2d 123 (La. 1982)
State v. Williams, 445 So.2d 1171 (La. 1984)
State v. Ancar, 508 So.2d 943 (La. 1984)
State v. McFadden, 476 So.2d 413 (La. 1985)
State v. Powell, 598 So.2d 454 (La. 1992)
State v. Howard, 626 So.2d 459 (La. 1993)

MAINE

State v. Knight, 43 Me. 11 (1857)
State v. Hilton, 431 A.2d 1296 (Me. 1981)
State v. Philbrick, 436 A.2d 844 (Me. 1981)

MARYLAND

Tirado v. State, 622 2d 187 (Md. 1993)

MASSACHUSETTS

Commonwealth v. Sturtivant, 117 Mass. 122 (1875)
Commonwealth v. Capalbo, 32 N.E.2d 225 (Mass. 1941)
Commonwealth v. Gordon, 666 N.E.2d 122 (Mass. 1996)

MINNESOTA

State v. Malzac, 244 N.W.2d 258 (Minn. 1976)
State v. Fossen, 282 N.W.2d 496 (Minn. 1979)
State v. Merrill, 428 N.W.2d 361 (Minn. 1988)
State v. Norris, 428 N.W.2d 61 (Minn. 1988)
State v. Robinson, 427 N.W.2d 217 (Minn. 1988)
State v. Moore, 458 N.W.2d 90 (Minn. 1990)

MISSISSIPPI

Dillard v. State, 58 Miss. 368 (1880)
Jordon v. State, 464 So.2d 475 (Miss. 1985)
Whittinger v. State, 523 So.2d 966 (Miss. 1988)
Fowler v. State, 566 So.2d 1194 (Miss. 1990)

MONTANA

State v. Mix, 781 P.2d 751 (Mont. 1989)

NEBRASKA

State v. Thieszen, 560 N.W.2d 800 (Neb. 1997)

NEW YORK

Lindsay v. People of the State of New York, 63 N.Y. 143 (1875)
People v. Comfort, 496 N.Y.S.2d 857 (1985)
People v. Murray, 537 N.Y.S.2d 399 (1989)

NORTH CAROLINA

State v. Simpson, 255 S.E.2d 147 (N.C. 1979)
State v. Willis, 426 S.E.2d 471 (N.C. 1993)
State v. East, 481 S.E.2d 652 (N.C. 1997)
State v. Clifton, 481 S.E.2d 393 (N.C. 1997)

OKLAHOMA

Farris v. State, 670 P.2d 995 (Okla. 1983)
Clayton v. State, 840 P.2d 18 (Okla. 1992)
Clayton v. State, 892 P.2d 646 (Okla. 1992)
Hogan v. State, 877 P.2d 1157 (Okla. 1994)
Taylor v. State, 889 P.2d 319 (Okla. 1995)

OREGON

State v. Luther, 663 P.2d 1261 (Or. App. 1983)
State v. Proctor, 767 P.2d 453 (Or. App. 1989)

PENNSYLVANIA

Commonwealth v. Goins, 495 A.2d 527 (Pa. 1985)
Commonwealth v. Duffey, 548 A.2d 1178 (Pa. 1988)

RHODE ISLAND

State v. Chiellini, 557 A.2d 1195 (R.I. 1989)

SOUTH CAROLINA

State v. Myers, 391 S.E.2d 551 (S.C. 1990)

TENNESSEE

State v. Melson, 638 S.W.2d 342 (Tenn. 1982)
State v. Cazes, 875 S.W.2d 253 (Tenn. 1994)

TEXAS

Guerrero v. State, 720 S.W.2d 233 (Tex.App. 1986)
Cortijo v. State, 739 S.W.2d 486 (Tex.App. 1987)
Lewis v. State, 737 S.W.2d 857 (Tex.App. 1987)
Salas v. State, 756 S.W.2d 832 (Tex.App. 1988)
Speering v. State, 763 S.W.2d 801 (Tex.App. 1988)
Mowbray v. State, 788 S.W.2d 658 (Tex.App. 1990), *vacated, Ex Parte Mowbray,* 943 S.W.2d 461 (Tex.App. 1996)

VIRGINIA

Compton v. Commonwealth, 250 S.E.2d 749 (Va. 1979)

WASHINGTON

State v. Perkins, 204 P.2d 207 (Wash. 1949)

Federal

Wilson v. United States, 162 U.S. 613 (1895)
United States v. Mustafa, 22 M.J. 165 (CMA 1986)
United States v. Mobley, 31 M.J. 273 (CMA 1990)
United States v. Hill, 41 M.J. 596 (Army Ct.Crim.App. 1994)
United States v. Holt, 46 M.J. 853 (N.M.Ct.Crim.App. 1997)
Smith v. Anzelone, 111 F.3d 1126 (4th Cir. 1997)

APPENDIX 4
Court Decisions Relating to Presumptive Blood Tests

Presumptive Testing Cases

State

State v. Stenson, 940 P.2d 1239 (Wash. 1997)
Ex Parte Mowbray, 943 S.W.2d 461 (Tex. 1996)*
Commonwealth v. Gordon, 666 N.E.2d 122 (Mass. 1996)
Young v. State, 871 S.W.2d 373 (Ark. 1994)*
Palmer v. State, 870 S.W.2d 385 (Ark. 1994)*
Robedeaux v. State, 866 P.2d 417(Okla. 1993)
State v. Bronson, 496 N.W.2d 882 (Neb. 1993)
People v. Clark, 833 P.2d 561 (Cal. 1992)
Marcy v. State, 823 P.2d 660 (Alaska 1991)
State v. Lord, 822 P.2d 177 (Wash. 1991)
State v. Moody, 573 A.2d 716 (Conn. 1990)*
People v. Coleman, 759 P.2d 1260 (Cal. 1988)
Smith v. State, 492 So.2d 260 (Miss. 1986)
Wycoff v. State, 382 N.W.2d 462 (Iowa 1986)
Riggle v. State, 585 P.2d 1382 (Okla. 1978)
People v. Talbot, 414 P.2d 633 (Cal. 1966)

Federal

U.S. v. Holt, 46 M.J. 853 (N.M.Ct.Crim.App. 1997)*
U.S. v. Burks, 36 M.J. 447 (CMA 1993)*

Luminol Cases

State

State v. Fukusaku, 1997 WL 570980 (Hawaii 1997)*
Ex Parte Mowbray, 943 S.W.2d 461 (Tex. 1996)*
State v. Workman, 476 S.E.2d 301 (N.C. 1996)
State v. Hyde, 921 P.2d 655 (Ariz. 1996)

---

* These cases address the issues of reliability and admissibility.

Jimenez v. State, 918 P.2d 687 (Nev. 1996)
Houston v. State, 906 S.W.2d 286 (Ark. 1995)
Smolka v. State, 662 So.2d 1255 (Fla. 1995)
State v. Zanter, 535 N.W.2d 624 (Minn. 1995)
State v. Campbell, 460 S.W.2d 144 (N.C. 1995)
Diffee v. State, 894 S.W.2d 564 (Ark. 1995)
Dansby v. State, 675 So.2d 1344 (Ala. 1994)
Young v. State, 871 S.W.2d 373 (Ark. 1994)*
Palmer v. State, 870 S.W.2d 385 (Ark. 1994)*
Robedaux v. State, 866 P.2d 417 (Okla. 1993)
State v. Bible, 858 P.2d 1152 (Ariz. 1993)
State v. Wages, 623 N.E.2d 193 (Ohio 1993)
Brenk v. State, 847 S.W.2d 1 (Ark. 1993)*
People v. Cooper, 809 P.2d 865 (Cal. 1991)
State v. Gonzales, 783 P.2d 1239 (Kan. 1989)
Lee v. State, 545 N.E.2d 1085 (Ind. 1989)
State v. Lewis, 543 So.2d 760 (Fla. 1989)
Thompson v. State, 768 P.2d 127 (Alaska 1989)
State v. McElrath, 366 S.E.2d 442 (N.C. 1988)
People v. Henne, 518 N.E.2d 1276 (Ill. 1988)
State v. Martin, 740 P.2d 577 (Kan. 1987)
Johnston v. State, 497 So.2d 863 (Fla. 1986)
People v. Hendricks, 495 N.E.2d 85 (Ill. 1986)
Green v. Superior Court, 707 P.2d 248 (Cal. 1985)
People v. Asgari, 196 Cal.Rptr. 378 (1983)
Waterhouse v. State, 429 So.2d 301 (Fla. 1983)
State v. Jones, 328 N.W.2d 166 (Neb. 1982)
State v. Brown, 293 S.E.2d 569 (N.C. 1982)
State v. White, 235 S.E.2d 55 (N.C. 1977)

Federal

U.S. ex rel. Savory v. Lane, 832 F.2d 1011 (7th Cir. 1987)*

U.S. v. Holt, 46 M.J. 853 (N.M.Ct.Crim.App. 1997)*
U.S. v. Hill, 41 M.J. 596 (ArmyCt.Crim.App. 1994)*
U.S. v. Burks, 36 M.J. 447 (CMA 1993)*

---

* These cases address the issues of reliability and admissibility.

Benzidine Cases

State

State v. Hyde, 921 P.2d 655 (Ariz. 1996)
Fisher v. State, 827 S.W.2d 597 (Tex. 1992)
Commonwealth v. Anderson, 537 N.E.2d 146 (Mass. 1989)
Clark v. Ellerthorpe, 552 A.2d 1186 (R.I. 1989)
Commonwealth v. Shea, 519 N.E.2d 1283 (Mass. 1988)
Wycoff v. State, 382 N.W.2d 462 (Iowa 1986)
Commonwealth v. Nadworny, 486 N.E.2d 675 (Mass. 1985)
Commonwealth v. Cuneen, 449 N.E.2d 658 (Mass. 1983)
Nathan v. State, 611 S.W.2d 69 (Tex. 1981)
State v. Clark, 423 A.2d 1151 (R.I. 1980)
Commonwealth v. Best, 411 N.E.2d 442 (Mass. 1980)
State v. Milho, 596 P.2d 777 (Hawaii 1979)
State v. Ruybal, 398 A.2d 407 (Me. 1979)
Riggle v. State, 585 P.2d 1382 (Okla. 1978)
State v. Swain, 269 N.W.2d 707 (Minn. 1978)
State v. Boyd, 359 So.2d 931 (La. 1978)
Chandler v. State, 329 A.2d 430 (Md. 1974)
People v. Johnson, 113 Cal.Rptr. 303 (Cal. 1974)
Commonwealth v. Appleby, 265 N.E.2d 485 (Mass. 1970)
Wilbanks v. State, 266 So.2d 609 (Ala. 1968)
Trotter v. State, 377 S.W.2d 14 (Ark. 1964)
People v. Schiers, 324 P.2d 981 (Cal. 1958)
Commonwealth v. Moore, 80 N.E.2d 24 (Mass. 1948)

Federal

Clark v. Moran, 942 F.2d 24 (1st Cir. 1991)
Real v. Hogan, 828 F.2d 58 (1st Cir. 1987)
Carillo v. Brown, 807 F.2d 1094 (1st Cir. 1986)
Marrapese v. State of R.I., 749 F.2d 934 (1st Cir. 1984)
Clark v. Taylor, 710 F.2d 4 (1st Cir. 1983)
U.S. v. Sheard, 473 F.2d 139 (D.C.Cir. 1972)

Orthotolidine/Ortho-Tolidine Cases/*O*-Tolidine

State

Commonwealth v. Gordon, 666 N.E.2d 122 (Mass. 1996)
Commonwealth v. Burke, 607 N.E.2d 991 (Mass. 1993)
Commonwealth v. Hodgkins, 520 N.E.2d 145 (Mass. 1988)

Federal

United States v. Hill, 41 M.J. 596 (ArmyCt.Crim.App. 1994)

Leucomalachite/Leuco-Malachite Green Cases

State v. Peterson, 494 N.W.2d 551 (Neb. 1993)
State v. Lord, 822 P.2d 177 (Wash. 1991)

Hemastix® Case

People v. Coleman, 759 P.2d 1260 (Cal. 1988)

Phenolphthalein Cases

State

State v. Fukusaku, 1997 WL 570980 (Hawaii 1997)
State v. Stenson, 940 P.2d 1239 (Wash. 1997)
People v. Bradford, 939 P.2d 259 (Cal. 1997)
State v. Workman, 476 S.E. 301 (N.C. 1996)
State v. Peterson, 446 S.E.2d 43 (N.C. 1994)
State v. Moseley, 445 S.E.2d 906 (N.C. 1994)
State v. Keel, 423 S.E.2d 458 (N.C. 1992)
Cheshire v. State, 568 So.2d 908 (Fla. 1990)
State v. McElrath, 366 S.E.2d 442 (N.C. 1988)
State v. Prevette, 345 S.E.2d 159 (N.C. 1986)
Wycoff v. State, 382 N.W.2d 462 (Iowa 1986)
Commonwealth v. Costello, 467 N.E.2d 811 (Mass. 1984)
State v. Brown, 293 S.E.2d 569 (N.C. 1982)
Riggle v. State, 585 P.2d 1382 (Okla. 1978)
Castleberry v. State, 522 P.2d 257 (Okla. 1974)

Federal

Clark v. Moran, 749 F.Supp. 1186 (D.R.I. 1990)

United States v. Holt, 46 M.J. 853 (N.M.Ct.Crim.App. 1997)
United States v. Burks, 36 M.J. 447 (CMA 1993)

APPENDIX 5
Trigonometric Tables — Sine and Tangent Functions

Degrees	Sine	Tangent	Degrees	Sine	Tangent
0.0	.0000	.0000	46.0	.7193	1.036
1.0	.0175	.0175	47.0	.7314	1.072
2.0	.0349	.0349	48.0	.7431	1.111
3.0	.0523	.0524	49.0	.7547	1.150
4.0	.0698	.0699	50.0	.7660	1.192
5.0	.0872	.0875	51.0	.7771	1.235
6.0	.1045	.1051	52.0	.7880	1.280
7.0	.1219	.1228	53.0	.7986	1.327
8.0	.1392	.1405	54.0	.8090	1.376
9.0	.1564	.1584	55.0	.8192	1.428
10.0	.1736	.1763	56.0	.8290	1.483
11.0	.1908	.1944	57.0	.8387	1.540
12.0	.2079	.2126	58.0	.8480	1.600
13.0	.2250	.2309	59.0	.8572	1.664
14.0	.2419	.2493	60.0	.8660	1.732
15.0	.2588	.2679	61.0	.8746	1.804
16.0	.2756	.2867	62.0	.8829	1.881
17.0	.2924	.3057	63.0	.8910	1.963
18.0	.3090	.3249	64.0	.8988	2.050
19.0	.3256	.3443	65.0	.9063	2.145
20.0	.3420	.3640	66.0	.9135	2.246
21.0	.3584	.3839	67.0	.9205	2.356
22.0	.3746	.4040	68.0	.9272	2.475
23.0	.3907	.4245	69.0	.9336	2.605
24.0	.4067	.4452	70.0	.9397	2.748
25.0	.4226	.4663	71.0	.9455	2.904
26.0	.4384	.4877	72.0	.9511	3.078
27.0	.4540	.5095	73.0	.9563	3.271
28.0	.4695	.5317	74.0	.9613	3.487
29.0	.4848	.5543	75.0	.9659	3.732
30.0	.5000	.5774	76.0	.9703	4.011
31.0	.5150	.6009	77.0	.9744	4.332
32.0	.5299	.6249	78.0	.9781	4.705
33.0	.5446	.6494	79.0	.9816	5.145
34.0	.5592	.6745	80.0	.9848	5.671
35.0	.5736	.7002	81.0	.9877	6.314
36.0	.5878	.7265	82.0	.9903	7.115
37.0	.6018	.7536	83.0	.9925	8.144
38.0	.6157	.7813	84.0	.9945	9.514
39.0	.6293	.8098	85.0	.9962	11.43
40.0	.6428	.8391	86.0	.9976	14.30
41.0	.6561	.8693	87.0	.9986	19.08
42.0	.6691	.9004	88.0	.9994	28.64
43.0	.6820	.9325	89.0	.9998	57.29
44.0	.6947	.9657	90.0	1.000	0.000
45.0	.7071	1.000			

Index

A

Accident reconstruction, 33–45
  airbag deployment, 45
  driver identification, 37, 42–43
  ejection/cast-off blood, 39–42
  expired blood, 35, 37–38
  hit and run, 38–39
  pattern recognition, 34–37
  pedestrian/occupant final rest position, 36, 37, 43–45
  pedestrian/occupant relative motion, 34
  seatbelt use, 36, 45
  throw distance, 36
Address of bloodstains/crime scene objects, 5–9, 14
Admissibility of evidence, 92–96
  Daubert standard, 94–96, 127–130
  example Motion in Limine
    cross-examination of expert witness, 240–253, 254
    direct examination of expert witness, 227–240, 253–254
    expert's qualifications, 227–234, 240–246, 248–249, 251
  Frye (general acceptance) standard, 92–93, 127, 129
  MacDonell's opinion, 236–237
  post-conviction analysis, 127–128
    historical background, 122–126
Airbag deployment, 45
Alpha angle, See Impact angle
American Academy of Forensic Sciences (AAFS), 98, 111, 229, 251
American Bar Association Model Rules of Professional Conduct, 112
Anatomical model, 87
Angle of impact, See Impact angle
Angular impact from horizontal motion, 164–165
Appeal issues, 127–139, See also Post-conviction analysis
  admissibility, 122, 127–128
    historical background, 122–126

expert qualifications, 131–139
standards of review, 128–130
Arcsin relationship, 21, 162, 163
Arterial spurting, 35
Attorney-client privilege, 103–105
Attorney ethics, 112–114, See also Ineffective counsel
Autopsy records, 76–77

B

Backspatter, 144, 146, 147
BackTrack/Win, 28–31
Benjamin, Steven D., 145
Benzidine test, 48, 50–51
  court cases, 263
  false positives, 51
Biology education, 240
Bird's-eye view, See Top-view projection
Blood dripped into blood, 36
Blood drop size, surface texture effects, 160–161
Blood drying time, 173, 185–186, 214
Blood presence, testing for, See Presumptive testing
Bloodstain pattern analysis
  address of bloodstains/crime scene objects, 5–9, 14
  admissibility issues, See Admissibillity of evidence
  case approach, See Case evaluation approach
  computer application, 17–32, See Virtual string method
  evidence, See Evidence; Expert testimony
  example of definition/explanation for the court, 237–239
  methods, See Impact angle; Point of origin; String method
Bloodstain pattern analyst, See also Expert witness
  objective mind-set, 72, 74, 84
  opinions, 72–73, 84, 86
  qualifications, See Expert qualifications

267